LAST MAN OUT

A Personal Account of the Vietnam War

James E. Parker Jr.

BALLANTINE BOOKS • NEW YORK

A Ballantine Book
Published by The Ballantine Publishing Group
Copyright © 1996 by James E. Parker Jr.

www.randomhouse.com/BB/

Library of Congress Catalog Card Number: 00-190008

ISBN 0-8041-1941-4

Manufactured in the United States of America

First Ballantine Books Edition: May 2000

10   9   8   7   6   5   4   3   2   1

More praise for
Last Man Out

"Few, like Jim Parker, saw the second Indochina War from start to finish. And few are qualified to conclude that 'even though we lost, we did the right thing by coming here to fight.' For those who did, that's the war's lasting legacy."

—COL. HARRY G. SUMMERS JR.
Editor, *Vietnam* magazine

"An enlightening story . . . Few others shared Parker's perspective on the war, and none has reported it quite the same way."

—*Library Journal*

"James E. Parker Jr. has written a thoroughly honest and compelling memoir. . . . *Last Man Out* is his unpretentious account of an American everyman's extraordinary service to his country throughout the Vietnam War, a tale told with humility and humor and packed with history and heroism. Refreshingly free of cynicism, self-pity, and self-aggrandizement, Parker's candid account of the human dimension of combat belongs on your bookshelf next to Moore and Galloway's *We Were Soldiers Once . . . and Young.*"

—COL. JOSEPH T. COX
Author of *The Written Wars: America's War Prose Through the Civil War*

"Parker is no run-of-the-mill war memoirist but a skilled storyteller with a knack for weaving quick tales with revealing punch lines. He introduces a memorable cast of supporting characters."

—*Publishers Weekly*

By James E. Parker Jr.:

CODENAME MULE: *Fighting the Secret War in Laos for the CIA* (also published as *Covert Ops*)
LAST MAN OUT: *A Personal Account of the Vietnam War*

To my father, J. Earl Parker,
who told me to make something of myself

We all went to Gettysburg, the summer of '63:
Some of us came back from there
And that's all,
Except the details.

—Capt. Praxiteles Swan, Confederate Army,
Complete Account of the Battle of Gettysburg

Contents

Acknowledgments

John J. "Jack" Lyons Jr.; Sgt. Maj. Cecil Bratcher, USA (Ret.); Robert M. Dunn and his former wife, Linda; Lt. Col. Larry D. Peterson, USA (Ret.); Col. John E. Woolley, USA (Ret.); and Lt. Gen. Robert Haldane, USA (Ret.), helped tremendously with the early chronology.

Col. Leonard L. Lewane, USA (Ret.), the former commander of the Quarterhorse; Col. Edward J. Burke, USA (Ret.), the secretary of the 28th Infantry Association; and Andrew Woods at the McCormick Research Center, 1st Division Museum, provided detailed background information on 1st Division operations.

Jerry F., Hardnose, Digger, Zack, Greek, Va Xiong, Nhia Vang, H. Ownby, Izzy Freedman, and George Taylor contributed to the early CIA days and the war in Laos.

Glenn R., Don K., Tom F., and Jim D. provided invaluable help in reporting on the last days in South Vietnam. Terry Barker helped with accounts of our experiences together in Vi Thanh. George Taylor corroborated details of the actual evacuation of the CIA contingent from Can Tho. Bonnie Myers, daughter of the captain of the *Pioneer Contender*, the late Edward C. Flink, located the ship's log and other official reports that expanded my recollections. Ron Ross of Alaskan Barge and Transport helped me to complete the story of Tugboat Control and the hectic scene at Vung Tau on 1 May 1975.

I extend special thanks to Doan Huu Dinh and Nguyen Ky Phong, proud former citizens and soldiers of South Vietnam, who provided information on the deaths of General Hung and General Hai.

I also thank Barbara Johnson, Paul Prester, Sedgwick Tourison, Ron Brown, Dr. Lewis M. Stern, Dr. William M. Leary, Dr. Matt

Oyas, and Henry W. Turner for their contributions to the overall manuscript.

Thanks go to my editor and close friend, Terry Belanger, a demanding, marvelously talented lady.

And most of all, I thank my wife, Brenda, who encouraged, criticized, and championed this work.

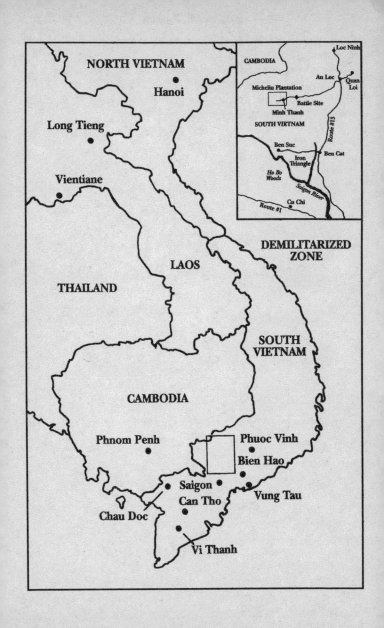

— ONE —

Army Recruit

Cottonpicker didn't think it was a big deal. This was Christmas 1963, and I was home from college. We were sitting on his back porch drinking beer.

"You don't die if you quit college," he said. "We ain't talking about the future of the world here."

Donald Lawrence, dubbed "Cottonpicker" by my father several years before, was my best friend while I was growing up. A big, brawny redhead, he was a paratrooper sergeant in the 82d Airborne Division at Fort Bragg Army Base near my hometown of Southern Pines, North Carolina, and lived with his wife and children in an apartment behind my house. During my early teen years, we had spent many late afternoon hours tinkering with his old car under a nearby magnolia tree. On weekends, we had hunted and fished deep in the woods of the Fort Bragg reservation. He taught me how to stalk deer and gig frogs and light a cigarette in the wind and cuss like a soldier. He had always done most of the talking when we were together. "I'm da Chief and you da Indian," was his way of putting it. I was used to taking his advice, so I listened carefully.

"You're what now, twenty-one? If you want to quit college and raise hell, well that's all right, I reckon. It's your life. Just don't go feeling guilty about it. Tell people, 'I ain't getting nothing out of college and what I want to do is get out there and holler, so get outa my way.' " He paused. "But, you know, you might want to have some plans, Jimmy. 'I just want to raise hell' don't feed the dog."

He looked at me and smiled in that lopsided fashion of his.

"The Army ain't bad. Been good by me."

My father had suggested that I stay in college while I was

making up my mind about my future because it was a better environment for decision making—more educated counselors, better choices. I had already dropped out once for a semester.

"If you drop out again," he reasoned, "you'll never go back. You are the family namesake. You have an obligation here."

When I returned to the University of North Carolina (UNC) after Christmas, I tried to study, but I just wasn't interested. And I felt alone. My friends had dropped out. That left me, along with maybe twenty thousand strangers at Chapel Hill, reading *The Organization Man* and in danger of becoming one.

I would sit at my desk in the dorm, a book open in front of me, and stare out the window, bored. I had always been more restless than my friends. As a kid, I'd stop and watch a train go by—or even a Greyhound bus—wanting to be on it, "getting on down the road." The journey had seemed as important as the destination.

My home was on the western edge of Fort Bragg. From a big tree in my front yard, I used to watch U.S. Air Force planes in the distance and daydream about flying those planes or jumping out of them. Cottonpicker had taught me the eight jump commands. Standing on a lower limb of the tree, I would recite, "Get ready. Stand up. Hook up. Check equipment. Check buddy's equipment. Sound off for equipment check. Stand in the door. Go!" I would jump to the ground and do the parachute landing fall (PLF), just as Cottonpicker had taught me. I'd climb back up the tree and fantasize about life as a soldier or a world traveler.

Those thoughts might have passed in time and I might have had a more normal adolescence and a less troubling college experience if I hadn't taken a trip during the summer of 1957, between my freshman and sophomore years of high school, that forever changed my life. My parents had sent me to Mars Hill College, my father's alma mater, to take college-level summer courses in hopes of jump-starting my interest in academics. Instead, I made friends there with a rowdy group of college sophomores. Two were from Cuba, one from Lake Wales, Florida, and one from Wilson, North Carolina. At the end of summer school, we developed an elaborate ruse to excuse my absence from home for a few days. My friend from Wilson and I then thumbed to Florida and went to Havana, Cuba. Three days and two nights there in the tenderloin area near the harbor—neon lights flickering off a Cuban bar at three o'clock in the morning, rumba music coursing the air, cigar smoke, fights, whores, rum were exactly what I had dreamed about in that tree in my front yard. I hated to leave, but we ran out of money. With a revolution going on in the hills, there were restrictions on just hanging around.

My parents were happy to see me when I arrived home, but in short order they sent me to a military school. That was a radical decision for them. They had grown up on farms in North Carolina and thought that only uncontrollably spoiled kids in California went to private military schools. They found it hard to believe that their son, raised in the rural heartland of the South, required special education, but they saw that unusual glint in my eye, the Cottonpicker influence, my total lack of interest in their goals, my trip to Cuba. I needed an attitude adjustment.

The structured environment of Oak Ridge Military Institute was not a bad situation, the instructors were more engaging and challenging than those I had known in public school. Also, there were some real characters in the cadet corps, and living like a soldier had a certain attraction.

I fell in love with an old 1903 Springfield rifle that I was issued for the drill team. We practiced almost every weekday afternoon, and I looked forward to getting into the armory and taking my rifle gently out of its place in the rack and twirling it in my hands. It was a handsome, no-nonsense war piece. I imagined that it had served our country in some previous war and had been retired to duty in a North Carolina military school. I had great respect for that rifle, and felt an uncommon rapport with it. In all the turns and twists required of us as the drill team marched along, that rifle never failed me. It was a solid weapon with a natural balance—a war tool.

After graduating from Oak Ridge, I enrolled in UNC. During my sophomore year, a couple of friends and I dropped out of school and drove a beat-up 1950 Willys Jeep through Central America to Nicaragua. We were looking for jobs there when we ran afoul of what would become the Sandinistas, and we had to get out. We flew to Miami, where I worked on the beach until the next semester of college began at Chapel Hill.

I still dreamed about "getting out there," living in faraway places. Hell, knocking around was a family tradition—my father should realize that, I thought. His father had never settled down. Grandpa had been a rural mail carrier but somewhat irregular in his work habits. Once during World War I, he was supposed to be on his delivery route but was holed up, drinking moonshine. Someone bet him that he couldn't drive his Harley motorbike up a nearby tree that was half bent over. He got up most of the way before he fell off. The motorbike was torn up pretty bad, plus the mail blew away and he lost his job. He and the family went back to Grandma's place and he tried to farm the forty acres they were given, but he just wasn't cut out to be a farmer. Every once in a while he left the farm and traveled around. He worked at odd jobs, once selling Fuller brushes in the eastern part of the state. Living in rooming houses and sometimes under bridges, he was different from all the rest but happy in his own way.

That's my heritage, I thought. I had heard genius skipped a generation, and I figured that held true as well for wanderlust. Maybe, like Grandpa, I was meant to be out there knocking around. It was my destiny.

I shook my head to clear away those thoughts, looked down at my book, and tried to study. Then I thought about Cuba again— that fight when two drunk sailors slammed into one another, knocking out teeth, breaking each other's nose, throwing blood over a group of whores standing nearby. The girls screamed and moved farther back, but no one tried to break up the fight. I looked back at my open, unread sociology book and yawned.

I didn't take many of my finals that January 1964. Midway through the exam period I packed all my clothes, left without saying good-bye to anyone, and drove my old junker station wagon back toward Southern Pines. In Sanford, I stopped at the Army recruiting office and signed up for three years in the infantry.

At home, I went into the kitchen and told Mother what I had done. When Daddy came in from the office, he stood in the doorway and smiled. Then he caught Mother's dour look and his smile froze. "I've joined the Army, Dad." I tried to sound upbeat, but my voice broke.

Dad walked over and slumped into his chair. The last rays of sunlight coming through the half-drawn blinds did little to brighten the gloom. Finally he said, "That's dumb." After a pause, he said, "Dealing with you is like trying to push a rope." Then he just stared out the window as if a great calamity had befallen the family.

On February 4, 1964, Mother and Daddy took me to Little's Gulf service station on the edge of town and we waited in the car for a bus to take me to the induction center in Raleigh, the state capital. They both cried. I told them everything was going to be okay, wondering as I said it why the bus was taking so long.

It finally arrived, coming to a stop in front of our car with a hiss of its air brakes. I kissed Mother on the cheek and reached over the seat and shook Daddy's hand. After boarding the bus, I looked out the window and saw the car parked off to the side of the service station. Mother was in the front and Daddy in the back, a sad, out of the ordinary sight. As the bus pulled out, Mother waved good-bye and I could see her smile. Daddy had his head down.

Grandpa's departures were probably just as melancholy.

The boys and young men sitting around the U.S. Army induction center in Raleigh looked like they belonged in the lost and found. I spent the afternoon mindlessly leafing through crumpled sports magazines that lay on tables by the worn Naugahyde couches. Eventually I was called to a desk where I signed my official enlistment papers. Later, everyone went into another room. An Air Force captain with a tired voice asked us to raise our right hand and officially swore us into military service. He then wished us good luck and added that he thought most of us would need it.

The next morning we went by train and bus to Fort Jackson, South Carolina, where we were processed into the Army. On the morning of the tenth day there—sheared to the skull, tested, vaccinated, wearing new ill-fitting fatigues, scared—my group fell into formation in front of the barracks with our duffel bags and boarded Army buses for basic training at Fort Gordon, Georgia. No longer "INductees," as we had been called at the processing center, we were off to become "boots."

At Fort Gordon the bus convoy pulled in front of our training company headquarters. "Company C" was painted on a brick-and-concrete sign out front. The doors to the bus opened, and I saw a "Smokey Bear" drill sergeant hat above a square-jawed black face rise over the two boys in the front row. Standing almost at attention beside the bus driver, the man slowly moved his eyes over the interior of the bus. Outside we heard the shrill shouts of other noncommissioned officers (NCOs) as they rushed recruits off the buses. There was a tense pause as the sergeant continued to look around. Finally he spoke in a low, smooth, and slow southern voice, "Welcome to Fort Gordon, Georgia, boys and girls. Ma name is Staff Sergeant Willie O. McGee. I am ya drill instructor. I'm going to make ya soldiers or ya'll find ya ugly asses run clean into this red Georgia dirt. Everyone stand up."

Everyone tried to push things aside and get to their feet. "Stand up, goddammit!" The voice suddenly became loud and frightfully mean. "Stand ya worthless civilian asses up, get off dis fucking bus, and form four ranks in da company street."

The recruits in front tried to get off quickly, but Sergeant McGee was blocking their way as he climbed slowly off the bus. As he moved aside, we fought one another to get out and into formation.

Standing before us, Staff Sergeant McGee was an impressive figure. Ramrod straight and deathly still, he moved only his eyes. His voice carried easily to the back ranks. He advised us to respond quickly as he "learned" us how to soldier. The Army "weren't" patient, didn't cater to individuals. The "onliest" way to act was to do exactly what he told us to—no more, no less. He picked one of the largest men, by the name of McDiarmid, to be the recruit platoon leader and four other large men to be squad leaders, and positioned them to the right.

He said he would not attempt anything silly yet, like trying to make us march or even fall out of formation in a military manner. He said, "Pick up ya duffel bags and go into da barracks behind ya, squads one and two on one side, squads three and four on da other and try to do hit without falling down."

Sergeant McGee followed us inside and paced the aisle while we claimed either a top or bottom bunk bed. Calling us to line up at attention at the end of our bunks, he walked by and corrected the stances of most of us. I stared off into the distance when he stopped briefly in front of me.

Finished, he told us that he graduated the best soldiers in the company, possibly in the whole training command. "Nobody skates," he said, "not no greasy Puerto Ricans," as he bent down close to one of the Puerto Ricans, "not no angry Negroes," as he put his nose close to the face of a very large black man, and "not no educated molly-wolly shithead," as he moved farther down the line past me and bent in close to a skinny country boy from Tennessee.

"I think I have made myself clear about what I expect, but I knows from experience dat some of ya ain't understood me, gonn'a be slow, won't follow orders, gonn'a want'a fall out. But listen here. Dis is my platoon. I own ya ass. You'll learn to do it right or I will get rid of ya." He turned to leave and then turned back. "Oh, and one more thing. I do not like ya, any of ya, and I don't want ya for a friend, any of ya. Don't try to be nice to me. Stay away. Do not talk with me. Do not come close to me unless ya have to. I do not want to know ya first names. I do not want to know about'sa dog or ya Momma or dat ya girlfriend's pregnant. Stay away from me. See the chaplain if ya want to talk with someone nice. I am Drill Sergeant Willie O. McGee. Stay da fuck away."

The recruit across from me made eye contact and bounced his eyebrows as Sergeant McGee left. I did not acknowledge him but turned to the task of making my bed.

Throughout that day and the next, McGee was with us constantly. Up and down the lines, shouting, cussing, correcting us in our dress and our drill. I stayed in the middle of the platoon, safely out of his way.

The second night, I was brushing my teeth in the latrine when the recruit who bunked across the aisle, the one who had bounced his eyebrows at me, came up to the next sink and started washing his face. "McGee is a rather persuasive fellow," he said. "Direct. I like that in a man."

I turned and smiled, possibly for the first time since I had arrived at the induction center in Raleigh. He said his name was Van Pelt and that he had signed on because he had lost interest in college. He was from Cape Canaveral, Florida, where his father worked as an engineer. He said he was doing fine in school until he got a little sports car and then something happened—all those beach parties and hangovers. He forgot to go to class one semester, so he joined the Army. But, finding the experience rather boorish, he was considering asking for the papers he had signed to see if there was an escape clause. Possibly there was a legitimate breach of contract here. He sought a more casual routine.

Coming into the latrine about the same time was a large black man named Tate [an alias], whom McGee had jumped on that morning for being too slow in reciting his serial number. Another black man going out the door bumped into him and Tate shoved him away, growling. Tate went in the shower room mumbling to himself. Several others came out of the shower quickly, some still lathered with soap, rather than stay in there with that very large, very black, very intimidating man.

The third day we were issued field web gear that we had to display over our lockers—packs, canteens, ammo pouches, canteen belts, and suspenders. We also received helmets, along with their protective steel outer shells called "steel pots." I noticed that one man was having difficulty putting his gear together properly and watched him for several minutes. Even with his GI haircut it was apparent that he was balding. He had a large head, a skinny neck, no shoulders, a pudgy middle, big butt, and short legs. He kept pushing his thick glasses up his nose as he tried to adjust his gear. I resisted an impulse to help him. The chore was so simple, and the fellow seemed so helpless. I decided he was exactly the reason why Cottonpicker had told me to mind my own business during basic training. Van Pelt went over later and arranged the man's web gear for him. He also helped adjust the webbing inside the helmet liner, and with the steel pot encasement in place, Van Pelt put the helmet on the man's head to check the fit. It fit too low and the man looked silly. His big glasses barely showed underneath, plus his neck was so skinny he had trouble holding his head up under the weight of his steel pot. His head wobbling from side to side, he looked like a turkey. Van Pelt continued to make adjustments until he got the helmet to fit properly. The man sat silently as Van Pelt worked. Van Pelt finally left and, after going to his bunk for a moment, came over to my bunk. Looking the other way, he said that he thought the "Professor," a draftee, was out of his element. He said the man smelt a trifle rank, too.

Later we were told to put on our web gear and fall out into formation outside—falling into and out of formation being a large part of our first few days. I noticed that the Professor had his web suspenders twisted in the back. They were the least of his worries, however, because he was having considerable problems as he tried to hold up his head under the steel pot.

Sergeant McGee came up to the formation from the rear and spotted the Professor's twisted suspenders. He walked up to the man and said, "How do ya feel, Molly-Wolly? Don't shake ya head at me, recruit. Do ya hear me, quit shaking ya frigging head!" McGee's face was contorted in anger. "I said goddammit quit shaking ya frigging head." I could see McGee's face soften after a while. "Is ya hat too heavy for ya, Molly-Wolly? Are ya so fucking weak dat ya can't wear a steel pot? Okay, I can understand dat. I can understand." McGee stood there for a moment and looked the Professor in the eye. "But ya know ya look like a smart young fellow to me. I gotta question for ya. How come ya fucking suspenders are twisted? Dat don't take no goddamned strength. Ya got to think, Molly-Wolly, think."

The Professor turned his head to one side, still wobbling from the weight of the steel pot, and I could see tears welling up in his eyes. McGee continued to look into the Professor's face, and he too saw the tears. I quickly turned my gaze to the front as McGee looked around to see who else was watching the man cry.

"Go inside now, double time, and get ya suspenders fixed, soldier, and come back out shere. Now, move out. Now. Go."

My first thought was that McGee was maybe a nice guy. A nasty individual, of the kind he had pretended to be, would have embarrassed the Professor about the tears. McGee told the squad leaders to check each member of their squads to make sure the equipment was on right, and he went into the barracks. The Professor soon came out and regained his place in the formation.

That night at retreat, the Professor fell out of the barracks with his shirttail out of his pants. McGee hesitated as he saw the man awkwardly run by to get in formation, but when he saw the Professor fall in without tucking in his shirt, McGee walked up to him. He told him that he was a disgrace to the platoon, the U.S.

Army, and the human race and, because of that, he was number one on McGee's list of people to watch.

Before lights out that night Van Pelt sat on my bunk and polished his shoes. He said, "Life's relative, you know. It's a proven scientific theory—the theory of relativity. You are judged against your peers. Like, for example, two men in the woods, surprised by a bear, were running away, the bear at their heels, and one man said he sure hoped he was faster than that bear and the other man said, 'I only hope I'm faster'n you.' That guy understood the theory. Wasn't necessary to be the fastest man in the universe there, only the faster of the two of them. The bear got the slow one. You see what I mean, things are relative. Life's relative to the situation. Here at Fort Gordon, it don't help if you're smart or rich, look like a movie star, or got the greatest little sports car in the world back home. Not relative. Takes primitive instincts here. Semideveloped playground skills and the muscle tone of a marathon runner don't hurt either. Don't think the Professor, relatively speaking, is packing the right gear here. He ain't playground material."

The Professor was sitting on his bed, awkwardly bent over, shining his shoes. He stopped often to push his glasses back up his nose. "You know," Van Pelt said with a smile, "it makes me feel better about myself here when I see how out of place the ol' Professor is over there. Relative to him, I'm okay."

I told Van Pelt that it was because he was basically a blunt instrument—primal man, comparable to Tate, the Neanderthal-looking black man. Van Pelt said that was a clever observation. "Not correct," he added, "but a good comment anyway, about a three on a scale of one to five. Above average. Maybe you should be the one dealing with the Professor since you're so clever."

"No," I said, "you are the one with the mother instinct. I'm here to learn to kill."

"You, my friend," said Van Pelt, "are the blunt instrument, but I like you anyway."

The next morning when we fell out for reveille, Sergeant McGee inspected the barracks. He came out and addressed us from the top of the stairs before we marched off to the mess hall.

"Okay, slimeballs, I walked into da barracks just now and hit smelt like a urinal. Like a goddamned piss pot. Ya hear me. A fucking piss pot. Someone peed in dere bed last night!"

McGee was talking so loud that people standing in formation by other barracks could hear.

"Then goddammit made da bed up on top of da stinking piss!" He walked down the stairs and up to the platoon. "My fucking platoon. We got ourselves a bed wetter. In da fucking Army." Softer, meaner, he asked, "Guess who it is?" He walked through the first squad line to the Professor. "Who Molly-Wolly? Who?" McGee fixed a hard, steady look at the man.

"Me, Sergeant," said the Professor softly.

"Ya go in dere while da rest of us are in da chow hall and ya get dat stinking mess and ya exchange it for clean stuff and ya have yar bed made before we get back. And ya take a shower. And, Molly-Wolly, I ain't finished." McGee grabbed his arm. "I am going to help ya get over dis. I'm going to stop ya from wetting da bed. Tonight. Ya'll stop. I'll show ya. I done it before."

That evening, Sergeant McGee walked into the barracks and everyone quickly braced to attention. The drill sergeant's footfalls were loud as he walked toward the Professor's bunk. McGee scowled at him a moment, then went down the line to Tate's bunk. He told the man who slept on the bunk over Tate to trade places with the Professor.

Van Pelt was standing across from me. He pursed his lips and squinted his eyes, as if in pain, when he realized what McGee was doing. Tate was possibly the most ill-tempered individual in the world. Not only did people leave the shower room when he entered, they were reluctant to stand behind him in the chow line for fear they might accidentally bump into him and set him off. He was an animal. No one even tried to get along with him.

After McGee left, Tate grabbed the Professor's T-shirt and told him in words that were hard to understand but whose tone was expressively clear what would happen to him if he peed in the top bunk. One of the black men suggested that Tate kill the honky "right now" rather than later, because he was sure to piss in his sleep again.

The last thing we heard that night after lights out was Tate's muttered warning, "Okay, mudder fucker, wet da bed and I'll knock ya fucking head off, ya hear?"

The next morning the Professor was up and dressed before anyone else. He looked tired. Van Pelt guessed he had not slept at all that night. And he did not sleep the next night. The Professor went on sick call the following morning after breakfast. When we returned from training before lunch, his equipment was gone. We never saw him again.

A couple days later we drew our rifles, the venerable M-14s. As we gathered outside the armory, I inspected my issue and tested its balance. It was an older rifle that had probably been handled by young recruits for years. Its stock had been restained and revarnished many times; the butt plate was scratched from hard landings in the manual of arms. The trigger mechanism was worn from a thousand training disassemblies and assemblies. The weapon looked like a tired old piece of rental equipment with no character, and I remembered the love affair I had with the Springfield at Oak Ridge Military Institute. The shoulder strap was old, tattered webbing, and I tightened it as much as I could so the strap would slap smartly against the stock when I handled it.

McGee called us into ranks and talked about the value of the rifle, the main tool of our trade. He said that before we learned to shoot it, we had to learn to respect it and handle it correctly. Our training for the next couple of days would be in the manual of arms—moving the weapon from the ground at our side, as we stood at attention, to "port arms" and then to "right shoulder arms" and "left shoulder arms" and finally back to the ground, "order arms." I stood in the middle of the platoon and thought about going through the manual of arms a hundred thousand times at Oak Ridge. McGee's description was like explaining the fundamentals of walking to an experienced hiker.

Taking a rifle from a man in the first squad, McGee demonstrated the movements. He gave himself the commands and brought the weapon up and then back to the ground again, with a bit too much waggle in his movement, I thought; he would have been reprimanded at Oak Ridge. Then he talked us through them slowly—count one, port arms; count two, right shoulder arms; count three, back to port arms; count four, left shoulder arms; count five, order arms—before giving the commands at regular speed.

The rifle movement felt familiar, and I slapped the rifle strap as I brought it up and down. I also snapped the butt plate with my thumb as I went to right shoulder arms so that it twisted quickly into the crevice of my shoulder. I was careful to move only my arms and to keep the rest of my body absolutely still, as we had been taught on the drill team. With some pleasure, I noticed that the men in front of me were awkwardly moving their shoulders and heads as they lumbered through the drill. McGee was counting cadence as we repeated the movement. He abruptly stopped counting in mid-movement, and the platoon finished with the random clamoring of metal butt plates hitting the company street.

Out of the corner of my eye I saw McGee looking in my direction. Without a word he came through the first two ranks and stood directly in front of me. He cocked his head to one side and eyed me quizzically.

My face flushed. I had been found out. I had not stayed out of sight, and I had come to McGee's attention. He looked at my name tag, then down at my M-14, and slowly up my uniform back to my face.

"Parker," he said, "do dat again."

I brought the weapon back to my right shoulder, but I did not slap the strap or snap my thumb on the butt plate. McGee told me no, do it again and make it pop, and I did. He told me to come out in front of the platoon and gave me the manual of arms orders there. When I returned the rifle to the ground, he came around in front of me and got very close to my face.

"What's going on here?" he asked. "Where'd ya learn to do dat shit?" I told him military school, and he said, "Huh."

He stepped away and ordered me to do a left face, right face, about face, and then the manual of arms again. I moved with precision. McGee moved in front of me and again said, "Huh."

It was altogether a grand moment, enhanced, I realized, by Van Pelt's explanation of "the theory of relativity." I forced myself not to smile. In the hot Georgia sun that day I had done a simple thing very well, and I felt good about myself.

"I would equate your little majorette act today as the high point so far in our little adventure here," Van Pelt told me. We were sitting on the barracks steps and smoking after the dinner meal. "Life will not be the same for you around here, my friend.

McGee actually said something nice to you. Who knows the consequences."

"What did he say? Tell me again."

"He said, 'Huh,' like in 'Huh, that's pretty good.' He's never said 'Huh' to anyone I know."

At the end of the second week we received classroom instruction on guard duties and the eleven General Orders. We had the weekend and most of the next week to memorize all of the orders. A test was scheduled for the end of the following week. McGee talked to us before we were dismissed that day and said that platoons in the company would be ranked against each other based on the test scores. The General Orders were just simple English sentences. He wanted the platoon to make the best scores in the company, and he ordered everyone to learn the General Orders perfectly. He walked up to Tate and said, "Even ya, fat lips, perfectly. I'm going to call ya out da morning of da test and ya going to recite ya General Orders. And if dis man can do hit—and he's going to do hit—each and every one of ya can learn dese eleven very simple little sentences."

It did not take long to memorize the orders, and I sat on my bunk during study time over the next week and read other manuals. I noticed Tate slowly, painfully reading his General Orders, over and over again. He moved his lips and occasionally squinted his eyes as he focused on a particular phrase or word. After supper the night before the test, he returned to the manual with dogged determination, but his efforts remained the same—slowly reading the orders over and over again. I walked down to his bunk.

"How's it going?"

He looked up quickly, angrily. "Ain't none of ya fucking business," he said. "Why ya wanta know?"

"I know that learning the General Orders can be tough, but there are tricks to memorizing things for tests."

"Fuck ya," he said flatly.

"Listen." I sat down on the end of his bunk, which I got away with because Tate was desperate. "Number one, you got to play games with your mind, Tate. Take General Order number one, for example. I say to myself, what's the first thing I do in the morning? I charge—Charge—out of bed and take a shit on government property. First General Order? To take charge of this post and all government property in view. The second thing I do is to walk—walk back to my bunk by that post near the head and look at everybody. That's the second General Order: to walk my post in a military manner, keeping always on the alert and observing everything that takes place within sight or hearing. First General Order, I charge. Second General Order, I walk. First thing I do in the morning, charge—government property. Second thing I do in the morning, walk—observe."

Tate looked away, but he was listening to me.

"First General Order, to take charge of this post and all government property in view. Come outside in the back and we'll go over the rest. I'm going to smoke a cigarette anyway."

I got up and walked out by the latrine. The only light outside came from the barracks door. I sat on the stairs and lit a cigarette. Tate soon appeared at the door and walked down the few stairs to where I was sitting.

"What's the first thing you do in the morning?" I asked without looking his way.

"I charge out da bed for a shit on government property."

We went over each order, making nonsense out of them, but connecting them in sequence. Slowly at first and then with confidence he repeated them in order, then randomly as I called out the numbers. I told him he would do fine the next day and went inside and went to bed.

The next morning McGee called Tate in front of the platoon and asked him to give the fifth General Order. Tate hesitated a moment, then spoke clearly and loudly, "To quit my post only when properly relieved, Sergeant."

McGee asked him the seventh and Tate responded quickly, "To talk to no one except in the line of duty, Sergeant."

McGee said "Huh" as he backed away from Tate and looked at him. He sent Tate back into ranks and walked up to Van Pelt. "OK, Molly-Wolly, what's da fucking tenth General Order?"

Van Pelt hesitated. Then in a short burst he said, "To give the alarm in case of fire or disorder, Sergeant."

"Asshole, dat's da eighth fucking order, you jack shit Molly-Wolly idiot!" Out of the corner of my eye I could see Tate smiling despite himself, as he rocked back and forth slightly on his heels.

At breakfast Van Pelt asked me if I thought being a "jack shit Molly-Wolly idiot" was hereditary.

The next week Cassius Clay was to fight Sonny Liston for the heavyweight championship of the world, and Tate and I decided that Liston would break Clay's smart-ass face. Liston was a three-to-one favorite, and it was hard to get a bet on Clay in our company. I offered five-to-one. Ten dollars on Clay would get fifty if he won, and I had some takers. No money passed hands before the fight, but Van Pelt kept the books. I had almost five hundred dollars of my money at risk, having taken in one hundred dollars in committed bets on Clay. I was slightly over-extended; we were making only eighty-four dollars a month as army privates. I would be about three hundred dollars short if Liston lost, but I saw no problem. Liston was absolutely a sure bet. Tate promised to help me collect.

We listened to the fight on the radio. Liston did not answer the bell for the seventh round—despite my desperate yells—and I was suddenly surrounded by people who wanted to collect on their bets. I had to scurry around that night and borrow money from McDiarmid, Tate, and Van Pelt to cover my losses. Van Pelt said it was a typical lowlife maneuver to lay long odds on a loser. He reckoned it did not bode well for my life as a risk taker, as in being a soldier or fighting a war. To do any soldiering, one needed to be lucky. He wasn't sure this line of work was up my alley—"You lost five hundred dollars—that's more than you make in six months, you dumb Molly-Wolly."

Tate became something of a shadow, sitting beside me in class and in the mess hall. He simply had no social skills, and I often acted as his spokesman. In turn, he provided security and an in-timidating presence to others when we were together, an enhanced status not lost on Sergeant McGee. I was awarded "Outstanding Trainee" at graduation from basic training. As we were packing up to go to separate advanced infantry training (AIT) companies, I went down to Tate's bunk. He was reading a comic book. I wished him well in life. "Yeah," he said, but he did not smile, as if our brief friendship was over and he was going back to his more hostile, antisocial nature, the only way he knew to meet the challenges ahead.

Along with many other recruits, Van Pelt and I put in for Officer Candidate School (OCS) during the last week of basic training. We were together in AIT and, during a slow training session, began exchanging notes. In one convoluted, pseudointellectual analogy, I took the position of a weed in life, ugly by urban standards but durable and adaptive. Van Pelt claimed that if I was a weed, he was a flower, cultured and beautiful—a more attractive standard. Our notes were crazy, surreal flights of fantasy, and we worried occasionally what our drill sergeants might think if they read them, especially when I found out my friend's entire given name and began addressing him as "Miss Elmer Lee Van Pelt the Third, the Flower Child."

Within weeks of starting AIT, people in our company began to get rejection notices on their OCS applications. The notices were form letters sent regular mail. This made mail call after retreat at night very tense. I looked forward to letters from home, but hated to hear my name called for fear it would be the rejection notice. It was like Russian roulette.

One night after supper I went over to Van Pelt's barracks. He was sitting on his bed writing a letter. As usual, he smiled broadly as we talked about our planned weekend together in Augusta, Georgia, home of the Masters and blue-eyed southern belles who "luved" skinhead GIs from Fort Gordon. I was leaving when he said, "Hey, weed, this came in the mail to me tonight." He tossed his OCS rejection notice on the bunk. He went back to writing as I read the form letter. He looked up after a while and shrugged his shoulders. I left without a word.

When AIT training was completed, Van Pelt received his orders to an infantry unit. I did not see him when he came to my barracks to say good-bye; I had been sent on detail across post. When I returned the following note was on my bunk:

Jim, You weed, you low, scummy, slimy, slob
of a worthless infectious grub. Despair ingrate,
the beauty and inspiration which you leaned on
like a crutch has left you, leaving you to wallow
in the crud of your mind, like a snake in the mud.
Crawl weed, wither and die. Love, beauty, fun,
happiness is gone. The flower has triumphed, herd

your miasmic children, change their pants, and tell
them their stories, you pimp, weed. Ugh! Leave
the world and all its charms to men, not nursemaids,
scouts. Ha! I despise you, fool. Wilt weed,
there is nothing left, don't try to retaliate,
it's too late. I tried to show you the light,
now you must burn. Weed, burn bright, and perhaps,
for once in your inglorious, dark, misery laden life
a bright spot might shine. Burn Weed. Burn.

After AIT almost eighty of us were still awaiting disposition
of our OCS applications. We were assigned to two barracks near
my AIT training company. I was given temporary corporal rank,
which I wore on a band around my upper-right sleeve, and assigned to a basic training company as an assistant DI (drill instructor) or "gofer," as in commands from the regular DIs, "Hey,
shithead! Go for this, or go for that."

Almost every day, someone in our group received a rejection
notice from OCS. When we came in at night another mattress
would be folded back and the bed coverings gone—like tombstones of the departed.

Five weeks after I graduated from AIT we heard that someone
across post in another holding company had been accepted to
OCS for the November 1964 class. Following that first accep-
tance, we all had new hope, but then came a spate of rejection
notices. Our eighty-man group was reduced to twenty. One barracks was closed, and we finally moved down to a single floor.
Every night another mattress was turned down. We continued to
hear of other candidates being accepted, but no one in our group
had been selected.

I came in one night from a long march with the basic training company and found a notice to see the first sergeant at our
holding-company headquarters. He and I had had a run-in during the previous week over the weekend duty roster, and he had
threatened to put a reprimand in my OCS application folder. He
was an unlikable, crass individual and I knew the message to see
him was related to extra duty that weekend. He was in the company commander's office when I entered the orderly room. The
door was open and the commander caught my eye and motioned

me into his office. I was sweaty and dirty from the road march and regretted not cleaning up before answering the first sergeant's summons, but I walked in and saluted. The commander stuck out his hand and said, "Congratulations." I had been accepted for the November OCS class.

—— TWO ——

Command Training

On November 15, 1964, after home leave, I drove my uncle's maroon 1949 Ford from Southern Pines to the Infantry Officer Candidate School at Fort Benning, Georgia. Parked across the street from the three-story barracks of the OCS company I was to join, I sat silently smoking as I watched new OCS candidates arrive. Immediately, they were set upon and summarily hazed by both the senior candidates in blue helmet liners and the more lethal commissioned officers assigned to the school as instructors. The officers, referred to as "Tac officers," were cool predators, hanging back in the shadows until they decided on a new candidate to attack. They walked up to a new man, called him to attention over some slight, got close to him and talked angrily—sometimes fast but sometimes, for effect, very slowly. Even from where I sat it was apparent that the comments of the Tac officers were hard-hitting, as they evoked painful grimaces from the candidates.

I resolved to ignore them—that had been Cottonpicker's advice. Show no emotion, take nothing personal, find out what you are expected to do, and do it. "It's not a personality contest," he had said. "OCS is a six-month test to find the fuckups. That's it. Don't fuck up. You got it more'n half licked getting to the school. That's the hard part. Don't fuck up. Don't try too hard. They'll try to break you down, you're going to get tired and sometimes you're going to want to quit, just keep on. Don't show emotion. Keep on. Don't fuck up."

I put out my cigarette, got my duffel bag out of the trunk, and walked across the street. As I expected, I was immediately attacked by blue-helmeted upperclassmen. I stood at attention and responded to their loud orders to get my chin in, suck in my gut, straighten up my back, get my gig line straight.

"I saw you sitting in the car across the street, candidate."

Someone had come up to my right side and was talking into my ear. His voice was lower but clearer than those of the upperclassmen yelling in my face about my shave and haircut. I could feel the man's breath.

"I do not know why you were sitting in your car for so long, but I do not like it."

The man moved in front of me, his nose a couple of inches from mine. The blue-helmeted upperclassmen moved aside, as if getting out of the way so the big dog could eat.

"I do not like sneaky people. The Army wants its officers to be upright. Men of character." He continued to speak in a low, soft voice. "You, I am going to watch very closely. This is no joke, candidate. I don't like you. I am going to get you out of here. You are finished before you start because you're a sneak. You're finished, I guarantee it. I'm going to kick your sniveling little young ass out. I'm gonna do it. I promise."

I looked straight ahead into the distance and did not focus on the Tac officer in front of me. I tried to show no emotion. He stepped back.

"Look at me. Look at my face. Look at my name. I am Tactical Officer Lieutenant Taylor. Every time you see me for the next week—every time you see me—drop down and give me twenty push-ups. You understand? It's going to be my way of telling you to get out."

"Yes, sir," I shouted.

"Drop now, and count them out loud."

I did the push-ups. When I got back to my feet beside my duffel bag, Taylor was gone.

Eventually I made my way into the orderly room and was assigned to the fourth platoon on the third floor. As I tried to go up the stairs I was constantly assaulted by blue-helmeted upperclassmen yelling, "Up against the wall, candidate," or "Give me ten, candidate."

Later that first day we were called out to formation, and the ever-yelling upperclassmen arranged us alphabetically, by platoon. Standing as still as possible to avoid harassment, I could see from their name tags that a Nesse was on my right and a Particelli on my left. I did not know or care to know the names of anyone else in the platoon.

After a time, the blue-helmeted men moved behind us and a slight, serious-looking young officer moved in front of the platoon.

"My name is Lieutenant Joseph C. Hailey," he said in a conversational tone. "I am the 4th Platoon tactical officer. The U.S. Army has asked me to find out who among you isn't qualified to be an officer. And you know what, most of you aren't. Not," he said, with emphasis, "because you aren't smart. You are all smart. Not," he said, again with emphasis, "because you don't want to be officers. You all do. No, most of you are not qualified because of," he paused for emphasis, "need. The U.S. Army just doesn't have much room in the officer corps right now. It doesn't matter if you are all relatives of MacArthur or Eisenhower, the Army doesn't need us to manufacture many second lieutenants. They're going to take the West Pointers and the ROTC grads first, and this year there're plenty. So there are not many openings. Sorry," he said. "It's just the way it is. Most of you are going to be weeded out."

At the end of the first week we were introduced to the most insidious aspect of the weeding-out process—the infamous "bayonet" sheets, in which everyone ranked everyone else in the platoon. Every Friday each member of the platoon submitted, on a single sheet of notebook paper, names of all the other men in the platoon listed in order, according to the way we judged their individual officer potential. The man we thought would make the best officer was number one, the man we thought was least qualified was last. The "bayonet" sheet got its name because of the knife job that one could do on his contemporaries. With thirty-five people in the platoon submitting a bayonet sheet every week for eleven weeks, a lot of evaluation was developed. The total process, called peer or student rating, counted for much in assessing the overall officer potential of each candidate.

There were exacting, almost impossible, housekeeping standards in OCS, certainly more demanding than anything I had known in military school, basic training, or AIT. We lived in two-man rooms. My roommate, an older, former noncommissioned officer, and I spent our first weekend shining every square of our linoleum tile floor with hard wax and spit. We cut cardboard within a fraction of an inch to fit inside our clothes on display in our wall locker and chest of drawers. We used a ruler to get our boots lined up properly under our beds and to get the right distance between items of clothing in the closet. We Brassoed the door hinges, washed the windows, polished our desks, and cleaned every piece of our equipment.

On Monday morning, Tac Officer Taylor came in and dumped our stuff in the middle of the floor. Despite myself, I pursed my lips and said "Shit" under my breath. Taylor whipped around.

"What did you say, candidate? Did I hear you say something? This candidate cursed me, I do believe. I will see you in formation."

There, he called me out of ranks and ordered me to run around the company as it marched toward Building No. 4, where we had most of our classes. This was not easy, especially when I had to cut across the front of the marching company. Taylor called me back into the rear ranks of the fourth platoon before we reached the building. When we stopped, one of the candidates near me said, "I think that man out there likes you."

"You want an introduction?" I responded.

"Nope," he half-whispered back, "I don't want him to know my name."

When we received the order to fall out to class, I looked at the candidate who had spoken. His name was Larry (Pete) Peterson, and I learned later that he was from Lincoln, Nebraska. Before coming to OCS he had been the PFC driver for the commander of a medical battalion at the Fort Benning hospital. Of medium build, he was wholesome looking, straightforward, and he cackled when he laughed.

Tac Officer Taylor's attentions continued. Pete thought it was because Taylor sensed—right or wrong—that I had a cocky attitude. Pete worked with me on appearing humble, but finally gave up. "You're just an asshole, I reckon, and Taylor seems to know that."

When I was assigned as platoon leader and had to march the platoon to an assembly area on the athletic field, Lieutenant Taylor walked briskly at my side. During most of the march he yelled obscenities, particularly as I prepared to give commands to the platoon.

Early the following week we had our first written test on leadership. Although it required reading during our study period at night, I had used my time to surreptitiously clean my equipment, that being Lieutenant Taylor's focus of the week with me. Just before lights out the night before the test, I told Pete I wasn't ready; I was just going to have to wing it. Ten minutes after lights out I heard a "psssss" by the door to my room. It was Pete. He told me to get the blanket from the foot of my bed and follow him into the latrine. As we huddled under the blanket in the showers, Pete shared his notes.

Because of Pete, I passed the test the next day.

Sometime later that week we made a pledge to help each other get through OCS. There was strength in numbers, we said. Thereafter I made him number one on my bayonet sheet. Pete ran interference for me whenever Lieutenant Taylor was around and tried to distract him. This often cost him push-up punishment. When Pete's roommate dropped out, I moved in with him.

We worked well together, Pete and I, though we both had a sense of fun and irreverence that was a liability. As the weeks progressed we became more accepting of the traditional OCS hazing and no longer took the constant harassment personally, except with Taylor.

Classroom instruction was interspersed with field exercises, with emphasis on leadership training. According to our instructors, our effectiveness as future infantry officers depended on our ability to motivate and lead men. Respect, fairness, humor, poise, determination, confidence, and empathy were characteristics of good leaders. Vanity, laziness, and sarcasm were not. Smart-asses don't make good leaders, we were told. Peterson looked at me and shook his head.

Veterans of World War II and the Korean War spoke to us about the demands on a small-unit commander in combat. One old gnarled NCO said personal courage was essential in leading men under fire. A good combat leader had to be a natural risk taker or he had to summon from within the will to get in harm's way—either way, courage appeared the same. To do their jobs in war, infantry officers must be courageous, and South Vietnam was our likely testing ground.

"South what?" someone asked.

"South Vietnam," the veteran said, "is a small jungle country in the Orient and American soldiers are fighting and dying there."

I had heard Vietnam mentioned occasionally during basic and AIT training, but it was never discussed outside the classrooms that I remember. However, it seemed more relevant now, and we talked about it among ourselves during the next break. Everyone pronounced it differently.

"What are we doing in Vieeet-nammmm, really?" someone asked.

"Killing Commies," someone else said.

"Okay, that's legal."

At the end of the eleventh week at OCS, all candidates faced an evaluation. Those who fell below a certain rating had to go before a panel, ostensibly to defend their records. In fact, candidates who were paneled were usually kicked out of the program or recycled to another company, regardless of what they said. It was the weeding-out process at work.

The panel was scheduled for Friday morning, 29 January 1965.

On Wednesday morning before the panel we fell out for a Physical Training run, although the rumor circulated that it was to test endurance and would have a bearing on those selected for the panel.

Wearing T-shirts, fatigue pants, and boots, we left the company area and shuffled along in formation. A candidate at the side led us in marching songs. It was a warm morning and Pete and I were shuffling along side by side, singing. Occasionally we would windmill our arms. Ah, it was good to be young and in shape. We could take the run.

We trotted out to one of the rifle ranges along a dusty tank trail. The dust became more of a problem as time went on. As we approached the rifle ranges, the candidate singing cadence fell back into ranks because we expected to take a break when we arrived. There were endurance runs, and there were death marches.

Several Tac officers, however, were standing poised in the assembly area of the rifle ranges. An ambulance was parked in the shade next to a couple of deuce-and-a-half (two-and-a-half-ton) trucks. It did not look good. "Damn if it don't look like an execution squad," I told Pete. "Them trucks for the dead bodies, you reckon?"

The Tac leading us fell out. Lieutenant Taylor took the lead and told the guidon bearer to follow him. He made a big circle on the rifle range, then headed the company back toward our barracks, almost seven miles away.

Taylor came back to the middle of the company file and told us that we were not to kill ourselves. An ambulance was right behind us, and the deuce-and-a-halfs would take the dropouts back to the company. "No problem," he said. "If you can't go on, stop. No problem." And he smiled at me. "I'm talking to you, Parker. Drop out, it'll be okay."

The formation began to break down. Some of the older candidates fell back as the young bucks moved to the front. Pete and I kept our places.

By the time we had run ten miles—seven out and three back—we were back on pavement again and the dust ceased being a problem, but we were thirsty and becoming more and more leg weary. "Keep going," Pete said. "We're almost home, more than half finished." Behind us, members of the company stretched out into the distance.

Taylor turned us off on a side road and then off onto a firebreak, and we started shuffling up a long, bumpy hill. Pete and I began to fall back—save our strength, we told ourselves. We didn't have to finish first.

As we made the hill, Taylor and some of the candidates pulled ahead, and we stumbled down the other side. Then we climbed another hill—and another and another—until we were on the paved road again. Taylor was five city blocks ahead of us.

Pete and I kept repeating that we could make it. We could see the barracks. We could make it. We were not going to be paneled. We were going to make it.

When Taylor reached the company assembly area, he dropped out and fresh Tacs led the first of the candidates around the barracks and out toward a PT field in the distance.

We were not stopping at the company. We were not almost finished. My feet suddenly felt ten pounds heavier. Pete cursed under his breath. I glanced at him. He looked like death—filthy, sweaty, bloodshot eyes, face contorted in fatigue, mouth open with dirt crusted around the edges. He started repeating, "We ain't quitting, we ain't quitting." I began to say it, but it took precious breath, so I stopped.

We stumbled through the company area to the PT field and around the quarter-mile track and then back to the company area, where the run mercifully ended. Pete and I fell out on the grass and gasped for breath. We came up on our elbows and smiled at each other. A deuce-and-a-half pulled up with the woebegone candidates who had fallen out.

After retreat the following day, two Tac officers took their platoons off to the side of the company assembly area and read out the names of the candidates being paneled the next morning. Two other Tacs posted names on the walls in the individual platoon areas.

Lieutenant Hailey, our Tac officer, wasn't around, and we found nothing posted in our area.

During supper, word circulated about the "panelees": it was a massacre. Half of the 2d, 3d, and 6th Platoons were going and almost all of the young guys in the 5th Platoon. I looked around the mess hall and could easily spot them. They ate with their heads down or were not eating at all, just looking straight ahead. No one talked with them. Those of us from the two platoons who hadn't heard anything were afraid to offer condolences because that would challenge fate. Didn't want to get too close to the panelees—bad luck. They were untouchables.

Pete and I finished our meal and went to our room. As we had always done, in order to protect the shine of the floor in the center of our room, we took one step in and then stepped onto my bed. Pete continued around the room by stepping on the desks and down to his bunk against the far wall without setting foot on the floor. Lying on our bunks, we stared at the ceiling and made wild comments ranging from dark and negative to confident and optimistic. We remembered Hailey's admonition that first day, that few would graduate, and agreed that we had to have an attitude about what was going on, something to cling to until we heard who was going.

"It's for the best, whatever happens, it's for the best, that's going to be our policy," Pete said.

At one point we were convinced that one or the other of us wouldn't make it, so we resolved that whoever stayed in OCS would not say he was sorry to the other. If both of us got paneled, we'd be out of the place that weekend and could get some girls, have some fun. It wouldn't be so bad. Cottonpicker would have said that the world wasn't coming to an end. Some mighty good people from the other platoons were paneled. We would be in good company.

Pete's bunk faced the door. Suddenly he yelled, "Attention!" He was unusually frantic in getting to his feet, and I followed quickly, wide-eyed.

Lieutenant Taylor stood in the doorway with the right corner of his mouth turned up in a humorless, mean half-smile. He looked me in the eye, turned, and left.

I did not say anything for several minutes. My stomach hurt. Pete told me to lie back down, that it was nothing to worry about.

"Hailey makes up the list," he said. "This guy is just trying to make your life miserable. Forget him."

I wasn't listening. I was thinking that it was all I could do to keep myself upbeat about the panel thing anyway, and Taylor shows up. He probably knew who was going from our platoon, and his smile, his "I've got the last laugh," made it pretty clear to me that I was on the list.

When the bell sounded for mandatory study, Pete and I got up and sat at our desks, but we continued to talk. Where was Hailey?

We heard someone come in through the swinging doors off the stairwell and walk slowly down the hallway of the platoon area. Our door was open. We thought we recognized Hailey's casual walk, but we did not look up. He walked down to the end of the hall and back toward our door. We heard him address one of the hardest working but least personable of the candidates in our platoon and softly ask him to come down to the first floor. Hailey walked to the stairwell, opened the swinging doors, and was gone. We looked up when the dejected candidate walked by our door. He was gone for what seemed a long time, but probably no more than five minutes. When he returned, he walked slowly down the hall to the room next to ours, told a candidate there that

Hailey wanted to see him, and then walked heavily to his own room. Next, we watched our neighbor make his way slowly past our door, and the process continued.

Thirty-three men were in our platoon when Hailey called out the first man that night. Pete and I agreed that the first ten men to go downstairs—all upstanding young men—probably were relatively low in the platoon ranking. The eleventh man to be called I had always placed toward the top of my bayonet sheet. Surely, I thought, he ranked higher than I did. If he's gone now, I must be next. A third of the platoon is gone. I'm next.

When he came back, he was crying. He walked quickly down the hall to a room near the end, and his voice broke as he called out the name of another candidate.

Pete's face immediately contorted in pain. That guy, also from the Midwest, was a friend of his. They had known each other before OCS, and Pete thought they stacked up somewhat equally.

Pete and I sucked in our breath when we heard the swinging door open five minutes later. The candidate walked slowly. Pete noted, in a tense voice, that he was walking on our side of the hall. We looked at each other without moving. The candidate stopped before he got to our room. He didn't call for anyone, but just stopped. Then he started walking again, came up to our door, and stopped again. He was looking in at us.

"Pete," he said, sadly.

But Pete was not paneled. His friend had stopped to say that he had tried as hard as he could and had no regrets.

We went on to graduate, Pete and I. In fact, not long after the eleventh week panel most of the hazing subsided and we focused more on field tactics. South Vietnam and guerrilla warfare were mentioned more and more, though our training was never tailored to nonconventional combat. Only when we received training in patrolling did we get a firsthand account of what was going on in Vietnam. Our instructor had recently returned from a tour as adviser to a South Vietnamese Ranger battalion. He told war stories, both in the classroom and during breaks, and said that the army did not train its troops to fight in the jungles of Southeast Asia—he didn't know why.

A few days after patrol training we had the opportunity to put in for additional schools after OCS. Thinking of Cottonpicker, I asked for paratrooper training.

Our assignments were posted on a bulletin board the week of graduation. I got jump school and an eventual assignment to the 1st Infantry Division at Fort Riley, Kansas. Pete was also assigned to the 1st Infantry Division, or as it was more commonly called, The Big Red One, because of its storied tradition as a bloodied combat unit.

Pete and I danced a jig. We were together, going to a tough line outfit. Others around us suggested that we get married.

Mother, Daddy, and my little sister Kathy came down for graduation. Maj. Gen. John Heintges gave the commencement address. He congratulated us on our commissions and went on to say something to this effect: "You have been specifically, individually selected to protect our Constitution and the dignity of our country against all enemies. You do this—you are charged with doing this, expected to do this—without any reservation. You must be willing to die to do your job. Your commission has no meaning without that commitment."

As excited as I was, trying to keep up with everything going on that day, I heard the general's words clearly, as if he were speaking directly to me. I was oblivious to the hundreds of people in that auditorium. No one else was there—only General Heintges on the stage, and me sitting alone in the middle of all the seats when he said, "You have been selected to protect the dignity of the United States. If necessary, die fighting . . . You . . . You."

Sitting in the auditorium as if I were alone, I thought, "Yeap, I'm your man. I'll take the risks. I'll do the job."

Later, Dad pinned second-lieutenant bars on my shoulders. The words of General Heintges still ringing in my ears, I stood tall and felt a tremendous sense of self-worth and dedication.

As a graduation present, Daddy and Mother gave me two thousand dollars. When I returned to Southern Pines on two weeks' home leave before jump training, I went out in search of a 190SL Mercedes convertible. Pete was a sports car enthusiast, had an Alfa Romeo, and had made the case a thousand times that dollar for dollar, pound for pound, the 190SL was the best sports car on the road.

So I looked for a 190SL. A used-car dealer in Raleigh had heard of one on a small lot in South Carolina, and I drove down in one of Daddy's trucks that afternoon.

I came around a curve on the country road. There on the edge of a field ahead was a 1957 190SL Mercedes convertible. It was love at first sight. Graceful, continental—what was it doing on a South Carolina dirt farm? The farmer/dealer said he had bought it at an auction and did not know its history. I bought it for fifteen hundred dollars, pulled it back to Southern Pines that afternoon, and was racing along country roads near home late that night with the top down and a beer between my legs.

I went out most nights during my leave and usually didn't return home until early in the morning, sometime after the sun had come up, but I hung around Mom and Dad and my sisters during the day. I took Mom shopping in the Mercedes. She squealed as we scooted along the streets and occasionally waved at the townspeople.

Returning to Fort Benning for jump training, I checked into the bachelor officers quarters (BOQ) at the school and played poker that night with some of the newly commissioned officers from my OCS company. We were now making the unheard-of amount of $242.42 per month. Some of the new officers lost a whole month's pay in the poker game. The following morning when we started airborne PT training, my former classmates and I realized that we were in better shape than anyone else. We ran the last leg of an endurance run backward and the jump instructors criticized us, but we found it was hard to be humble and intimidated after a half year of OCS training.

We did become humble, however, when we started tower training prior to our first airborne jump. We became even more humble the first time out of a plane. I was in the middle of the "stick" of men along one side of the plane for my first jump. I ran out the door and do not remember anything until my chute opened, jerking me back to my senses. The ground came up so quickly that I froze and landed with a bone-jarring thud. The next time out I had a sense of doom as I jumped. I felt little relief when my canopy opened, because I knew that I still had the thud ahead. The third time, unfortunately, I was the stick leader. As we neared the drop zone, the jump master went through the jump commands. When he reached "Stand in the door," I stood with my hands outside the door frame, helmet hitched tight, loaded with parachute main and reserve plus combat gear, one foot slightly in front of the other, head up to watch the red light under the wing outside, ready to jump when it turned green, and I waited and waited. I looked down and the sky was filled with chutes as jumpers from other planes were descending to the ground, and then I looked back to the light, but it stayed red and the jump master yelled that we were too far over the jump zone and had to come around again. I stood in the door as we flew over trees and a lone country blacktop road and some houses. My legs, tense from standing at the ready, began to ache and then started to shake, so I relaxed them and continued to look down. I began to lose the feeling that anything could stop me from falling out of the door to the ground below, and I suddenly lost all enthusiasm for jumping. I stood there paralyzed with fear and the drop zone came into view and the jump master yelled for me to get ready, but my grip on the door remained loose and I swayed back and forth. The light turned green, the jump master yelled "Go!" and I just stood there, and the jump master yelled again "Go! Go!" and something hit me squarely on the butt. I was out the door, tumbling, then jerked up when the canopy opened, and the ground rushed up and I landed with the most jarring thud yet. I hit so hard that my teeth hurt. Mercifully, no one ever mentioned my hesitation. Cottonpicker would not have been proud.

The Saturday after our third jump I was at the bar in the main officers club when President Lyndon B. Johnson delivered a speech to the nation. Sitting at his desk in the Oval Office, he began by saying, "My fellow Americans, we have been called on to stem the tide of Communist aggression in Southeast Asia. I have today ordered the 1st Cavalry (Airmobile) Division at Fort Benning, Georgia, to Vietnam."

Some officers in the bar cheered. A colonel bought a round of drinks, and the bar buzzed with excitement. Men came in from the dining room and were told the news. Some scurried out to make telephone calls; others, especially those from the 1st Cavalry (Cav), left for their units.

I tried to call Pete at Fort Riley to find out if the 1st Infantry Division was on alert, but couldn't get through. The next day Fort Benning was alive with troop movements. Tanks moved through areas they had never been in before. Truck convoys clogged the streets.

Monday started our last week at jump school. We had two more jumps to make, one at night, but they were anticlimactic. The real interest was in the buildup of the 1st Cav for deployment to South Vietnam. The base was on a war footing. There was a sense of breathless anticipation.

We made the last two jumps. Neither of mine was noted for artistic performance. Both hurt when I landed. I was proud to get my wings, but I was sure that I had developed a fear of heights and had no interest in making future jumps. Graduation was on a Friday afternoon. By nightfall I was on my way to Fort Riley and assignment to the 1st Infantry Division.

I went over again and again what I planned to say to the men of my platoon at our first meeting. Though we had had numbing hours of lectures on leadership at OCS, I thought back to conversations with Dad and Cottonpicker, and remembered lines I had heard in movies and read at college. As I developed phrases that seemed appropriately firm and yet reasonable, I remembered General Heintges's comments at OCS graduation and felt a sense of destiny.

I drove with the top down most of the way and the radio turned up. Occasionally I would just howl with joy and pump my fist at the moon.

Arriving at Fort Riley late Saturday night, I got Pete's BOQ room number from the post locator and woke him up. We went to a seedy after-hours beer joint in nearby Junction City, Kansas, and talked. Pete said that the entire division was on alert, although most of the able-bodied men had been grouped into the 2d Brigade, which was being readied as the first for deployment to Vietnam. Pete was in the 1st Brigade and had asked an old enlisted friend who worked in division personnel to have me assigned to his battalion.

Early Monday morning I was not surprised to learn at 1st Division headquarters that I had, in fact, been assigned to Pete's battalion, and by mid-morning I was checking in with battalion

Sgt. Maj. William (Bill) G. Bainbridge. Friendly but firm, his look clearly said, "Second lieutenants do not outrank me, so mind your manners." Respectfully, I asked him for a platoon beside Pete. The sergeant major looked at me for a long moment, shrugged, nodded his head yes, and within minutes I was walking down to Company A, 1st Battalion, 28th Infantry Regiment, 1st Brigade, 1st Infantry Division—Capt. John (Jack) E. Woolley, Commanding.

The buildings in the company area were built during World War II. Four barracks, two stories each, on the right of the company street, orderly room and mess hall on the left. An old oak tree provided shade for the orderly room. Woolley was behind his desk when I walked into his office and saluted. He greeted me warmly and said that I had the 3d Platoon, Peterson had the 4th, Joseph L. Duckett the 1st, and Ray A. Ernst the 2d.

At sunrise the following morning I stood under the oak tree and smoked as the men fell out for reveille. Captain Woolley, tall and tan, was already on the scene. At breakfast, Pete pointed out some of the men in my platoon—they looked sloppy, undisciplined. My platoon sergeant was an old World War II veteran who was sleepwalking, according to Pete, and rarely spent time with the platoon. Pete thought that, in all, there were only about a dozen sick, lame, or lazy men in my platoon. All the able-bodied soldiers had already been pulled out for the 2d Brigade. Not much of a first command, I thought, disappointed.

I met the other platoon leaders over breakfast. Duckett was a large black second lieutenant from Philadelphia who had driven a cab to pay his college tuition. He was quiet but not shy, and had a toughness to his manner that was unfamiliar to me. Ray Ernst was a small, deliberate South Dakotan. He was, surprisingly, a natural companion to Duckett. They just went together, like a longtime married couple.

Captain Woolley joined us at the head of the table and easily, naturally, assumed the leader role. He expected deference to his rank and position, but he listened when we spoke and had a reassuring confidence about himself. A friendly, articulate man who led through the strength of his personality, I immediately felt privileged to be under his command.

After breakfast, as I walked down to the 3d Platoon's barracks, I went over my introduction speech. I had added, since seeing some of my men at breakfast, that I did not tolerate sloppy attitudes and expected close attention to military deportment. We faced the prospect of imminent deployment to a theater of war; beginning this morning we were going to shape up.

I took a deep breath on the barracks steps. Another benchmark in my life, I thought, as I went in to "meet my men." Tough but fair was the image I wanted. I walked in with a stern expression on my face.

Loud music coming from a radio in the latrine competed with another radio on another station to the rear of the bay area. Nine men were lounging around. A few turned and gazed disinterestedly at me. A fat private got off a bunk to my right and called attention, but it produced little response from the others. One soldier lying on a bunk with the mattress folded back closed his eyes and made snoring sounds. Another, cigarette dangling from his hand, continued to lean on a broom. A Latino wearing a towel and combing his hair came out of the latrine, looked at me and then around at the other men.

"My name is Lieutenant Parker," I began, "your new platoon leader."

"Who's this guy?" asked the Latino.

"Shut up, everybody," from the fat guy.

I turned to him. "You want to wake that guy up down there and go turn off those radios?"

He walked away, shaking the snorer first, then headed to the radio at the rear. I heard someone say, "Touch my radio and I cut your fat ass."

The Latino said, "Can I get dressed before you start talking, siirrr?"

It wasn't starting out the way I had in mind, but Manuel, the fat guy, eventually turned off the radios, the Latino got dressed, the snorer got to his feet, and the man with the broom put it down and finished his cigarette. I asked them something about themselves. Each had a reason for not being sent to the 2d Brigade. Some were finishing their enlistments and leaving service within a month or so, others were awaiting court-martial, some were sick and lame, or claimed to be. Manuel was fat.

I had a speech ready, so I let it go, but it was lost on this audience, except for Manuel. I ended by saying, "No one skates anymore in this platoon, even if you have only a week left in the army. Until you receive your orders, you belong to me." As I turned to leave, someone turned on a radio.

I told Pete that my group couldn't fight a cold.

—— THREE ——

Marshaling for War

Troops from U.S. Army units in Germany and Korea arrived at Fort Riley. The misfits in my platoon and throughout the battalion were sent to a holding company at the hospital. Sgt. Cecil W. Bratcher arrived and was assigned to my platoon as 1st Squad leader. Slightly stoop shouldered, he had a facial tic that tensed the muscles in his neck and jerked his jaw to the right. He reminded me of Cottonpicker, however, when he walked up closer to me than necessary, saluted, smiled, and introduced himself. Within days I had Woolley transfer my original, timid platoon sergeant to company headquarters so that Bratcher could take over the job.

One morning after a load of new replacements arrived, Woolley called me to his office.

"Got a new rifleman here that I'm going to assign to your platoon, but, ah, he, ah, he's, I'm not sure how long he's going to be around." Woolley continued to look down at a paper on his desk as he talked. Not yet completely comfortable around the company commander, I stood awkwardly in front of his desk.

"He's scheduled for a dishonorable discharge. Just got out of the brig for shooting a man—apparently he was dorking this man's wife and got caught. He's an ex–M.P. Sergeant E-5 before his court-martial. He's here, best I can tell, because of some administrative mistake—all the bodies being moved around, he got out of a line to get kicked out of the service into a line of replacements for the 1st Division. His name is Private Wiler Beck. Keep an eye on him until we decide what to do with him."

I called Beck off to the side shortly after Woolley ̶ ̶ ̶signed him to my platoon to tell him that he proba̶ ̶ ̶ould not be around long, that as far as I knew his dis̶ ̶ ̶ ̶rable discharge was still being processed. A big, burly man in his mid-twenties, he stood as tall as he could and with a stoic, implacable look on his face, said, "Sir, I bribed my way here from the holding company at Fort Leavenworth. I don't want a DD. I want to go to Vietnam with the 1st Division. I won't let you down."

Beck was, in fact, a very good soldier, though he was assertive by nature and tended to be the first and the loudest with an opinion—a private with a sergeant's attitude. He carried an M-79 grenade launcher like a war club.

A month after I arrived the battalion was at full strength. President Johnson gave another televised talk beginning with "My fellow Americans." Pete and I were at our favorite bar in Junction City that night and didn't hear the broadcast live. When we got back to the BOQ around midnight, people gathered in the dayroom were talking excitingly.

"We're going to Vietnam," someone told us as we walked in. He was excited to be telling someone who didn't know.

"Who?" I asked.

"The whole damn 1st Infantry Division. President Johnson just said so. We're going to join the 1st Cav. We going to war, boy." With his close-cut hair and flushed face, the young officer looked a little zingy. Pete looked at me and said, smiling, "War!"

I repeated it, "Waarrrr!!"

The day after that announcement the battalion left for a planned cavalry exercise with the armored personnel carriers (APCs) assigned to the battalion. It was great fun racing across Kansas prairies kicking up a rooster tail of dust. Peterson peered out of the turrets of an APC on my left, and Ernst and Duckett were on my right. We were all yelling "Yahoo!" as the tracks took dips and then bounded over the tops of rises. Vietnam in an APC wasn't a bad proposition, I thought. On our return to garrison, however, the APCs were turned in. We were going to Vietnam as "straight leg" infantry, not as a mechanized infantry battalion.

Robert M. Dunn from Portland, Oregon, and George McCoy from Munster, Indiana, other platoon leaders in the battalion, th̄med with Pete and me on our nights out in Junction City and at was a gōd officers clubs on base. McCoy was quiet but funny. He word, the type oꞁ ꞁ̄ner and, true to his midwestern roots, a man of his ꞁ̄ ꞁon you wanted at your side in combat.

Dunn was also good to have around. His loud laugh could burst streetlights. He had a quick wit, but he was also quick to fight. His father had played pro football for the Green Bay Packers, so Dunn probably came by his physical nature honestly. Orphaned when he was thirteen years old, he went to live with an older brother who was also a minor. That arrangement actually worked out pretty well and gave Dunn a certain freedom in growing up that most other kids his age envied. While he was in the tenth grade, however, he ran afoul of the law for selling false IDs. That led the social service people to place him with an older married sister, who insisted on more responsible behavior, and he eventually graduated Seattle University ROTC. Because of his loud wit and the fact that he did not bluff, nothing was calm when he was on the scene. Though he probably would never hit one of his men, if a fellow officer irritated him he'd hit the officer flush in the nose. He'd do it without a second's thought, and that came across in his manner. We didn't mess with Dunn.

One night in a remote club, I went outside to pee and then staggered across the Kansas plains, more to keep my balance than to see the countryside. I ended up at a stable. When I turned around I could see the officers club behind me in the distance. Several horses were in their stalls. No one was around, so I got a saddle and bridle from the tack room and had opened the door to the first stall when a strong right arm landed on my shoulder. A friendly, mustached sergeant told me not to mess with Chief, he was the Army's last cavalry horse, a local institution. "Ah, Chief," I said, having no idea that this was the most famous horse in the Army.

"Chief," the sergeant repeated. "I'll take you back to the O club."

In the club parking lot, Dunn was pushing someone around in the middle of a ring of young officers. I broke through the crowd and tried to separate the two. One of them hit me square upside the head, and I fell to my knees. Dunn and the other man continued slugging each other above me. One of their blows came down on my crown like a club, and I fell forward, face down in the parking lot.

McCoy helped me to his car. When P

us, Dunn looked none the worse for wear. I told him that sometimes it sure hurt having fun with our crowd.

More staff and equipment arrived every day. Our platoon received two very heavy antitank guns, which we assumed would be turned in with the APCs. Incredibly, we learned that we would take them to Vietnam, although we hadn't heard much about Viet Cong tanks. Bratcher said that if we were taking the guns to Vietnam, they would be good for something. You've got to believe in the Army, he said, plus something about those heavy guns made him think they were going to be valuable.

Dunn left for Oregon to marry Linda Lowe, the daughter of a dentist. On weekends Pete and I raced each other north to his home in Lincoln, Nebraska. He pushed his Alfa Romeo faster than I wanted to drive my Mercedes, and he'd often go out of sight in front to wait for me, sitting high on top of a ridge ready to race down and pass me again.

Back at Fort Riley, training intensified. I was pleased to see that most of my men were good marksmen, whether they came from the city or the country. A fair shot myself, I challenged the high scorer from the platoon for a shoot-off at the end of rifle practice. Sometimes I won, but usually the marksman of the day beat me.

We also marched across the Kansas prairies on field exercises. As we walked along I had a chance to talk with the men in the platoon. Sergeant Bratcher's father in Tennessee had a business fixing jukeboxes, a business he planned to join when he retired from the Army. Jo Ann, his wife, had recently broken both her arms, but was moving the family from their last post back to Tennessee.

"She's a good woman," he said. "Good soldiers have good wives. I see it all the time."

The majority of the NCOs in my platoon were black. On average the riflemen were eighteen years old. Most had bad teeth, many had tattoos, and few had graduated high school.

Sgt. Miguel Castro-Carrosquillo from Puerto Rico was one of the platoon clowns. PFC Gilbert P. Spencer was a tall black man from an urban ghetto who led the "Angry Negro Coalition." ~t. Antonio De Leon, a college graduate, had been sitting out a ～～make money for graduate school when he was drafted. ～～trick was a lanky Texan who had gone through a series of civilian jobs before joining the Army. Sgt. Roosevelt S. Rome was a burly squad leader who rarely spoke. Pvt. Harold G. Ayers was a large, barely literate eighteen year old from the Midwest. Sgt. Ray E. King was a redheaded noncom who led the 3d Squad. Pvt. Warren J. Manuel, who carried a machine gun, had been in the platoon longer than anyone. He was the fat guy who was in the platoon when I arrived. PFC James E. Newsome carried my PRC-25 radio. Pvt. John J. (Jack) Lyons Jr. from Pittsburgh, Pennsylvania, was a draftee, Pvt. Beck's best friend. Together, Lyons and Beck formed an alliance that was seldom challenged in the platoon.

Most of the men had personal situations to settle prior to departure, and most requested leave to go home, except Ayers. Pay allotments had to be taken out, wives and families settled, cars sold, and personal equipment sent home or thrown away.

We received movement orders in mid-August. Our battalion was going by train to the west coast and by ship across the Pacific. Departure was tentatively set a month away, mid-September. Training activities increased. Lt. Col. Robert Haldane, a West Point graduate, was battalion commander. He had an intelligent, educated manner, spoke in a low, resonant voice, and had that intangible quality usually referred to as "presence." By reputation, he was the finest battalion commander in the 1st Division. With his sidekick, Sergeant Major Bainbridge, he often led the entire battalion on PT runs in the morning.

Men continued to arrive, and most of them immediately went on leave to take care of personal business. Once a day, it seemed, I was called to the orderly room for a telephone call to exclaim, "You have to do what?" or "You're where?" It was hard to believe some of the twisted situations in which the men—boys mostly— of my platoon had found themselves. Some returned from leave with broken noses, or drunk or broke, in taxis, on buses, thumbing, with pregnant girlfriends or dogs, with chest colds or venereal disease.

"Is there something about going to Vietnam that makes people crazy?" I asked Bratcher.

"Yep," he said, "there is some of that, but most of these guys are crazy anyway." Bratcher smiled, and the muscles in his neck tightened and his head jerked to the right.

The platoon was unanimous in its disapproval of war protesters. The men talked about them as we marched out to the rifle range.

"They don't have anything to complain about," Beck said. "Hell, we're the ones going to get shot at. What are they protesting about? Soldiers are real men, dope-smoking hippies are slime."

But De Leon said, "That may be true, but those hippie girls do it with the lights on, sometimes in groups."

Lyons said, "Hippies are pinko Commies."

"They protest about this fucked-up society, man," Spencer said.

"Shut up, Spencer," Beck responded quickly. "I get tired of your whining. Bitch, bitch, bitch. Ain't you ever been satisfied, man?"

"Yeah," Spencer replied, "with your sister."

Beck shifted his M-79 and slowed his gait as he glared at Spencer.

"Tell you what," Bratcher quipped as he walked up near Beck, "if I hear any more bickering, I'm going to take your young asses out there and tan 'em. I'm looking for about ten minutes of quiet here. Don't nobody say nothing. No body. Shut the fuck up."

Even I was quiet, which I didn't particularly like. Bratcher had a way of taking over—he was very strong-willed. He had the respect of the men because he was tougher than they were. My problem was that platoon sergeants often usurped the authority of young officers and turned them into mascots. They had the network of sergeants in the platoon on their side. If it came down to a popularity contest, the platoon sergeant won. During those first few weeks, as we prepared to go overseas into God knows what, Bratcher and I had been sizing each other up. I liked the Tennessee sergeant, though. He reminded me of Cottonpicker, and I believed that we could develop an effective division of labor in leading the platoon. But we kept an eye on each other.

Out of nowhere I received orders to Little Creek, Virginia, for loadmaster training, to help the battalion liaise with the Navy during sea travel.

I had decided to leave my car with Pete's dad. The weekend before I left for Virginia, Pete and I raced over the Kansas/Nebraska line to Lincoln. I opened up the Mercedes and for miles on miles we raced side by side, bumper to bumper.

While we were in Lincoln, Pete suggested that we visit one of his high school classmates, now an insurance agent. Each of us bought a ten-thousand-dollar life insurance policy. The agent said we could not name each other as beneficiaries because initially, in drafting the policy, the beneficiary had to be a family member. We could take out the policies with our mothers as beneficiaries, and after a period of time, say a month, we could change our beneficiary to each other. Fine, we said, that's the plan. We paid a nominal amount for the first premium, got receipts and change-of-beneficiary forms, and went to a bar to discuss what we had done. In a back booth at the Diamond Bar and Grill, I said, "If anything happens to you, Pete, I will be surely sorry. I want you to know that I will be sad like I have never been sad before. But this ten-thousand-dollar policy, I think, will almost make it all right."

"You know, Parker," Pete said, "you could have saved money on your premium, 'cause I would have been happy with a buck fifty if something happened to you."

After attending the ten-day naval training class, I flew to North Carolina to say good-bye to my parents. While I was there I took my old 12-gauge shotgun out of the broom closet and carried it to the back porch. As I had done years before when preparing to go hunting with Cottonpicker, I checked to see if any shells were in the chamber. Then I bounced it in my hands, feeling for its center of balance. It felt comfortable. I brought it to my shoulder quickly and laid in on a distant tree. Dead center. No wasted movement. The gun knew where to go, like the '03 Springfield I had used at Oak Ridge.

A good weapon is important in a war. The shotgun and that '03 were the best that I had ever had in my hands. The shotgun was an extension of my body. I had been firing it since I was a kid. If I had a way of taking it to Vietnam, I would. And I suddenly remembered the antitank weapons. I could pack my shotgun with them. Bratcher was right. Those weapons were going to be useful for something—to carry my very own shotgun to Vietnam. I disassembled it and put it in my duffel bag without telling my parents.

Later I went to Fort Bragg, home of the Special Forces, and bought a jungle hammock from the post exchange. It was made for Vietnam, and I wondered why the battalion hadn't been issued similar types. If I could pack a 12-gauge shotgun in those antitank weapon boxes, then I could squeeze in a hammock. I put it in the duffel bag along with the shotgun.

When I was ready to leave, my parents told me to be careful. I laughed and said, "Okay."

"Come home," Dad said, shaking my hand. Mom, with tears in her eyes, twisted her mouth to one side and looked off to the side. I put my arms around her and she looked at me, tears now rolling down her cheeks. She kissed me and said softly, "Please come back."

I went to Pope Air Force Base to catch a space-available military aircraft hop to Fort Riley, but was bumped and rerouted twice. In Chicago the morning after I was supposed to return to base, I finally got Pete on the telephone. He said, "You are where?" and added that Woolley was pissed. Movement had been rescheduled and we were leaving within the week. Woolley himself had taken a forty-eight-hour pass to go somewhere, and I had better be there when he returned.

At reveille the next morning, I was back under the oak tree by the orderly room. The battalion was moving out to Vietnam in five days.

Railroad tracks ran beside the highway dissecting Fort Riley. For days passenger cars and engines came through the base to make up a train to transport the brigade to Oakland Naval Base, California.

I had the company armorer take off most of the barrel of my shotgun. It changed the balance, but I thought that the weapon would have a broader shot pattern and I could point it quicker at close range. Bratcher, King, and I packed it with the jungle hammock in an antitank weapon box. King called it the "lieutenant's survival kit."

There were surprisingly few problems in packing out the company. We did not have that much equipment; the infantry operates with what it can carry. The antitank weapons and mortars were our biggest pieces, and after those were packed we killed time doing PT, waiting for the last of the platoon to return from leave.

Captain Woolley and I were at battalion headquarters one morning doing administrative chores when the sergeant major motioned us into Colonel Haldane's office. "What are we going to do about this guy, Private Beck?" Haldane asked.

Woolley, in his usual good-mannered way with the battalion commander, said, "Well, sir, Beck's a pretty good soldier according to Parker here. We think he'll do okay."

"The sergeant major says we can get him paroled to the 1st/28th. But if he proves to be disruptive or criminal, what's the point?" Haldane looked at me as he finished.

"He'll do fine, sir," I replied. I briefly considered telling the colonel that the man had bribed his way to the 1st Division, but that sounded loopy as I thought about it, so I continued to hold the colonel's gaze without further comment.

"Okay, we'll do what's necessary here. He's the only man in the battalion in this kind of situation. He's supposed to already be out of the service with a DD. How did he get here, anyway?" Haldane asked. I looked at Woolley and he shrugged.

Later I told Beck that he was going to Vietnam because I had stood in front of the colonel and vouched for him. "You better not make me look bad."

Standing as tall as he could, Beck said, "I won't let you down."

When the train was finally assembled, formal movement orders were posted in the battalion area. We were to leave at 1500 hours on 17 September 1965.

Pete and I packed out of our BOQ the night before and left our gear in the orderly room while we went into Junction City for one last beer at the seedy bar we had gone to my first night at Fort Riley. Pete and I sat on the edge of a damaged pool table and watched the colorful mix of prostitutes, drifters, and other patrons going about their Thursday night business, which probably wasn't much different from any other night. About to start a trip halfway around the world, we had no idea what awaited us. The common night crawlers who frequented that bar couldn't have cared less, and we smiled about that.

"We gotta remember this scene," Pete said. "It means something. I don't know what exactly, but I think this is America, if we're ever going to wonder about that later. I mean if we're ever going to try and put our finger on what we're doing over there, who we're fighting for, just remember this lineup at the bar."

A bum came over and begged a dollar to buy a beer.

After he left, Pete and I agreed that we might very well be that guy in a few years. We were just going through a phase, our short-haircut phase. I wondered aloud what lay ahead—the adventures to come, the danger.

"Any last-minute things that we needed to do?" I asked Pete.

"Well," Pete said, "we'll mail those insurance forms on the way back to base and that's it. We're set to go warring."

Earlier that afternoon we had filled out the change-of-beneficiary forms for our ten-thousand-dollar policies. If I were killed, Pete would get ten grand, tax-free. If Pete died, I would get the same amount. The change-of-beneficiary forms were in my jacket. On the way back to Fort Riley, I got out of the car and walked to a mail drop, but then the devil overcame me. I put Pete's change-of-beneficiary form in the drop but put the envelope with my form back into my jacket. If I died, Mother would get the ten thousand.

There is something very rotten about this, I thought, but then I smiled. Naw. Walking back to the car, I figured the people back in that beer joint would have given me a hand; it was their kind of thing. Naw, I thought, this is rotten. Later. I'll mail it later. It made me smile, because we did not expect to die, neither one of us. We were doing it for bragging rights with Dunn and McCoy. Plus I could always say I was worried that Pete might shoot me for the money. . . . I'd just give it some time to make sure he was honest. Then I'd mail it in.

All the men in my platoon had returned except Sergeant Castro. He had called from Puerto Rico the previous morning, and I had told him to be back by 1200 hours the next day or he'd miss movement. I had trouble understanding his accent, but I thought that he had only one thing to do and he'd be on his way. I said, "You're in Puerto Rico—you're out of the country—you've got just a few hours to get to Kansas and you've got something else to do before you leave?" There was no answer. "Castro," I said, "are you crazy?"

"I be there, I be there, I be there," he kept saying.

He still wasn't back by 1500 hours the next day as we started to assemble in the company street. I had Bratcher bring out Castro's duffel bag and put it in formation. Castro was the only man missing in the 3d Platoon. We stacked arms, loaded our duffel bags into trucks, and milled around. At 1600 hours Captain Woolley called us to attention and said, "Let's go kick some ass."

We were marching out of the company area when a taxi screamed up and Castro leaned out the front passenger window. Bratcher told him that his uniform was on his bunk, we had already packed his duffel bag. Castro motioned the taxi driver to drive on.

The train cars stretched out of sight in both directions. Air hissed from brake lines. Everyone in my platoon was talking and laughing as we marched along the tracks. I stopped the platoon beside our assigned cars and had the men climb aboard. From across a nearby congested parking lot, Castro's yellow cab, speeding dangerously, made its way in our direction and stopped almost at the tracks. Castro was putting on his field uniform as he got out of the cab. Everyone in the platoon cheered. He paid the driver and waddled past me quickly to the train. I followed him up the train stairs. The men clapped their hands in unison and shouted.

"I told you I be here!" he called out to me before he slumped down in a seat.

Children on the shoulders of their parents, old people, farmers, and businessmen lined the road. People in cars drove slowly by. Some late-arriving wives and girlfriends raced by us on foot and asked soldiers leaning out of windows what unit they were with. One soldier down the line reached out and kissed a girl for a long time. She finally stood back with tears in her eyes. Another GI reached down and took a small child into the train and played with him for a few minutes before returning the boy to his crying wife. The division band was playing at the front of the train.

The sun had begun to set over the western prairies when, without warning, the train lurched and started to move. It went slowly at first, and the well-wishers easily kept up with it. Then it picked up speed and only a few people could keep pace. As our section of the train pulled through the main post area we saw signs that read, "God Save America," and "The Big Red One." Well-dressed civilians stood by large cars in the parking lot of division headquarters.

We stopped at Laramie, Wyoming, where the snow was two feet deep, so the men could disembark and stretch their legs. Back under way, we traveled over the Rocky Mountains. Somewhere east of the Oakland Naval Terminal the train came to a stop again. Scuttlebutt sourced to battalion headquarters in the front of the train was that a large demonstration of peaceniks blocked the train tracks into the terminal.

"Hell," Lyons said, "put me on top of the engine with some live ammo and I'll clear the tracks."

On Monday, 20 September, three days after leaving Fort Riley, the long train pulled into a railroad terminal inside the naval base. Sections of the train were pushed down a pier beside an enormous gray World War II troop carrier, the USNS *Mann*. We had to lean out the window and look up to see the deck. After waiting for hours to disembark, we walked in single file along the pier toward the gangplank with our duffel bags over our shoulders. Grandmotherly-looking Red Cross workers stood smiling behind tables filled with pastries and coffee.

The endless line in front continued up a gangplank to the deck, across a passageway, and down into the bowels of the ship. Once we arrived at the fifth level down, we found the company's area in a large compartment with bunks stacked five high. There was barely enough room to pass down the rows of bunks. The men were happy about leaving the train, and began settling into the smaller spaces of the ship in good humor. A card game, started on the train before we left Fort Riley, picked up again in the latrine. I noticed that there wasn't much air circulation. I was thinking it was going to be a long Pacific crossing for me down in this hold, when a Marine told me that the officers' quarters were above. I wished Bratcher well, told him it was better he than me down here, and left. Pete, McCoy, and Dunn had already secured a four-bunk stateroom off the main officers mess. I stood inside the hatch and looked at our plush, spacious cabin.

"Goddamned if I don't feel a little guilty about this," I said. "Those men are crammed together like cattle down below."

Dunn reminded me that in the U.S. Army, a second lieutenant took what was given to him and said thank you.

Troops boarded the ship all that day and throughout most of the night. Eventually twenty-eight hundred soldiers of the 1st Brigade, 1st Infantry Division, boarded the *Mann*.

Around two o'clock the next day the ship's horn blew and I went out on deck. Halfway down the pier a military band stood at the ready. The Red Cross women were cleaning up around their tables. Longshoremen disengaged heavy ropes from cleats on the pier. Fewer than a dozen civilians stood below looking up at the huge ship. Another whistle blew and the band started to play. The women stopped picking up trash and looked up. One out in front waved, and then the others joined in. The longshoremen heaved the ropes away, tugs moved the ship from the pier, and, under her own power at last, the *Mann* headed into San Francisco Bay.

We sailed under the Golden Gate Bridge and headed out to sea.

—— FOUR ——

Sea Voyage

The second day at sea I began preparing and delivering training classes on small-unit tactics and field hygiene to the company. Later, support personnel from brigade headquarters delivered a series of lectures on Vietnam and its history. These were held on the open deck where movies were shown at night. The movies were better received.

When not involved in training, the men waited in line for meals, for the PX, for the latrine, for space on deck. If a soldier wanted to see a movie, he had to get in the mess line for dinner at 1600—everyone was supposed to go through the chow line for every meal whether or not they ate it—in order to be finished in time to get in line for the limited movie seats on deck. The card game in the latrine never stopped, and I often stood and watched. Conversation was biting, with much bragging, much bluffing, and some shouting. Friendly smiles were few. Stakes were high. New players came and went, leaving their money behind with the regulars. Not a game for sissies.

I often used Bratcher's bunk for my office/couch when I was in the hold. Once I was sitting with him, wondering out loud what kind of operations we were going to be involved in.

"It's no big deal," he said. "It's a police action. Stopping cars, checking ID cards. The U.S. Army, the U.S. Navy, the U.S. Air Force, the U.S. Marines against one little pipsqueak country. Come on, Lieutenant, get serious. We'll blow 'em away." He smiled and his jaw jerked to the right.

The officers mess had clean, starched white tablecloths at each meal, and Filipino stewards served us. We had plenty of seats for our movies, and coffee, soft drinks, and sweet cakes were on a table should we want refreshments. We had the run of most of the ship. At night Dunn, Peterson, McCoy, and I often climbed to one of the uppermost decks to talk and joke. Dunn was the master of ceremonies.

Late in the morning of the eleventh day at sea I went down in the hold to see Bratcher, but he wasn't around. I picked up the platoon roster from his bunk and went over to Spencer's bunk to read it. Spencer was reading an old, dog-eared letter.

Directing his comments to no one in particular but speaking so that only I could hear, he said, "Da man is coming down to the slave quarters to look after da field niggers, huh?" He smiled faintly. Although not educated or well-read, Spencer was probably the brightest man in the platoon. Aware of what was going on in the States in the mid-1960s, he was angry that his country had tolerated segregation for so long and felt that the law of the land was still stacked against him—that he didn't have the same opportunities that the white man did. "Discrimination is as American as apple pie" was his phrase before something like that became part of the national black/white dialogue. Spencer was angry and sassy and was, in our platoon, the king of jive.

"Spencer, you know I didn't make the reservations for this cruise. You've got a right to complain, I reckon, but then so do a few thousand other good men on this boat."

"It seems strange to me that it's never anyone's fault. It ain't the man's fault, he was born white, it's his society, his laws. Problem sure ain't the black man's fault, he ain't never had nothing. Don't have no stuff, don't have no voice. We got ourselves a society that is fucked up, dude, and there ain't no one to blame, no one to fix it. White man likes it like it is. Negro ain't got no power. Nothing ever's going to change. You understand what I'm saying? In our society Negroes don't get due consideration, though I note we're more than well represented in this group being sent to some godforsaken place to get shot at 'cause it's what some white man has decided to do. Ain't nothing in it for me or my kind. Understand, Lieutenant?"

"Nope, Spencer, I don't," I told him. "It ain't my job. You'd be surprised all the things I don't understand. All I know for sure is that, for whatever reason, we're on this boat together, going somewhere where we have to work together. Shit you're talking about don't matter. I didn't ask to be born white, you didn't ask to be born black—you just supposed to make the best of what you given. That's what I know."

Bratcher walked up and sat down on Spencer's bunk with us. He and I talked for a few minutes about a class coming up, and then I left. Later I told Bratcher in passing that Spencer had made some point about our changing social consciousness, and that I understood his frustrations.

"What da fuck is that, Lieutenant?" Bratcher exclaimed. "Spencer is a private, E-3. Rifleman. Period. That is all you should think of when you see that person. Rifleman. Do not let him talk to you about nothing that doesn't have to do with him being a rifleman and you being the platoon leader. Not now on this boat and certainly not in Vietnam. Don't be his friend. Don't listen to his shit. Let another rifleman listen. Don't make this any more complicated than it is. Sitting on that private's bunk talking some intellectual-sounding bullshit don't help you do your job, and it don't help me, and it don't help him. You understand the concept here, Lieutenant?"

Bratcher was glaring at me, his jaw twitching. His points were well taken, but he was testing the limits of our relationship. I couldn't let him take over.

"Sergeant," I said, mustering as much authority as I could, "let's understand each other. If I go down and hold that man's hand and talk about poetry, that's okay. Because it's my fucking platoon. Not yours. I set the standard. I talk about whatever I want to talk about. You don't tell me what to talk about. Be careful giving me advice when I don't ask for it. You understand this concept, Sergeant?"

Things were chilly for a couple of days with Bratcher, but they returned to normal by the end of the first week at sea when we heard about the 1st Cav's first skirmishes in the A Shau valley.

Rumors began circulating over breakfast regarding an operation by one of the 1st Cav brigades in the central highlands of South Vietnam. It was the first big engagement of an American unit in the war. Some companies, we heard, had taken heavy casualties.

Later in a briefing to the officers and senior NCOs, we heard that the 1st Cav had "gotten their noses bloodied," which was an understatement. That afternoon we read that whole units were wiped out. All of the officers in one company were killed in the first few minutes of a firefight. The North Vietnamese had surrounded some units and attacked in waves. Weather was bad and air support limited. Under the jungle canopy, it was apparently difficult to fix exact positions of the ground forces and artillery fire support was imprecise. When it was on target, overhanging foliage often dissipated it. The battle evolved into hand-to-hand combat, and with the American units separated, the North Vietnamese moved against the smaller straggling units and decimated them.

"So much for your opinion that the U.S. Navy, and the U.S. Air Force, and the U.S. Marines, and the U.S. Army can whip up on this little pipsqueak country," I told Bratcher. "This doesn't sound like any police action I've ever heard about. This sounds like combat. And I want to look at those men of ours again and think about who's going to handle the heat, who's going to get the job done, and who's going to break and run."

"A lot's going to depend on you, Lieutenant," Bratcher said. "The men are getting the word about this 1st Cav thing through the grapevine and every soldier's going to make it sound worse. Don't let our men start off thinking they're going to get their asses shot. You need to go down there and tell 'em the 1st Cav was suckered in them mountains. Tell 'em we ain't going to walk into no traps. We're going to keep our head on our shoulders and we're going to kick some ass. Doesn't matter exactly what you say, you just gotta say something with confidence. They're down there now and don't know what to think. You've got to step in and give them an attitude they can believe in, live by, fight by. First Cav fucked up, but we're tough. Dinks attack us, we're going to kick their asses. If you say it with enough conviction, they'll believe you."

Bratcher wasn't looking at me as he talked. He was looking out over the ocean. I'm thinking this guy is right, but hell oh mighty, Pete, who's going to lead this platoon, me or him? I had told him not to give me advice when I didn't ask for it. But then I'm thinking again, he's right, the men need to be reassured. And it's my job. We'd work out the command-and-control thing later.

We walked down to the compartment where my platoon was

bunked, and Bratcher called the men together. He moved aside, and I recounted the dispatches we had received on the 1st Cav. Then I started winging it.

"We're going to do just fine," I told the men, "because we aren't going to make the same mistakes. The 1st Cav screwed up, but we are going to cover our asses and we're going to be tougher. And when you're more determined, you're luckier in battle. It's a well-known fact, you can will victory. You can beat 'em with a tough attitude. And I ain't just whistling through my teeth—the officers in the 1st Cav died faster than anyone else, and I personally am looking forward to my chances out there. You'all should be looking forward to what lies ahead. We are going to walk through the valley of death and, like the captain said when we left Fort Riley, we are going to kick some ass. You have nothing to worry about."

As I finished I looked around; Beck, Spencer, Castro, Manuel, Patrick, Lyons, and Ayers were standing close by, and I could see they believed me. Behind me, Bratcher told the men that he wanted every man to bring his weapon by his bunk for inspection before going to chow. On my way out, I noticed the poker game was still going in the latrine, the players nonplussed about the 1st Cav reports.

After supper, Dunn, McCoy, Pete, and I went to the top deck and talked about the 1st Cav news. Without giving Bratcher any credit, I repeated parts of my speech about the probably clumsy execution of 1st Cav in the mountains, but that we were tougher and would survive.

"Well, that's just hogwash," Dunn said. "You have no idea what went on out there. Fact is, people get killed in combat. You just accept the fact that it's not going to be nice and live with it. Some of our men are going to live and some are going to die. Maybe one of us ain't coming back. You just accept that and you don't misrepresent the situation with some kind of double-talk."

McCoy agreed. He said, "War isn't so difficult to deal with really when it comes down to the basics. You make the best of it day to day. Learn as you go. What can happen? One, the worst is you get killed. But hell, you get killed, you're dead. It doesn't hurt anymore. Somebody else has a problem with that, then it's their problem. You're dead. You're at peace. And the next worst, what's that, you get wounded and you get sent back home. Not too bad there, getting sent back home. Hell, you can get on with your life. What does that leave? You don't get wounded or killed. You finish your tour, you go home. It's that simple. One, you die, but dead you're in no pain. Two, you get wounded, you go home. Or three, you don't get wounded. But no matter what happens, it's okay."

"The important thing isn't living or dying," Pete said. "None of us think we're going to die anyway. The important thing is how we handle ourselves over there. We platoon leaders are the ones who have to get the men moving when bullets are flying and bombs are going off, when there is noise and confusion. That's the time. Right then. Will we have the presence of mind, the good judgment, the courage, and the luck to do the job? Or will we freeze and hug the ground? Can we hold ourselves responsible for the death of our people and keep on going? What's it like, really, to get shot at? To give orders that get people killed?"

We were lost in thought. I looked up at the stars and thought about freezing in the door of that airplane during jump training. Would combat be different? I had started this conversation by saying we were going to get through the next year's walk through the valley of death by just being tough, but I worried about my personal courage.

"You know what?" McCoy finally said. "I think the worst here is not knowing exactly what to expect. I think we're going to be okay. What we should hope for—and there ain't nothing more to do right now but hope, 'cause we can't change shit—we should hope that we got what it takes to be strong and that we are courageous in front of our men and that we have good judgment. That we just get it right, regardless of the consequences." He turned to Dunn. "But as for who's going die—since we don't know—you want to flip a coin and see who might likely be first."

We laughed, even Dunn, and lapsed back in silence.

As I sat there I could see clearly in my mind's eye some of the skirmishes I had read about in the dispatches. I tried to imagine what I would do, what my platoon would do, if we were surrounded by drum-beating, whistle-blowing, Oriental fanatics crawling forward in the jungle. No air force, no artillery, no mortars—us and them in dense jungle at night. My stomach tightened and began to hurt. Don't get in the fix in the first place, I thought. Think tough. Cover your ass. I was right to start with. We can will victory here. Tough is a state of mind. Stay tough. Think tough. And hope, like George said, that we're lucky.

Nine days out from Oakland we passed near Midway Island. Rumors began to circulate that we would stop at Guam to refuel, be allowed off the ship for a day on the beach, and that the Guam National Guard was going to host a beach party for the ship. Snorkeling, Polynesian girls, bonfires, free beer, clean air. Vietnam could wait. Guam was ahead.

The mood below deck was jubilant, but the poker players were unaffected. Guam came into sight off the starboard bow early on the morning of Sunday, 3 October. Men abandoned the chow line in a rush up to the deck for a glimpse of the approaching island, green and lush in the distance. Native fishermen in fishing boats passed close by the ship and the men on deck waved. Some yelled, "Where're your sisters?"

The port was now in sight and tugs had come out to guide the *Mann* to the dock.

The commandant of troops, speaking over the PA system, said that, despite the rumors, we would be allowed no shore leave. Repeat, he said, no shore leave. The ship was docking only to take on fuel and supplies, and we would be on our way the following morning.

I was on deck watching the tugs work and did not turn when the commandant spoke. What he said was not surprising. It seemed improbable that the thousands of men on board could be allowed onto the small island, entertained, and returned to the ship in any reasonable amount of time. They would overwhelm the island.

The men, however, were not understanding. The rumors about shore leave had been detailed, some aspects even discussed by the Navy crew. The troops thought army brass had decided among themselves against letting them off. An angry rumble drifted up from the hold and grew louder. Men ran up the steps from the troop compartments. Clusters of soldiers stood on the deck and talked conspiratorially. Somewhere below, a soldier slammed the butt of his M-14 into the side of the ship. The noise increased as more and more men grabbed their weapons and started thumping the bulkheads.

Pete came up and we stood together waiting, listening. It was mutinous. The banging of weapons continued as the tugs pushed the ship into place beside a long concrete pier.

A gangplank was lowered from the ship. We watched the commandant and Sergeant Major Bainbridge leave with an entourage of staff officers. When some of the men on deck saw them leave, they yelled that the top dogs were going ashore, leaving the troops to rot on the ship. Men ran below to spread the word. The banging got louder.

The sergeant major soon returned and a meeting of all officers was called in the officers mess.

The banging stopped.

An officious lieutenant colonel addressed the group. Without reference to the previous message over the PA system, he said that the port authority had offered some old dry docks a few miles from the pier so the men could stretch their legs and drink some beer. But he said everyone had to be back on board by midnight because we sailed for Vietnam at first light. It was then almost 1300. As he was giving instructions for off-loading, we heard a roar from below. The men apparently had heard through their own sources that they were going ashore.

Disembarking by companies, almost three thousand soldiers marched off the pier and down the island road toward the dry docks. Four abreast, they sang, waved their arms, and clapped their hands as they marched.

The dry docks, four large wooden bulwarks three stories high and in varying degrees of disrepair, stood amid a variety of smaller buildings. Once inside the gates, the men fell out from the column to explore or stood around in groups and talked. An officer climbed on top of a shed near the gate and announced that the Guam National Guard would arrive in a few minutes with beer on the back of flatbed trucks. The beer was ten cents a can, and each man could buy twelve, no more. After giving further instructions about what the men could not do, he said that the opportunity for the men to stretch their legs was done on the authority of the troop commander, who wanted the men to form up at 2200 and march, by companies, back to the ship.

The men were milling around as he spoke. Peterson opined that not everyone had paid attention. He guessed that before the day was out there would be a few violations of the rules.

Captain Woolley gathered his platoon leaders—Peterson, Duckett, Ernst, and me—and said that two of us had to stay with the men at all times. The others were allowed to go to a nearby officers club. Duckett and Ernst agreed to take the first shift. Pete and I would return by nightfall.

As we walked out the gate, two dump trucks laden with beer pulled into the compound. The men behind us let out a roar and began to form up in lines. McCoy and Dunn were in the officers club when we arrived. They had staked out an area overlooking the beach and had their drinks on a side table. Pete and I downed a starter set of drinks quickly before settling down to more reasonable drinking. We became boisterously happy and made preposterous toasts. "Larry Moubry" [alias], the battalion supply and transportation platoon leader, came over and loudly joined us in making toasts. He had a reputation for being very religious and we found his drunken behavior unseemly, maybe because he was a little drunker than the rest or because he wasn't funny or clever or invited. He was, in fact, obnoxious and his mood turned morose quickly after we had gone through a series of toasts. He imagined that many of us would die in Vietnam, a sweltering, Oriental hellhole. He said the Viet Cong were godless demons who killed without mercy, had no regard for life, and ate their dead.

He finally stumbled off, and after watching him barge into another group Dunn commented that he was a righteous son of a bitch.

Dunn noticed Woolley, carrying several drinks, across the room and called to him to join us. Woolley made his way through the crowd and placed his drinks on a nearby piano. Dunn said it was fair to tell him that Parker and Peterson didn't think much of him. Dunn said the good captain looked pretty damn good in his uniform and everything, and Dunn liked him a lot personally, and that was why Dunn was going to tell him something in confidence. "Keep your eye on Parker," Dunn said, "especially when we get live bullets."

Woolley threw back his head and laughed. Dunn reached over and got one of Woolley's drinks from the piano.

"Mr. Parker's going to be in front of me most of the time, pulling point, I think," Woolley said.

"Pulling point?" I asked. "Odd-sounding phrase."

Suddenly Ernst burst into the room and ran over to Woolley. "They're rioting at the docks!" he yelled. "They are out of control. They've turned trucks over, burnt buildings. They've gone crazy. Crazy, Captain, crazy. It's a riot."

Maj. Robert J. Allee, the battalion executive officer, came in and talked with the troop commander. The commander stood up and said everyone was to return to the dry docks and begin policing up the men. He was canceling shore leave as of that moment.

Not far from the officers club, groups of men were wandering off in all directions. The gate to the dry docks was clogged with people trying to get out. Most were heading toward the ship, but many hundreds were making their way inland. In the half light of dusk we could see some small buildings on fire inside the dock area. I found a few of my men and told them to go back to the ship. Down by the gate, Moubry was telling men who appeared to him to be heading away from the ship to drop and give him fifty push-ups and then go on to the ship. To their credit, most told him to fuck himself and walked away as he screamed, "Give me fifty, give me fifty, soldier!" Dunn told Moubry to go to the ship or he was going to break his nose because he was giving all the officers a bad name.

Sergeants Bratcher and King were sitting on top of some lumber inside the gate, a couple of cases of beer between them.

"I thought twelve beers a person was the limit," I told them.

"King can't count good." Bratcher said. "Want a beer, Lieutenant?"

I sat down beside them and opened a beer. The scene resembled Sherman's sacking of Atlanta. Some buildings were on fire and others had been torn down. King said that too many men were standing on the roof of one building and it just collapsed, so the men built a bonfire.

High up on the off-limits bulwarks, men were happily walking about. Others were sitting with their legs hanging over the side and drinking. Some men were swimming in the lagoon. Hundreds of beer cans were floating in the still water.

Bratcher said, "It was the lines. They made the men form up in lines and they weren't that interested in more lines. Plus it was the ten-cent beer and the twelve-beer limit and the fact that not everyone had the right change and it took a long time sometimes for one person to get his beer and get his change and then, maybe the most important, was the fuck-you attitude of the National Guardsmen, who weren't hardly going on to Vietnam themselves. They didn't show enough respect. Not necessarily smart on their part, when you consider that they were inside a barbed-wire enclosure, outnumbered a thousand to one or more."

I told Bratcher and King to stay behind at the dry docks while I went to the ship and made a head count. They were to send any stragglers from the platoon down and come back themselves when they were convinced that none of our people remained at the dry docks.

King said, "Good plan, Lieutenant." He opened another beer.

By midnight, my men were all back on the ship. That was not the case everywhere; men staggered back all night. Two swam up to the ship from the sea side. Several got on the wrong ship. One group tried to board a submarine. The local police returned another group that had crashed a local high school football game, run out on the field, and stolen the game ball. Policemen also found 1st Infantry Division soldiers on people's roofs, under cars, and in churches.

The ship slipped her mooring at midmorning the next day and the tugs pulled her to sea. Under her own power, the *Mann* continued her westward journey toward Vietnam. As Guam disappeared behind us, the holds were awash with puke. The Navy stopped issuing sheets. Everyone stayed on deck as long as they could.

By the second day out the platoons began to organize their equipment. That night battalion officers met for a briefing on what lay ahead. After landing at the port city of Vung Tau we would move to a staging area north of Saigon for outfitting and then overland to an area farther north where we would set up a battalion-size base camp. When that was built, our battalion would join other division units securing the area north and north-west of Saigon. We received maps and intelligence briefings about known or suspected enemy activities in our tactical area of responsibility (TAOR). Small Viet Cong units were active in the coastal and central regions, mainline North Vietnamese units were on the Cambodian border. Some friendly Army of (South) Vietnam (ARVN) units were scattered throughout our TAOR, although irregular forces that had U.S. Special Forces advisers comprised the principal Government of South Vietnam (GVN) presence along the Cambodian border. Our area was primarily jungle, but it included a number of rice fields and rubber plantations. We would go ashore on U.S. Navy landing craft. The beach area was reported to be secure, and no hostilities were anticipated.

"Reported to be?" I whispered to Pete. "Anticipated? Sorta vague, don't you think? You reckon we ought to call him on it?"

"Everything's going to be okay. Cool it." Pete whispered back out of the corner of his mouth. "This is a good briefing."

"Good my ass," I said as I leaned toward Pete as if retying my bootlaces. "We're heading into a combat zone and this guy doesn't 'anticipate' hostilities. I don't think he knows what he's talking about."

"Just shut up. There'll probably be a brass band playing when we get there."

We arrived off the coast of Vietnam on 8 October, eighteen days after leaving Oakland. The next morning at first light we would go over the rail of the ship and down rope ladders to the Navy landing craft.

I was up long before dawn, packed my gear, and went down into the hold to wait with my platoon until we received orders to go on deck. We were among the first out, with Vietnam before us and the sun coming up behind us. Still some distance from shore, we couldn't make out many details there. The fading night lights from a coastal town were visible to the north. I asked about the ammo and was told that it would be in the LSDs (landing ships, dock).

Small landing craft were bobbing on the ocean. Some were tied up to the *Mann* and others waited in the distance. Alpha Company, amidships, would be in the first wave over the side and among the first to reach the beach.

When word came to board the landing craft, I hitched my

helmet strap one last notch tighter and slung my leg over the rail. The loose rope netting jerked around as men all along the side of the ship climbed tentatively down to the waiting LSDs. The *Mann* moved up and down as if trying to shake us off. We were laden with equipment. Anyone who lost his grip would fall backward into the landing craft below.

Reaching the boat, I was helped aboard by Rome. In turn I helped Ayers. The landing craft bobbed up and down like an empty paper cup. Men continued to board our small craft, but there was a breakdown in unit integrity. Not all of my men were in the LSD with me. Men from Peterson's and Ernst's platoons were there, plus other soldiers I didn't recognize. I was considering an attempt to make contact with the craft on either side to find the rest of my men when we cast off. For a time, the *Mann* loomed large above us and then disappeared. We couldn't see over the side.

The ammo was in boxes in the middle of the LSD. Bratcher and I discussed whether we should obey the order not to break the cases. He was in favor of doing everything possible to protect our asses, such as issuing some ammo, but I didn't comment. I was afraid to say yes or no—bad sign. My first decision and I couldn't make up my mind. So we left the ammo crates unopened.

Most men held their weapon close to their chest to protect it from the spray. Some looked around nervously; others kept their eyes down. No one talked. The pounding of the waves on the bottom of the landing craft increased. We were coming through the surf, I thought, and would be landing soon. I looked at the big door ramp in front, which would drop into the water at any minute. We were getting ready to make our entrance into the war zone. I had a flashing recollection of John Wayne and *The Sands of Iwo Jima*. The Navy driver yelled something. As I turned to look at him the ramp fell forward. Beck was the first soldier off, bravely running down the ramp into waist-high water. Surprisingly, Spencer was right behind him.

On the back of a U.S. Army flatbed truck ashore, the 1st Infantry Division band was in midstanza of "God Bless America." Several U.S. military officers were standing in a group off to the side and waving at us. Vietnamese civilians were farther away. Some smiled, but others appeared apprehensive. A column of deuce-and-a-half trucks was parked on a blacktop nearby. My platoon gathered around me on the beach, looking confused.

And the band played on.

—— FIVE ——

First Firefight

We were trucked to a staging area near Bien Hoa and off-loaded near medium-size tents inside a concertina-wire enclosure. Wet and sandy from the beach landing, we had dried out in the truck ride. When we moved our equipment into tents, we burst out in sweat and our uniforms were soon drenched again—our first taste of the "now-you're-wet, now-you're-not" cycle of life in the Vietnam countryside.

The staging area was on a hill near some local government buildings. To the south, sectioned rice fields stretched almost out of sight. Grazing water buffalo dotted the green landscape. This peaceful, bucolic scene, with a cooling, earth-scented breeze coming up the hill from the rice fields, made it hard to believe that the country was the site of so much turmoil and fighting.

A paved, heavily traveled road was to the east. In front of huts scattered along the roadside, produce was displayed for passing motorists. To the west were office buildings and to the north was jungle.

The heat was suffocating. As we acclimated, we drew special jungle equipment that included claymore mines and, for night firing, starlight scopes. Not only were the scopes cumbersome and heavy, they didn't work because the oddly shaped batteries were missing. Not believing the Army would issue us incomplete equipment, we tried without success to make them work and became frustrated. Moubry thought it was irresponsible of the men and officers to make such a fuss over something so small. When he said that the Army would provide in time, McCoy told him it was entirely possible that the Army could be fucked up. Woolley sent a sergeant from company headquarters into the large supply depot at Bien Hoa to barter for the batteries we needed, and

Bratcher came up with a half dozen for our two scopes on his own. Moubry reported to Haldane that men were going outside channels to get material.

During our fourth afternoon in the staging area, Woolley ordered me to take my platoon on an ambush patrol behind a village across the paved road that night. Before leaving we test-fired our weapons and drew grenades. In planning the route to the ambush area, I decided to take the men down a stream that led away from the staging area to the north, then over the road to the east, and back along a hedgerow to the high ground behind the village, where we would set up the ambush at a trail junction.

My platoon was up to its full strength of forty-five men. In addition to Bratcher and the radio/telephone operator (RTO), Newsome, I had three eleven-man rifle squads and an eight-man heavy weapons squad. Each rifle squad had two five-man fire teams and a squad leader. The heavy weapons squad had the squad leader, two-man machine gun teams, and three men carrying disposable antitank rockets called LAW, in lieu of the heavier and more impractical antitank weapons that had come over in crates. Our platoon organization was suited for a conventional war, but, as I prepared the platoon for the ambush patrol, it was apparent that the four-squad structure wasn't appropriate for the jungle work that lay ahead. Castro was one of the best fire-team leaders, so I had his team lead the patrol. Ayers, a rifleman in Castro's fire team, would be at point. He would be followed by another rifleman, then Castro. I would be midway in the single file, just ahead of my RTO. Bratcher would be at the rear.

That evening, Bratcher stood by the concertina fence and checked that each man had his weapon locked and loaded before he stepped through the wire. There was a steady clamoring of bolts as rounds were loaded into the chambers. We were armed, ready for combat—our first patrol.

We walked cautiously along the zigzag path through the minefield of the staging area and out into the jungle. Avoiding trails, we cut through the jungle until we reached the stream I wanted to follow. It began to rain softly as we waded into the water. We passed several houses and could hear the Vietnamese talking inside. Occasionally a baby cried or we heard someone laugh or cough. We got to the road and crossed it without detection. We were in position on one side of the trail behind the village by 2100. From where I was, halfway down the platoon, I could see the lights from the village. It was supposedly friendly, but, in fact, we didn't know who the friendlies were. What we knew for sure was that the Vietnamese had a 2100 curfew. Anyone moving around after that could be taken for a Communist, either a Viet Cong or a Viet Cong sympathizer. We were to shoot to kill, which didn't leave much room for error.

Lying on my stomach, I looked down at the village and wondered if any innocent schoolboy ever came along there at night after seeing his girlfriend or delivering something for his mother. What if a woman, or child, came down that trail? What if a family appeared? Could we tell the difference? It was such a peaceful-looking village below. There was no sense of danger. Just quiet, friendly night sounds. Please Lord, I prayed, don't test us tonight.

A Vietnamese walked into the rear of the ambush sometime after midnight. He saw us, turned, and was gone before anyone fired a shot.

In the morning, on the way back to camp, we passed the village near the highway. The villagers, up and going about their early morning farm chores, stopped what they were doing and silently watched us pass.

I thought that everyone had been lucky the previous night—the men in the platoon and that guy who had stumbled into us. No blood, no foul.

The men expressed regret as we walked along, however, that we did not get the "gook." I didn't tell them how relieved I was for fear they would think I wasn't tough enough for the job ahead.

McCoy and Peterson were waiting for me near my cot. I gave them a detailed report of the patrol. Peterson suggested that he cut off the tail of my shirt, as is done in hunting parties to men who miss a shot.

A few days later the entire battalion moved out of the enclosure in single file down the highway, past a few villages, along a side road, and across a rice field. We were going to "sweep" a wooded area between two villages. As we walked alongside the highway, cars slowed down and people looked at us. If there were any Viet Cong out there we weren't going to sneak up on them, I told Bratcher.

We crossed the open field and the men lined up along the wood line, shoulder to shoulder. On order from Haldane, we chambered rounds in our weapons and moved into the jungle. We were to stay spread out all the way to the next village, three and one-half kilometers away.

This was not my idea of releasing the dogs of war.

A dozen steps into the jungle, my RTO fell in behind me.

"This ain't the way it's supposed to be," I said. "I ain't breaking trail."

Then, some men fell in behind the radio operator.

"Okay," I said, "none of this. You men get out there on the flank like you were, and let's get back on line."

"What if we just looked over at the flank, Lieutenant. Ain't that enough? I mean, we don't have to actually walk every step of this goddamn jungle, do we?" This came from Beck, who, unfortunately, had a good point.

I told him to get in front of me. Off to the left, Ayers, strong as a horse, was breaking through the jungle. Several men had fallen in behind him. Bratcher was leading some men on the right. "Who's fucking idea is this, anyway?" he asked.

Peterson called on the radio and asked where I was.

"How in the hell do I know where I am? I'm in the Vietnam jungle somewhere. That's all I know," I said. "And my platoon's all over the place. You see any of my people, send them my way. Over."

"I don't know where you are, so I wouldn't know where to send your people if I came across them. I want to know where you are because I hear some people moving up ahead of me. Is it you or the bad guys? Over."

"Assume it's me. Don't shoot. Over."

Shortly afterward Woolley asked for my location. I gave him my best guess. If I was right and if Peterson's guess was accurate, he was on the opposite side of me from where he had been when we started. Then shortly I saw one of Duckett's men beside the group behind Ayers. They should have been on the other side of

Ernst, who was to my left. Bratcher's group moved closer to mine. The jungle was so thick we couldn't see ten feet in any direction.

"I think this is going to be a long year," Beck said.

Suddenly, off to the left came the sound of movement through the undergrowth, crashing, charging toward Ayers's group. Ayers fired a burst from his M-14 fully automatic. As he fired he yelled that we were being attacked.

Whatever, or whoever it was, turned and began making its way to the right. Spencer joined Ayers in firing at the retreating sound.

I got on the company radio and warned the other platoons that we had contact with something when a group opened up on the right. Stray bullets zipped over our heads. We hit the ground. People opened up to our left, to our right, in front of us, behind us. Rounds were going everywhere. My radio operator kept repeating, "Holy shit, holy shit, holy shit." Grenades went off. M-79s went off. More automatic fire.

Then someone started yelling, "Hold your fire! Hold your fire! Hold your fire!"

And everyone stopped.

Woolley came on the radio and said it was a deer.

I told Bratcher I thought it was World War III.

It was absolutely miraculous that no one was hurt.

Over the course of the afternoon, the battalion staggered out of the jungle in twos and threes and sevens and eights. Haldane was the first to admit that we needed to staff out that tactic before we tried it again; it was a reasonable idea, but its implementation needed work.

A week after arriving in the staging area, the battalion moved by truck convoy to Phuoc Vinh, the area selected for the battalion base camp. The town and airfield were considered pacified, and the men lounged in the shade there without much concern about security. I joined the command group moving up the hill north of the airstrip to reconnoiter the area where we would build the battalion base camp. Bratcher was with me, and we tied handkerchiefs to jungle vines to mark our area of the perimeter and then returned for the men. As the sun set, the platoon cut down the underbrush to our front and cleared fields of fire for the platoon's two machine guns.

It was quiet that night. I washed down a C-ration supper with warm iodized water from my canteen, checked each position after dark, and slept hard, even though it poured rain toward morning.

For the next four days we cut the trees and scrub to improve the fighting positions and connect them with a trench. Three bulldozers arrived the following day and graded circles around the entire battalion perimeter. We received the crates of antitank weapons that contained my shotgun and jungle hammock. I hung the hammock in a small cleared area behind the command bunker. The men ran telephone landlines from the platoon area to company headquarters. Truckloads of concertina wire were stretched and connected in three strands in front of the area. The men worked hard, mostly with their shirts off, sweating in the Southeast Asia sun. Morale was high and there was much friendly banter.

We posted a lone sentry out by the wood line as we worked, causing Spencer to say, "Man, I feels like I'm on a Louisiana chain gang, whacking weeds and a guard sitting over there with a gun."

"Spencer," Beck said as he stretched out a strand of wire, "I've been on chain gangs. This is good work here. Plus, look'it. We're making nine dollars a day, got all the grub we want to eat . . . dry hootch, air mattress, smokes, mail. Shit man, this is fine."

Spencer began singing in a good baritone voice, "Beck's been working on the chain gang, all the livelong day. Beck's been working on the chain gang, just to pass the time of day. . . ."

Beck, off-key, joined in, "Don't you hear the whistle blowing, rise up so early in the morn. . . ."

Lyons, from across the field, "Oh my bleeding ass, shut the fuck up, you two."

"Fuck you, Lyons," from both Beck and Spencer.

The next day the mines arrived.

Medieval, ugly, they smelled like death. Appropriately, the wooden boxes they came in were marked with a skull and crossbones. We were issued three types: "Bouncing Bettys" that jumped up and exploded about waist high to maximize casualties, foot jammers that blew feet apart, and swarthy, lethal antitank mines.

We dug row upon row of potholes between the concertina-wire loops in front of our positions. The following morning we placed the mines by the holes and marked them on a map. At midday, King, Rome, and I, lying on our stomachs, lifted the mines, one by one, put them in the holes; covered them with dirt; tied out trip lines; and, finally, removed the safety pins.

I had Castro replace me when we finished the first row. I sat on top of Spencer's bunker the rest of the day watching the men as they slowly and carefully laid the minefield. The following afternoon they placed the last mine. We were the last platoon in the battalion to finish. A safe lane was marked through the field with reflectors that could be seen from the inside looking out. If a friendly patrol arrived back at the outer concertina strand, someone from inside would have to go out to escort it into the area. Our safe lane came down right in front of the M-60 machine gun.

There was nothing funny or cute about laying a minefield. It lay like death at our front door.

For meals we had C rations, which included a canned meat such as boned chicken, turkey loaf, ham and eggs, beans and franks, roast pork, chipped beef, or ham and beans; a dessert such as fruit cocktail, fruitcake, or chocolate; peanut butter and crackers or jelly and bread; plus chewing gum, cigarettes, matches, salt and pepper, coffee and cocoa, powdered cream and sugar, and toilet paper. Altogether a C ration was not a bad box lunch. We all had our favorite meals. I always got first pick, so I took what I wanted. Lyons once told me that wasn't necessarily fair. I told him he was right. Life's a bitch.

Castro, who had been in the Army longer than anyone in the platoon, knew how to turn regular C rations into gourmet meals. Two days after we finished the minefield, I invited him to my command bunker to fix a communal stew. He propped a steel pot half filled with water between three rocks and put several boxes of heat tablets beneath it. He lit the heat tablets; while the water was coming to a boil he put in several portions of different meats. From his pack he brought out some Tabasco sauce, garlic, onions, and red peppers and put them in the pot along with some greens he had cut as we cleared the area. After adding salt and pepper, stirring the stew with a wooden spoon from his pack and spitting in it to add real Latin flavor, Castro ladled out rich, aromatic portions.

It was so hot my eyes watered, but it was, all in all, the best meal I had had in Vietnam.

I had a cigarette and beer later when Bratcher and Castro had gone to their bunkers, unlaced my boots, and leaned back against a tree. Night was falling, the moon was out. With the bunkers built, the land cleared, and the barbed wire and mines laid, I felt safe. Everyone in the platoon was becoming more acclimated to the heat and more accustomed to living in the jungle. It's not such a bad place, I thought as I put out my cigarette, crushed my beer can, and threw it toward the trash hole. I stood up, stretched, and walked over to my jungle hammock. After unzipping the side, I bent down and inward, turning so as to sit on the hammock inside. I took off my boots and put them on the ground, put my belt inside one boot and reached out for my pistol inside the holster of my web gear. My shotgun was on a peg nearby under my poncho. I zipped shut the mosquito netting, put my pistol under the clean set of fatigues I used as a pillow, took a deep breath, and fell asleep.

A couple of hours later, a Viet Cong sniper crawled up behind an anthill on the edge of the wood line beyond our last strand of barbed wire. Kneeling, he rested his rifle on the top of the anthill and scanned the bunkers along the perimeter. Other Viet Cong were taking positions around him. They intended to wait until their companion in the middle drew fire from our different positions so they could pick out individual targets from our muzzle flashes. The Viet Cong gunman in the center continued to scan the line. He finally focused on the command bunker and then at the irresistible hammock to the rear. The moon glistened off the rain roof.

He aimed for the center of the hammock and fired. The first bullet went through the rain roof over my head and the second through the mosquito netting beneath me.

I woke from a dead sleep when the first bullet whistled by and was desperately trying to get out when the second round passed under me. Frantically, I clawed at the zipper, and the hammock rotated 180 degrees as another round zipped by. The Viet Cong in the middle ducked behind the anthill after firing his three shots, seconds before men in the bunkers opened up on the anthill. I heard automatic fire from a dozen M-14s and a long burst from the M-60 machine gun, punctured by explosions of M-79 grenade rounds.

In a frenzy, I couldn't find the zipper to get out of the hammock. Upside down, I literally didn't know which way was up. Outside, it sounded like a full-scale attack by hundreds of Viet Cong, and here I was suspended in the air, captured in a hammock death trap. Where was the frigging zipper? Which side was up?

"Aaauggggg!" My yell was not heard over the din of battle.

I'm sure one of the other Viet Cong, watching the reaction along the perimeter to his companion's three shots, debated between firing at the machine gun bunker or at the strange bag jiggling wildly in the middle. He would have time for one shot, or at most two, before having to duck. The machine gun or the hammock? The hammock, he decided, since it was like a sitting duck.

Captain Woolley was calling on the radio to find out what was happening. Newsome, my radio operator, crawled over to my hammock and yelled out that Woolley wanted to talk with me.

I was still thrashing around inside, my hands wildly searching, legs pumping. The hammock flipped on one side, then the other. My pistol hit me in the head. Mother of Jesus! *Where is the zipper?*

Then, incredibly, one end of the hammock dropped to the ground and I tumbled down to the bottom.

Another round zipped overhead.

Newsome reached over from the base of a tree, unzipped the hammock, and pushed the handset toward me as I squirmed out. Rather than chance standing up, he had cut one end of the hammock down.

"Hate to wake you up like that, sir, but we got a shoot-out going here and the captain wants to know what's going on," he yelled.

I told Woolley that we were under attack, did not know about casualties, and I'd get back.

Bratcher yelled out, "No attack, just probing. We're okay."

"Hold your fire, goddammit, hold your fire!" I yelled.

Gradually the firing stopped. No more rounds came in. It was absolutely quiet, although my ears continued to ring. My heart seemed to be beating in my ears.

I radioed Woolley that we had been probed, but the enemy had pulled back. I didn't think we had any casualties (hoping this was true) and promised to report if we discovered any wounded.

As I finished my radio transmission, Peterson's platoon fired mortar flares and the whole area was illuminated. The wood line beyond the concertina looked eerie but unoccupied.

Everyone had been looking toward the front when the firing started, and no one in the platoon saw me wrestling to get out of the hammock. I had no comments the next morning when the radio operator put his fingers through the bullet holes in the rain roof.

"Close, man," he said.

Peterson, Dunn, and McCoy dropped by the next morning.

"You know, Parker, it's people like you who keep the average high on second-lieutenant casualties in combat," Dunn said.

McCoy looked at me a long moment and just shook his head. "Correct me if I'm wrong here, but weren't you the one saying you were going to be the meanest bastard in the valley of death?"

"All right, all right. Anyone want to buy a hammock?" I asked.

Colonel Haldane found no humor in the incident and chastised us for opening up with all our weapons against an unseen enemy. Because he felt we had given away our positions, he had us relocate every foxhole and bunker. He issued an order that we could not initiate counterfire at the perimeter unless we clearly saw a target.

The order specifically talked about rifles. It did not mention the large 106mm antitank weapons.

A few nights later, Duckett's men thought they saw Viet Cong out on the edge of the woods, and Duckett conferred with his platoon sergeant. Soon there was a "kaboooooom!" as the 106mm fired, then "whaaaammmmmm" as a large tree fell over.

The next morning Haldane came to the perimeter. "Duckett, look at me," he said. "When I say you don't fire your individual weapons, I'm also talking about that 106 millimeter. You hear?"

Pete came out later, fuming. He said, "Duckett, we used that tree to register and adjust our mortars. What we going to do, now you've blown it away?"

At lunch Duckett told me, "You know, you can sure get in trouble shooting your gun in this war."

— SIX —

Shadow War

Two nights later, the group of Viet Cong returned and sniped at our position. Some of the men saw them clearly, and we returned a tremendous amount of fire. Peterson's platoon fired flares more quickly this time. Interdiction rounds from our mortars flew over us and landed in the jungle well beyond the perimeter. The noise, the tracers, the fluorescent half-light from the flares were surreal, like Halloween.

Woolley was yelling on the radio, "What's going on? What's going on? Red Cap Twigs Alpha November Six?"

I hollered to the men to stop firing. In the rear we could hear fresh mortar rounds "whoof" as they left their tubes, whistled overhead, and exploded in the jungle in front of us. There was no other sound except low half-whispers from our men discussing the attack.

"We were probed again. It's quiet. Nothing more. No casualties," I reported to Woolley.

The next day we went out to the anthill on the other side of the concertina wire. There was no evidence that anyone had been there the night before. We could find no expended cartridges; the grass was not matted down. When I talked to Woolley later, I found myself defending my platoon's actions. Why were we the only ones probed? Woolley asked. "Well, maybe," I suggested, "because there's that trail that comes near my part of the perimeter from the village. Maybe that's it."

Bratcher and I later decided to put some men in the jungle in front of the perimeter for a few nights in hopes of catching the probers. There was a point of honor here. Had we been firing at ghosts? Spencer and Beck were drafted to man the listening post. At mid-afternoon I took two squads for a small patrol out to the trail leading from the village. I carried my shotgun with the sawed-off barrel. Woolley knew about the gun. In fact, he had smuggled a shotgun himself to Vietnam—a Browning 12-gauge automatic.

On the way back to the perimeter, near the anthill, Spencer and Beck dropped into a thicket where they would spend the night in hopes of catching our visitors if they came calling. Spencer gave me a resigned look as he disappeared into the bamboo.

That night, I sat on top of my bunker and suddenly felt a breeze. I remembered Cottonpicker talking about spooking game when the wind was in his back. Creatures living in the woods can smell creatures that don't. The wind was blowing away from the perimeter, taking Spencer and Beck's scent into the jungle. How good are the Viet Cong? I wondered. Then it started to rain. Beck cursed the next time he called in. He was cold, wet, and sleepy. I told him to shut up and do his duty.

When the rain stopped, I went back out on the bunker. Clouds covered the moon. I squinted to make out images in front and listened closely. Focusing on the jungle, I strained to hear any footfalls of Viet Cong moving behind Beck and Spencer. Rain dripped off leaves and branches, and a slight breeze caused some of the foliage to sway. I could almost make out images of people along the wood line and hear footsteps. Once, I was sure I saw a man holding a gun across his body as he stood by a tree between us and my two soldiers. I asked the RTO if he saw anything. He looked for a long time but could not see anyone. When I looked again the image had changed into a tall bush.

Beck and Spencer were at the wire at first light. Patrick went out through the safe lane to escort them in.

Later that day we went out by the anthill and cleared away some bushes that I had imagined to be Viet Cong the night before. Bratcher hid two directional claymore mines behind the anthill and ran wires along the safe lane to the machine gun bunker. If someone climbed up behind that anthill and fired, we could just mash a button to detonate the claymores and the entire area behind the anthill would be a killing zone.

Bratcher was in the machine gun bunker that night. I instructed the men not to fire for any reason until the claymores went off. If the sniper came back and fired, Bratcher would take him out.

Showers continued on and off all night with the moon breaking out of the clouds periodically. Several times I thought I saw movement by the anthill. The more I watched, however, the clearer it was to me how the eye can be fooled.

There were no sniper attacks that night. The next day most of the men in the platoon worked to clear an area where we were going to build a tent city for the battalion. It would include an aid station, ammo dump, supply area, latrines, showers, and mess halls. After we staked out the streets the area began to resemble a Wild West frontier town.

Bratcher manned the detonators for the claymores that night and the men had instructions again not to fire until the mines went off. Near midnight a single round zipped over the perimeter. I was instantly wide awake and expected to hear the mines. After a few minutes I called out to Bratcher. He said he was waiting. He hadn't seen where the shot had come from, and wasn't sure it was from the anthill. Somebody down the line thought he saw a muzzle blast off to the right. The moon was out, and the anthill was clearly visible on the edge of the jungle.

Fire again, you son of a bitch, I thought. Fire.

There were no more rounds during the night. Ayers, Castro, Bratcher, and I went out to the anthill the next morning. Ayers stood guard near the jungle as Castro, Bratcher, and I looked around. At first we saw no signs of anyone having been there the night before.

"Lieutenant," Castro suddenly said, "look at this." He was standing by the area where we had hidden one of the claymores two days before. It had been moved, turned, and aimed back at our machine gun position at the end of the safe lane.

The other claymore was missing. The wire had been cut.

"Very cute," Bratcher said, his neck tightening. "If I had detonated the mine we would have gotten splattered. As it is, the guy still got one of our mines."

"Clever little bugger," I said, although there was some gratification in knowing that there were VC operating outside our lines and we weren't shooting at shadows.

That same day we received orders for a battalion-size patrol operation twenty kilometers to our north. My platoon led the battalion north, and at dusk four hundred infantrymen of the 1st of the 28th Infantry were in position along a VC supply trail.

Around three o'clock in the morning Lyons crawled over to the tree where I was sleeping. He shook me awake and said he thought some men were carrying things down the trail. I couldn't fathom what was going on. Lyons didn't see things that weren't there, and it hadn't been raining. If Viet Cong were walking down the trail, units on either side should have fired at them. The whole battalion was near the trail. I told him to go back to his position and if he saw anybody else walking down that trail, shoot him. Lyons crawled away and disappeared in the dark jungle. I had just decided to follow him and see these men on the trail for myself when he started firing his M-14 on full automatic.

The night was suddenly filled with tracers and the thunderous sound of automatic rifle fire. It finally died down and then stopped completely as the word circulated: "Hold your fire."

In the quiet that followed we heard a man groaning. He called out in Vietnamese. Around him, from my platoon and down the line, men fired toward the sound. I yelled to stop the firing. There was quiet. Then I heard the man groan again. A long painful wail. Some men fired again. I yelled again to stop the firing.

Colonel Haldane and Captain Woolley crawled up with a Vietnamese interpreter. Out in front the man babbled Vietnamese. Haldane asked the interpreter what he was saying.

"He says he is shot and he says he hurts. He asks us to help."

Woolley and Haldane exchanged looks without comment.

"I think . . . I think, maybe trap. Maybe other Viet Cong around. He has gun for sure," the interpreter offered.

"Yeah, well what's he saying?" asked Haldane.

"He says he hurts a lot," the interpreter said after a pause.

"Continue talking to him. Try to find out if he is really alone," Haldane ordered in a hushed voice.

In the jungle to our front, the groans had no accent; the tremor in the low wails were an international human expression of pain. But could that be faked? Were we being baited to come out of our perimeter?

The moaning continued for an hour or so, but became gradually weaker. It stopped before the sun came up.

At first light my platoon moved out toward the area where the sound had come from. The young Vietnamese man was dead. He had taken off his watch and tried to hide it in some bushes near his outstretched hand. A bag of rice lay some distance away. The man was unarmed. The first Viet Cong killed by the battalion was an unarmed porter. We had come halfway around the world to kill a laborer.

"Ain't war fun," Spencer said, standing near the dead man. Surprisingly, I did not feel much remorse, although I had listened to the man as he died. It had been frightening in the darkness, not knowing if other VC were around us, getting ready to attack. Plus I had been frustrated by our lack of catching the VC who had probed our part of the perimeter at the base camp. Last night, in the dark, we had reached out to get the enemy and had only gotten a porter, but it was a start. We had much to learn about jungle fighting.

I walked away from the dead man without looking back, saying under my breath, "Don't probe my perimeter anymore."

The battalion swept the area from the trail down to the river and uncovered a large store of rice. Some of the bags had the sign of clasped hands across the ocean on them, which indicated that the rice was part of U.S. aid to the region.

While burning down a hootch near the rice cache, Patrick was standing by, lighting a cigarette, when suddenly he heard a shot. He dropped to the ground, brought his rifle to his shoulder, and looked around wildly for the enemy. The rest of the men in his squad did not react.

"The bamboo," De Leon said. "It's the bamboo burning. Sections popping. Get up. Nobody's shooting at you, sweetheart."

The bamboo continued to pop as Patrick got to his feet.

Later when we broke down into platoon patrols for the move back to the base camp, a grenade on Manuel's web belt came unscrewed and fell to the ground. The firing pin was still on his belt.

"Grenade!" he yelled, as he dived away.

He lay there, his mouth wide open and his eyes shut tight, waiting for the explosion that would take his life. After a minute the men around him got to their feet. Bratcher walked up and saw the fuse, pin, and handle still on Manuel's belt, who continued to lie on the ground with a confused look on his face.

"Good God almighty," Bratcher said, "how can we be expected to fight in this war when we got dumbbells for soldiers? Get your fat ass up, Manuel. You ain't going to die. Fix your frigging grenade and move out."

Over the course of the next few days the platoon was assigned to work details to fix up the company area, erect tents, dig latrines, and string wire. Ernst, Duckett, Pete, and I moved into a tent next to company headquarters, near the mess hall. My platoon was in two similar-size tents down the company street. We changed our routine from having the whole platoon on the line each night to posting a small twenty-four-hour guard detail.

Periodically at night, the mortar platoons, including Pete's in our company and the 4.2-inch mortars at battalion, shot harassment and interdiction (H&I) fire at randomly selected road junctions or trails. The purpose was to keep the Viet Cong, if there were any out there, on their toes and wary of mindless wandering near our position.

One night one of the battalion's mortar platoons misfired an H&I round into a group of huts northwest of the friendly village of Phuoc Vinh. The local ARVN unit advised our battalion about the accident early the next morning. Company A was sent out to investigate.

The huts were separated from the main part of the village along a river, and the mortar round had landed directly on top of a hut in the center. A woman and two men had been killed and several other people wounded, including some children. The dead were lying in the shade by the side of a hut when we arrived, their bloodstained night clothing only partially covering the gaping holes in their bodies. The villagers were wailing and crying. Most of the wounded had been evacuated to a hospital in town, but a few of the lesser wounded were standing around, displaying fresh bandages. Through an interpreter, we took information about the time of the accident, the number of casualties, and the exact location of the huts.

The hit occurred at approximately the same time that an H&I round was fired by the battalion 4.2-mortar platoon at a road target near the huts. Our unit had killed the civilians. It was a mistake, and everyone was sorry.

"Things like these happen in wars," Bratcher said, twitching his jaw. "We just got to hang in there and learn how to do it right. War ain't never been easy. Or error-free."

Two nights later to the west, near the huts we had accidentally hit with our mortar fire, several rockets were laid in wooden V wedges and ignited by a small group of people, probably Viet Cong. The rockets soared up and into our base camp and landed in Company B's area. The west side of the perimeter was probed at about the same time.

Within ten minutes from the time of the first rocket explosion, everything became quiet. I reported to Woolley that there was no activity in my sector, but I continued to stand in the command bunker and scan the edge of the jungle line. There was no conversation on the radio. Finally the field telephone rang. My RTO said it was Lieutenant Peterson.

"Dunn's wounded," Pete said. "He's at the aid tent."

I took a flashlight and made my way to the aid tent near the center of the base camp. Haldane and Allee were just coming out through the blackout curtain. Haldane said Dunn was going to be all right. Inside the tent, three men were lying on stretchers on the floor. Dunn was on the operating/examination table. He was talking fast to the battalion surgeon, Dr. Isaac Goodrich, and the corpsmen attending him.

"Goddamn that hurts. Quit it. Goddammit. Quit it. Quit it."

"Lieutenant," said Goodrich, "if you don't shut up, we are going to quit it and leave you alone to sew up your own mess. Shut up."

Dunn had shrapnel wounds on his chest, arms, stomach, and legs, but they did not appear to be life threatening. The corpsmen were probing in the open wounds to find the shrapnel, occasionally extracted bits of metal, and dropped them in a stainless steel pan on a nearby table.

"Owweeee," Dunn moaned, though not very seriously. "Don't you have some laughing gas or opium or something? Aren't there supposed to be some female nurses around here? Owweeee."

"Bob," I said, "I just talked with some of your men. They did it. Threw grenades at you. Don't like you. Tried to kill you. They're standing around outside, some of them, taking bets on whether you live or die. Only no one wants to take bets that you live."

"Owweeee, Jimmy. Ohhhhhh, Jimmy. I don't like this. You gotta help me."

I took out a .45-pistol round and put it in his mouth. "Bite on this," I said. "It's the way they do it in the movies."

Dunn was flown out to the 93d Field Hospital in Bien Hoa the following day. The doctor opined that he would be back in the unit within weeks. He had lost some blood and had some nicks, but he was going to be all right.

Shortly after Dunn left the battalion received orders to provide protection to a truck convoy traveling between Phuoc Vinh and Bien Hoa. We were deployed along the road in advance of the convoy and spent several days in relaxed platoon-size positions as the trucks sped by. We received mixed reactions from the civilians in the area. Some of the older men and women ignored us and stayed out of our way. Others, especially the children, were fascinated and watched as we approached, smiling when we smiled. Rumors circulated that we should not buy drinks from the locals because glass and poison had been found in Cokes sold by children in other areas.

After the convoys passed we were trucked down to the edge of Bien Hoa, where we were to camp while the trucks were loaded. We expected to be in the bivouac area for several days. The day we arrived there, Pete, Duckett, and I borrowed a Jeep and went into Bien Hoa. I went to a furniture maker and placed an order for a bar for our tent at Phuoc Vinh. The furniture maker promised to have it finished by the next afternoon.

We wandered from the furniture maker's shop down to a strip of bars and noticed that we were dirtier than most of the U.S. soldiers we passed, who we assumed worked at the Bien Hoa logistic command.

"It's like the Wild West movies, you know," Pete said. "These here are townies and we're just in from the range, covered with trail dust."

An Armed Forces Radio station was on in the bar we finally entered, reporting on an upcoming Bob Hope concert. We envied the way the local GIs seemed to know their way around the bar, playing darts and talking with the girls. One of the soldiers came up to Duckett and asked if he had any souvenirs for sale.

"Beg your pardon?" Duckett said.

"Viet Cong stuff, flags, AK-47s, hats," the soldier clarified. "Big price for it at Bien Hoa, though they make VC flags in some of the shops better than the real thing."

"Nope, we ain't got none of that," Duckett said as McCoy came in the bar and joined us.

"I tell you what," he said. "This is the way to do the war—inside work, light lifting, air conditioners, bars, girls, cold beer."

"You're going candy ass, George?" I said.

"Ah, the romance has gone out of being in the infantry," George said. "A little logistic command assignment, two or three months down here—I could do that."

We noticed a drunk soldier, with pressed fatigues and shined boots, groping at a bar girl.

"Well, I don't know," George said. "Maybe it is better out in the boonies. The beer tasted better when you could get it cold. You're thirstier, you know what I mean? Didn't have to worry about dressing up for any Bob Hope concert."

The next day I commandeered an empty deuce-and-a-half truck and, with Manuel driving, returned to the furniture maker. The bar was everything I had expected. Nicely curved on one end with adjustable shelves behind. A water-resistant top. We took it back to our bivouac area and put ponchos over it, more for protection against the possibility of rain than to hide it. When the convoy was assembled the following day, I located a driver who was taking supplies to our battalion, and he agreed to put the bar on top of his load. I assigned Manuel as the bar guard and told him to ride in the back and protect that bar with his life.

I was standing by Woolley as the convoy passed. Manuel was on the back of one of the first vehicles. The bar, obvious to me because of its shape, was under wraps. I waved to Manuel. Woolley put his head to one side as he looked at me, quizzically.

Manuel had the bar in our tent when we finally arrived three days later. Woolley came in and asked where it came from.

"Damned if I know, but it sure is pretty," I said. "Something to come home to from those long camping trips we take around here."

An hour later Colonel Haldane and Major William E. Panton, the battalion G-3 (operations officer), walked into the tent, looked at the bar, then at me, and walked out without comment.

I wrote to several liquor companies at the addresses on their bottles and asked for bar accessories, napkins, shot glasses, anything to give our bar a professional touch. Within weeks I began to get packages. Each liquor company responded and was generous with gifts. Our bar soon had all the machinery of a first-rate neighborhood gin mill.

Mail call was the most important part of the day to most of the soldiers. Late in the afternoon Bratcher picked up the platoon's mail from the company clerk. He called the men into the company street and yelled out the names on the packages and letters. Ayers was always in the front, but he never seemed to get any mail. Bratcher said that it was painful for him, when he had to tell Ayers that he got no mail; the big lug always looked so hurt. It wasn't that Ayers didn't write to anyone. Every couple of days he gave the company clerk a painfully addressed letter to someone in the Midwest. As far as we knew, no one ever responded.

Ray Ernst also had a man in his platoon who didn't receive mail and, like Ayers, stood in the front during each mail call. Ernst wrote to a preacher friend, who organized an Operation Alpha Company. Members of his congregation sent personal letters to men in the company, including Ayers. Bratcher was also careful to call out Ayers's name for boxes addressed to "Anyone in Alpha Company, 1st/28th Infantry." We were soon receiving care packages from other churches, civic organizations, and grammar school classes. We got a lot of Kool-Aid; some newspaperman somewhere must have written, "Those boys over there need Kool-Aid to win this war," 'cause we got Kool-Aid packages by the hundred. No one ever used them.

Dunn returned from the field hospital within a month. We had a "welcome home" party for him at the bar.

We continued to widen our area of operations in November and December, sweeping farther and farther from our base camp. In late November we had returned from a battalion-size sweep when we were visited by a congressional delegation led by Sen. Jacob Javits. The officers and NCOs of the company were standing in a loose formation near the company headquarters when the senator arrived. As he came down the line, he asked me if I needed anything or if there was anything he could do for me back home. I told him that we had a bar in our tent, but we needed a picture of a nude behind it.

"I am trying to upgrade the ambience of the place," I added.

"A nude?" the senator asked hesitantly, as though my request was slightly uncongressional.

"Yes sir," I said.

I did not look at Woolley or Haldane, because I knew they were glaring. Second lieutenants should not be forward with congressional delegations. Certainly they shouldn't ask for pictures of naked women. Javits smiled and wished me well.

In late November 1965 my platoon was on patrol south of the base camp. Private De Leon and Sergeant Rome were on point. As they broke out of a bamboo thicket De Leon dropped to one knee and Rome lifted his arm in the air, stopping the platoon. Rome turned, made eye contact with me, and called in a loud whisper, "Lieutenant!"

Rome moved off to one side behind a tree and I joined him there. We looked through the jungle toward a small Vietnamese village in front of us. Off to the side of the village near an open field, several women wearing straw cone hats were sifting rice, separating it from the chaff. Several old men and a few children were moving around among the huts. Smoke from two cooking fires drifted up.

"No men," De Leon observed. "Don't look right."

A chicken crowed from inside the village and then, closer to us, some pigs snorted.

I leaned against the back side of the tree, wiped my brow, and pulled a map from my side pocket. Sergeant Bratcher walked up. When he took in the scene and saw me studying the map, he turned and motioned for the platoon behind us in the thicket to get down and rest.

The village was clearly marked on my map, as was the nearby rice field where the women were working. The map indicated that a path ran from the village across our front to a road five kilometers distant to the west. On the other side of the village from us was another rice field.

We had been in Vietnam now for seven weeks. Although my men had killed the VC rice porter—and had been probed at our base camp—the platoon had not been fully engaged by the enemy. We were coming together as a unit, however, and becoming comfortable in the jungle, more sure of ourselves, as we gradually extended our patrols farther away from other friendly units. We looked jungle tough. Because we carried our weapons with us every minute we were in the field, they became extensions of our bodies. Our field uniforms and web gear were becoming faded; the coverings to our steel pots were personalized with identifying marks—girlfriend names, personal mottoes, and so on. Most of us carried our C rations in extra socks hanging off the back of our packs. Although we looked like pack mules with all of our gear, we did not clank when we walked. On patrol, every day, we moved more silently as we learned to traverse jungle obstacles, but we were tired of trudging endlessly through the jungles. We wanted to engage the Viet Cong, and we felt that we were getting closer. Newsome, my radio operator, in fact, had remarked during our last break that he felt we were being watched.

It was mid-afternoon but still hot. We heard no sounds from the women, old men, and children in the village, only the distant steady thumping of threshing rice and the whirring of nearby insects.

I reached for the handset to the PRC-25 radio. "Red Cap Twigs Alpha Six, this is Red Cap Twigs Alpha November Six, over," I said, calling Captain Woolley in a soft voice.

There was a short pause. Then, "Yeah, November Six, this is Alpha Six, what's your location, over?"

After giving a coordinate from the map, I turned to look at the Vietnamese people working to my front and said, "We're near this village, and there ain't no men that we can see. Maybe twenty women, children, old people. I think they know we're here, but they ain't looking this way. Just going on about their business. Don't like it. What you want me to do, over?"

During a long pause, I stared at the back of an old man in black pajamas who was sitting in the shade of a hut, stiffly staring away from us. I sensed he was listening intently. He probably had heard the distinctive sound of the radio-breaking squelch.

"Alpha November Six, this is Alpha Six. Go on around the village; don't go mixing it up with civilians. You're out there looking for VC. Go on, you got another few klicks to go anyway to tie up with Alpha Mike Six before sundown. Circle the village and continue on. You copy, over?"

I acknowledged the order and handed the handset back to the RTO as I pushed myself away from the tree. Sergeant Rome had also heard the company commander's order. He rose from his squatting position and turned to me. I motioned with my head to stay well within the jungle and pass the village to the left. As Rome and then De Leon started moving, a dog in the village began barking. I stood by the tree and watched the village as my platoon slowly filed by. The dog continued to bark loudly. The old man sitting in the shade did not move.

Falling in near the end of the patrol, I walked alongside PFC Joaquin S. Cipriano for several minutes, although my attention was still on the village we were passing. Cipriano had not been feeling well lately. "I'm sick," he said. "Stomach, plus I'm hacking up some crud. Feel like I got bugs or worms or something. Really, I ain't making this up."

I heard him, but my focus was to our right. Finally I looked in his direction and we made eye contact.

Cipriano smiled. "Back home, feeling the way I do, my momma would make me some soup."

Smiling at him, I made no comment and moved up the patrol line to fall in near Newsome with the radio. Ahead, De Leon and Rome cautiously came to the path leading across our front to the village. De Leon stuck his head out into the pathway, looked both ways, and took three quick steps to the other side. Rome followed and then a few more soldiers. I crossed the path, and one by one, the rest of the platoon began to cross. Up ahead, De Leon was approaching the second rice field, and I strained to see if there was anyone working in the field.

With fearful suddenness, a sharp sound cracked through the air. For a second, an enormously loud blast consumed us. Shrapnel shredded the foliage around us, and everyone hit the ground.

"Owweeee," someone in great pain yelled immediately. De Leon began firing his M-14 on full automatic. I fell to my knees behind an anthill, but couldn't see anyone between us and the rice field.

"What the hell's happening, De Leon?" I yelled.

Behind me, near the path, I heard again, "Iiioooooowwwwweeeeee," and then, "Oh Mother of Mercy, oh God, oh God, oh God, I'm dying. Iiiioooooooowwwweeee."

"Nothing just yet, but I ain't letting no one come up on me," De Leon answered. Behind at the path, more screaming. "Medic, medic, medic! God, where's the medic?"

Quickly moving back, I saw Cipriano lying facedown at the side of the path. He had a large, bloody wound in his back, above his pack, near his neck. He kept yelling for the medic. Nearby on the path was a hole surrounded by fresh dirt blown away by a mine. Two wires sticking out of the hole led back toward the village. Someone had touched off the mine as Cipriano passed. A patrol member applied a bandage to the wound. I told Cipriano to be still and it would be all right.

Crazed with fear and pain, he kept looking around as he said, "I'm dying, Doc. I can't feel nothing. I can't feel my legs or my arms or nothing, Doc. And goddamn it hurts. Don't let me die. Please don't let me die."

Newsome had followed me back to the path. He had called in a medevac helicopter, and I took the radio to report to the company commander. As I finished, the air ambulance chopper was arriving; it must have been very close by. I sent men to surround a nearby clearing and throw purple smoke into the field. Within minutes, possibly less than fifteen after the mine had exploded, Cipriano was on the chopper heading for a hospital. He was still conscious, but he had bled a great deal and bloody bandages covered his back. Lying on his stomach in the back of the helicopter, he looked in our direction with eyes glazed in pain. As the helicopter rose out of the field, the corpsman on board was clearing Cipriano's weapon. Helicopter gunships buzzed the tree lines on either side.

Then it was quiet again, and we went into the village.

I sent some of the men to the far side, and they herded the women from their rice chores back into the center of the village while the rest of the platoon searched the huts. Shortly, all the villagers were collected near me in front of one of the cooking fires. There were no young men—just women, old people, and children standing in a huddle as they fearfully looked around at us. But I knew that one of them had set off the mine that had wounded my man, or perhaps killed him or maimed him for life. Or, if one of them had not set off the mine, they were hiding the person who did.

Rome, Bratcher, De Leon, and the others had stopped their noisy search of the small village and gathered around to look at the Vietnamese. The loud dog, beaten off by one of my soldiers, continued to bark at the side of a hut.

To let the Vietnamese go free would certainly mean that they would shield attacks on other Americans patrolling their countryside, looking for their Viet Cong brothers, fathers, and sons. Allowing them to go without punishment would not further our ends or vindicate the attack on Cipriano. They were the enemy—directly or indirectly. I felt something needed to be done.

None of us in the platoon spoke their language. We could not threaten or interrogate them or make them understand why we were here. What could we do?

De Leon walked up with a VC flag he had found in a tree on the edge of the village.

Beck picked up the old man who had sat silently in the shade of the hut and shook him. The old man did not show fear, and I told Beck to release him.

A few moments later I ordered the men to move out, and we left the villagers alone, unhurt. It is not pleasant to be the conventional force in a guerrilla war—maintaining high moral standards of conduct when the enemy is engaged in total war. It is a hard war to win.

—— SEVEN ——

At Home in the Jungle

Peterson was transferred out of the company to take over the battalion reconnaissance (recon) platoon when we returned from the field. Expected to be the eyes and ears of the battalion, roaming in the front and on the flanks during conventional field operations, the recon platoon had been heretofore in Vietnam no more than battalion staff security, and the colonel wanted more aggressive leadership. I hated to see Pete go. He was my best friend and I wanted him at my side in battle. Pete, however, was eager to get out of the mortars and into a maneuver element. Plus he wanted to work directly for Colonel Haldane. So I was happy for him, but sad to see him go. I thought about the insurance policy, remembering that I hadn't ever sent in the change-of-beneficiary form. I looked for it, couldn't find it, and then let it go. Helping Pete move his gear over to battalion, I started to mention the insurance, but I was embarrassed and told myself I just had to find the form or write the company for another.

During the next battalion operation, Pete's first as recon platoon leader, we went across a large river to the west of our base camp and broke down into platoon-size units. Battalion staff officers, assigned to spotter helicopters, looked for signs of VC fleeing in front of the platoons.

From their elevated vantage the spotters could not see men moving on the ground as well as they could see trails, villages, and clearings. They had never served on the ground themselves and did not realize how difficult it was to move through the jungle. Sometimes we faced swamps and deep crevices beneath the jungle canopies, so the observers often miscalculated the time it would take us to move through a particular area.

"Okay, Red Cap Twigs Alpha November Six, you, ah, you, ah,

are where? Throw smoke?" Pause. "Okay, I got it. What are you doing there, you're supposed to be another klick ahead. They're waiting on you up there."

Down below, Bratcher would say, "I think I am going to shoot that REMF, next chance. Next opportunity I have at that clean, good-smelling, staff shithead, he's dead."

Ayers and Beck, stinking from their sweat, would be out of breath from breaking trail in the dense jungle, and we'd hear the helicopter way off in the distance. The staff officer would come back on the radio telling us to double-time to meet up with the other men. Once Moubry told Duckett's unit that they were off line. Duckett ignored him and soon thereafter called Woolley with a request to stop for the night. His men were exhausted. He invited Moubry to come down with some supplies, such as cold beer.

For the most part we were not successful in initiating contact with the VC during that operation. We did have one encounter, however, when Bratcher was at the head of our column. The platoon was walking down a trail. We often avoided trails because of the chance of mines and ambushes. Breaking new trails through the jungle was safer, but we had been beside the path earlier in the day and we were not going to stay on it for long. As he was looking down for trip lines, Bratcher almost ran into a couple of VC who were coming in our direction around a bend in the trail. He dropped to one knee, but by the time he got his rifle to his shoulder and fired, the VC were gone. Beck was running after them when I ordered him back.

Although we were unsuccessful in finding the VC during the day, they came at us at night, probing our positions. As we lay in a tight perimeter, tired and wanting to sleep, they crawled in and threw grenades or sniped at us. They also tried to steal our claymore mines; however, we planted trip flares around them so if a VC slipped in to steal them, the flares went off. One night a work detail of VC crawled along the perimeter, figured out how the trip flares were planted, and stole the flares and the mines. The next night, McCoy planted flares beneath the claymores. At midnight he heard movement out by the claymores just moments before a flare went off. One of his men squeezed off the detonator. In the morning McCoy guessed that there had been three VC, but it was hard to tell from the bits of flesh blown over the area.

My platoon suffered no casualties in the operation. Duckett was not so lucky.

Duckett was a stern taskmaster. He told his men he expected them to get out there and fight. He pushed hard at the enemy whenever we had contact, and he was the last platoon leader to call in dust-offs (medevacs) for his wounded. That was different from some of the other platoon leaders. When we took casualties, some platoon leaders stopped everything to look after their wounded; Duckett's first job always was to kill VC. Duckett did not wear socks or underwear, so his early weeks in Vietnam were painful. But after a short time his feet and crotch toughened up and he felt no discomfort from the lack of underclothing. He also wore a flak jacket he had picked up from a cavalry friend. Because he was Duckett, people did not question this. Most of us would not have worn a flak jacket if they were available; they were heavy and wore down the body. But Duckett got used to his flak jacket and never left base camp without it. Eventually it saved his life.

Early in the operation he and his platoon deployed some distance from the company in an area north of a village thought to be sympathetic to the VC. After dark he posted a two-man listening post (LP) among some rubber trees halfway between the village and the thicket where the platoon had dug in. Soon the listening post reported hearing movement to their right. In a low whisper, they suggested that a small group of people might be moving from the village toward Duckett's position. Duckett alerted the platoon, and everyone waited quietly.

A light rain began to fall. Suddenly out of the dark, a shot zinged in.

As the men tensed, Duckett's platoon sergeant hissed loudly, "Don't fire." He thought that other VC might be waiting in front for the muzzle flashes to give away their positions.

He was right. The VC in front, soon tired of waiting, began firing at the platoon. Duckett called for mortar flares as his men returned the fire. Illumination rounds burst over the rubber trees and the VC pulled back. Within minutes the listening post reported the VC running back toward the village.

Everything was quiet until early morning when the two men at the listening post reported hearing movement all around—the VC had returned. Duckett told them to calm down; it could be the rain dripping off the trees. They did not acknowledge his call but quickly, breathlessly reported seeing men maneuvering directly at their position. Before Duckett could answer, he heard small-arms fire to his front. The listening post yelled into the radio that they were pulling back to the platoon.

Duckett called down the line to his men, "Get ready, the LP is coming in. VC in the front. Be careful, don't shoot the LP!"

The men lay silently in their holes as they scanned the jungle toward the rubber trees. Duckett, who shared a foxhole with his RTO, ducked into the hole, called for more flares over the radio, and drew his .45-caliber pistol. As he came back up, he aimed it over the top and took a deep breath. Woolley came on the radio and asked about the situation. Duckett bent down into the hole again to talk with Woolley.

The RTO saw movement in the front. He pulled the pin on his grenade. Footfalls came closer in the dark. Forms began to take shape into men, running headlong toward them. The RTO pulled back his arm to throw the grenade, then he saw the distinctive steel pots on the heads of the men and yelled down the line, "LP coming in. Don't fire! Don't fire!"

The men from the LP were running as fast as they could in the dark.

A shot ran out behind them, the round whistling over their heads. Another round zinged through the jungle. The men lunged toward the hole as Duckett came up after talking with Woolley. He barely avoided a head-on collision.

The radio operator, the grenade still in his hand, ducked into the hole. As more rounds from the pursuing VC passed overhead, the two men landed on top of the RTO, the grenade was knocked from his hand, and it fell into the hole. The radio operator tried to get out of the hole and became frantic, but the LP men forced him downward as they desperately sought cover from the enemy fire. The two men, also excited, continued to worm their way into the hole.

Duckett was trapped on the side of the hole. As the three men wrestled beside him, he fired his .45 into the dark, toward the VC.

And the grenade went off.

The radio operator and one of the men from the LP were blown apart. The other man from the LP had shrapnel wounds over most of his body. Duckett was covered with bits of clothing, web gear, and flesh, but his flak jacket had protected him. Although he was not wounded, he was blinded by the blast and could not hear anything except a ringing in his ears. By morning he had regained his sight but had lost the hearing in his right ear.

Duckett and the wounded LP man were evacuated, along with the remains of the other two men. After a night at the field clearing station, Duckett was sent to a U.S. Army hospital in Japan.

When we returned from the operation, Sp4. Burke, who carried one of Colonel Haldane's radios, sought me out. He said that he had heard, although he could not confirm it firsthand, that an oil painting of a nude had arrived at division headquarters in Di An. It was from Senator Javits's office in Washington, D.C., and was addressed to the unidentified 1st Infantry Division field officer who had built a bar in the jungle. A division support officer, an REMF, had it in his office, but he was not, as far as Burke knew, making any effort to find the intended owner. I thanked Burke and went looking for Captain Woolley, who had not been pleased when I asked Senator Javits for the painting. He might not approve any effort on my part to retrieve it. I found Woolley behind his desk in the company headquarters tent and asked him for a day's leave to go down to Di An on a personal matter of some importance. He smiled. I smiled.

"And?" he asked.

"And what, sir?" I replied.

"What is the personal matter?" he asked, not smiling as much as he had.

"I'd rather not say, sir, exactly, other than to say it is important to me."

Woolley gazed intently at me for a moment or two and then said, "Okay, but this better not have any blow-back. You understand me?"

At Di An I first went to the post office and talked with the NCOIC (noncommissioned officer in charge), who remembered the package. He'd sent it to G-4 (logistics). The NCOIC was there, in fact, when the officer opened it. "Damned nice piece of work," he told me.

I thanked him and went to the logistics Quonset hut. I was clearly aware of the difference in my appearance from that of the staff people whom I encountered along the way. My fatigues were worn, and I had a strange tan—my forehead was white from wearing my steel pot, but my cheeks were ruddy and showed briar scratches.

As I made my way toward the rear of the Quonset hut, I looked into each office as I went, sometimes interrupting conversations and work activities. Finally, in a major's office I spied an oil painting of a nude woman, looking out a window from behind a curtain, as if she were waiting for someone to come home. I was staring at the painting when the major looked up from his paperwork at me, then at the painting and back at me.

"Senator Javits?" I asked.

"I beg your pardon," the major said.

"Did that painting come from Senator Javits to an unidentified 1st Infantry Division field officer?" I asked as I walked into the room.

"Who are you?" asked the major.

"That officer," I said.

There was a pause. Then the major asked, "How am I supposed to know that?"

"I just told you, that's how you know. Last month, Senator Javits visited our position at Phuoc Vinh—I'm with the 1st of the 28th—and I asked him for a picture of a nude. That one. So I'm here to pick it up."

"No, you're not," said the major, leaning back in his chair. "You are going to have to get me some proof from your battalion commander or someone who can verify the fact that Senator Javits was sending you a painting. How am I supposed to know this is actually meant for you? Maybe you've just heard it's here and are trying to talk me out of it. I've got a responsibility here."

My first thought was that I didn't know how Woolley or Haldane would react. But then I thought, that isn't the point; this REMF major is a horse's ass, sitting here in an air-conditioned office with my painting hanging on his wall.

"Major," I said, "I don't know about your responsibilities, but I know that's my painting and that I've only got one day down here. I'm a little hurt you don't want to help me with this."

The major continued to lean back in his chair; I wasn't going to win any war of words. Without thinking it through, I changed tone and said, "So listen here. I'm just going to take *my* painting off *your* fucking wall and if you so much as touch me, I'm going to hurt you. And I'm still going to take it."

With that, I walked over, took the painting off the wall, and left. The major did, in fact, file a report which eventually reached Woolley, saying that I had threatened him and stolen a painting off the wall of his office. By the time the letter arrived, the painting was a fixture behind our bar and the story of how it came to be there was part of Alpha Company folklore. Woolley destroyed the letter.

Ernst returned from an operation in December with what was diagnosed as dengue fever. Over the next few days he became gaunt and tired easily, but he did not go on sick call. Some "dingy fever" wasn't manly enough to call him out of the field. He'd leave if the medic said he had *typhoid* fever—but not "dingy." "Get outa here," he said. "It's just Jimbo and me to help the good captain." Peterson and Duckett were both gone.

He had in his platoon a young man who never stopped talking. And he was funny. Shortly after picking up the dengue bug, Ernst and his platoon were on patrol south of Phuoc Vinh. He and the comic were walking close together when the platoon was ambushed. A bullet hit Ray in the hand. The young man was splattered with shrapnel. They had to be moved several kilometers to a clearing for a medevac. Wounded in dozens of places, the young man walked most of the way out. He was lying by a tree when the medevac helicopter arrived. A corpsman walked up with a bandage in his hand but paused because the man had so many wounds. "Just put a bandage on me anywhere," the young man said. "You're bound to cover a wound." As the corpsman worked, the youngster borrowed a cigarette from someone standing by and lit it himself. Exhaling, he asked the corpsman, "You know the names of any nurses in the hospital where we're going?"

Ernst, on the other hand, had to be carried on a makeshift

stretcher all the way from the ambush site to the open field. He was in great pain. Eyes sunken from the dengue fever, his hand torn open, he looked like a corpse. He was a good man, popular with his men. They knew that he was leaving them, and they feared he would have to have his hand amputated. As the corpsmen were carrying Ernst to the helicopter, several of his men grabbed the sides of the stretcher. When they lifted the stretcher to put him inside the helicopter, it came apart and Ernst fell through it to the ground. He landed on his head.

The youngster, already on board, said, "Not necessarily the helping hand the lieutenant was looking for."

Ernst was finally righted and put on the helicopter. With his good hand, he gave a thumbs-up to his men. He was eventually evacuated back to the States and we never saw him again.

For a short while I was the only platoon leader left in the company and then a new second lieutenant, "Brad Arthur" [alias], arrived. Woolley gave him Ernst's platoon. Arthur was loud. When some other replacements whom he knew dropped by, he repeated the stories he had heard about Ernst's medevac, but with the wrong emphasis, I thought. He hadn't earned his spurs yet and didn't have the right to laugh.

The new M-16 assault rifles arrived and, like Arthur, they did not make a good first impression. I had handled guns all my life, but I instantly disliked that light aluminum and plastic toy with its designer lines. It didn't feel right, made silly little sounds when a round was chambered, had no recoil when it was fired, didn't come up naturally to the shoulder, and had a handle on the top. For what? It made sighting awkward. I told the men I didn't know about this thing that looked like it was made by Mattel. Didn't look like the kind of gun that would win wars. Didn't want any of my men holding it by the handle, like a woman's pocketbook.

I told Bratcher I was keeping my shotgun. He nodded and asked when I had last fired it. I figured about three or four weeks before. Bratcher said that he had noticed a lot of rain and wondered how waterproof that gun was, how well it might be able to handle, say, firing all seven rounds without jamming.

Newsome, my RTO, had covered it with oil, and I had cleaned

it religiously every time we returned from an operation. It seemed to be in good shape.

On Bratcher's suggestion, however, we took it down to the perimeter. Standing on top of Spencer's bunker, I put it to my shoulder and fired. The gun jammed after one round. I tried to clear it and heard something break inside. The bolt stopped working altogether. Bratcher looked at me with his eyebrows raised. I tore the gun down as much as I could and found several pieces, weakened by rust, broken or bent from firing that one shot.

"Not many spare parts around here for a Stateside rabbit gun," Bratcher said.

I threw the shotgun and the parts into the minefield, then went back to the company armorer and drew an M-16. I tried to like it, but the more I handled it the cheaper it felt. Where was the wood, the weight? Sure, we could carry three times more ammo, but everyone would fire the thing on full automatic and no one would aim. It was not a woodsman's gun.

And the magazines? The guns might be high-tech, but those magazines were mass produced and cheap. The spring wires were smaller than coat hangers. I could bend them with my finger.

I raged against those M-16s and the magazines, but no one listened seriously.

So I resigned myself to life with the M-16. Like everyone else, I put twenty rounds in each magazine, as we had been told to do, and then one more for Mother. If we squeezed down tight on that thin wire spring, we could get twenty-one rounds in. For many people that last bullet was a tragic mistake because the springs in the early-version magazines rusted together. Also, because they were so light, men taped two, sometimes three magazines together so they would be at the ready in a firefight. This extra weight on the light latch that held in the magazines caused the magazines to droop just enough to cause misfires. Plus, the guns were not hardy and would not function with any dirt in the workings. And there was a lot of dirt in the jungle. We had to give up the durable M-14 and got a light, faster, cheaper replacement. Initially we certainly suffered more from its disadvantages than we gained from its lighter weight and higher speed.

At about that time, Mother and Daddy sent me wire spectacles and a commode seat. I had asked for the latter item because the company latrine had uncomfortable holes cut in flat wood. I took great pride in my ass, I told my friends. The civilized man looked after his toilet facilities. It was what separated us from the animals that crapped in the jungle. Woolley said he wondered about me sometimes—the bar, the toilet seat. He wondered if I was queer.

I kept the toilet seat near the bar and took it with me on each visit to the latrine. No one made any catcalls. That might have been because I usually carried the toilet seat in one hand and a .45 in the other.

One day I was walking down the company street toward the latrine with the commode seat. I saw Spencer sitting in front of his tent. He looked at me and the seat and then smiled. I tried to look ahead and ignore him. I was wishing I had my .45. As I walked in front of Spencer, he followed me with his smile. I passed by.

"I can't think of a damned thing to say, Lieutenant. Goddamned I'm trying hard and I can't."

Just before Christmas, Jim Newsome, my RTO since Fort Riley days, rotated back to the States. I went down to his tent to say good-bye. I picked up his PRC-25 radio and walked over to Spencer. Bratcher, Castro, and Rome were standing by the entrance to the tent.

"No sir, goddamned, no sir, goddammit, no. I ain't carrying no fucking radio. I ain't. I don't have to." He appealed to Bratcher, "Tell him, Platoon Sergeant."

"I don't care what you think about this thing, Spencer. Get the freqs and call signs you need from Newsome before he leaves." I had a half smile on my face, but my eyes were serious.

Spencer looked at me and said, "Ah, shit."

Initially I had thought about making De Leon my RTO, but as we became more experienced in the field it became apparent that Spencer, in addition to being bright, was very cool under fire. And, I could not explain it, this black youngster from a northern ghetto, and I, a white man from a small southern town, were in sync together in the jungle. Bratcher and I had uncommonly good rapport, but he was usually at the rear of the platoon file during operations. Beck and Spencer were, for whatever reason, always near me when things were happening. Beck's attitude was to go get 'em. Don't matter 'bout nothing. Get' em. Spencer had just as much courage, but he was more deliberate. He would always hesitate a moment before acting. For all of my initial concern that he would be disruptive and hard to control, he was effective in combat. Plus, he was smart and I liked him. So he was my RTO.

Woolley initially questioned this selection because often the RTO spoke for the platoon leader, and Spencer was known to be irascible. Plus his thick inner-city diction was initially hard for most of the other white college-boy RTOs to understand. But in short order Woolley, and the other RTOs, realized that Spencer always knew what he was talking about. And when he spoke for me, he always got it right.

We stayed in the base camp from shortly before Christmas through New Year's. Each night different platoons were sent out on ambush patrols. Woolley told Arthur that he had the patrol for Christmas Eve night.

I told the captain how much I appreciated that. "I'll be able to spend Christmas in camp, probably because I'm your favorite, been around the longest."

"Nope," Woolley said. "It's because I want you on patrol New Year's Eve. If there is any man I want out away from the base camp New Year's Eve parties, it is Red Cap Twigs Alpha November Six, the proprietor of the Company A bar."

Christmas was pleasant. The company cook made a wonderful holiday meal. We cut down a small shrub for a Christmas tree and put homemade ornaments on it. On Christmas Eve, Peterson, McCoy, Dunn, and I opened presents together. Just like home, we opened them in turn, one at a time, so that we could comment on each gift and stretch out the evening.

On New Year's Eve, I was lying on my belly in the jungle by a bridge south of town. Around midnight the soldiers on the perimeter of the base camp behind us began firing tracers in the air. I started singing "Auld Lang Syne" softly and the men on both sides of me joined in. With the tracers still going off in the ~~nce~~ our voices carried over the water and into the village on ~~side.~~ The locals must have wondered.

~~Colonel Haldane and his staff went to division~~ ~~ve new operational orders. They left in the~~

morning and we expected them back by early afternoon; the trip had never taken more than a couple of hours. They didn't return until after sundown, and all officers and top NCOs were called to the operations tent at 2100.

Colonel Haldane began by saying that during the twelve weeks we had been in-country, we had learned how to fight in the jungle, had engaged elements of every VC unit operating north of Saigon, and disrupted their ability to control the territory. We had also taken casualties, and we had lost men to disease and through termination of service. Only 50 percent of the men who had left Fort Riley for Vietnam were still with us, but we had received replacements. We were still an effective fighting organization.

"Operation Crimp will launch in three days. It will test our ability to live up to the 1st Infantry Division tradition," Haldane said. "We are going to attack an area the VC and North Vietnamese have controlled for decades. It is the Ho Bo woods north of the town of Cu Chi. It is where the Ho Chi Minh trail ends inside South Vietnam. We will be up against hard-core Viet Cong combat units supported by local villagers. The VC own this territory. The only significant South Vietnamese military presence in the area is inside the town of Cu Chi. Turn the first bend in the road west of town and you are in territory of the VC's 7th Cu Chi Battalion, a unit that has never lost a battle. We know from the French that their tactics are to bend away from frontal attacks but slap back on the sides and attack from the rear. They do not run away. They fight. Our mission is to attack the center of the area, secure a base, and clear it from the inside out. Once we have pacified the area, the 25th Division, presently en route to Vietnam, will move in and control it."

The plan was to move by Caribou airplanes from our base camp to Phu Loi, a staging area some distance east of the operational zone. On 7 January 1966, we would conduct a helicopter assault into Landing Zone (LZ) Jack in the middle of the Ho Bo woods. The landing zone area would be prepped by artillery and then Air Force fast movers (jet airplanes) and finally Air Force prop-driven slow movers. Leading the troop-carrying helicopters ("slicks") would be helicopter gunships. 1st/16th Battalion would go in first. We would be in the second wave. My platoon was to be in the third, fourth, and fifth helicopters of the second lift into the LZ.

The briefing went on until midnight. We picked up new map sheets on the way out.

As we walked back to the company area, Bratcher said, "It looks like we got ourselves an operation here. We're going to get after them Commie bastards, rather than just hanging out the way we been doing, acting a lot like bait. You want to do business, go where the customers are. Am I right or what?"

The following morning we loaded onto the ugly Caribous for the short flight to the staging area. Dunn's company had already arrived there and had set up poncho shelters at the end of the runway, near where Alpha Company was assigned. The next day more units came in. Helicopters and planes were flying overhead constantly. Round rubber bladders of aviation fuel were positioned at the end of the runway. Fresh ammunition, medical supplies, and batteries arrived. The whole assembly area was alive with activity.

Before dusk Dunn and I went over to an old building built by French plantation owners. A basketball hoop was attached to the back of the building and someone had found a basketball. We joined a half-court game and wore our fatigue pants, combat boots, and T-shirts. Dunn played basketball the same way his father had probably played no-faceguard football for the Green Bay Packers. Very tough. One guy, who was much quicker than Dunn, was driving around him when Dunn hooked him around the neck, throwing him to the ground. He was angry and getting up in a hurry when Bob pushed him down again. Dunn moved quickly to stand over him and said, "Get up, asshole, and I'll knock your fucking head off."

I grabbed Dunn and said, "Hey man, save it for tomorrow. That's a good guy. You gotta know the difference. This is just a game."

— EIGHT —

Tunnel to Hell

The following morning we were up before sunrise. The mess units flew in hot breakfast. After eating, we were standing in groups of ten along the runway when we heard the first rounds of artillery fire in the distance. Not long after the sun came up we watched a large formation of helicopters, seven groups of ten helicopters each, heading our way carrying the first wave of the 1st/16th. Ahead and below them were the gunships.

As the helicopters came closer, I followed them through my binoculars. Crammed on board were soldiers in olive drab. Some were sitting with their legs hanging out, and most were clutching their M-16s in both hands. Artillery fire increased as the helicopters passed. We heard the jets before we saw them, streaking by toward the west. The artillery stopped, and the jets began working the area. More explosions came from the west, then the ground shook as B-52s bombed the fringes of the operational zone.

We figured it would take twenty minutes for the helicopters to fly from our area to the LZ. In forty minutes they should be back to pick us up. I was anxious to get started. The waiting reminded me of the ride on the landing craft when we arrived in-country. This time we would not be greeted by a brass band. The lead gunships came back first. Two moved off to the bladders of fuel. Others landed at the end of the airstrip and picked up more ammunition. Shortly, the first lift of ten transport helicopters came in low over the tree line.

I got the men up and in line. My platoon would be boarding the second group of helicopters.

Only seven came in. Where were the other three? I had not

imagined that some of the helicopters would not return. Maintaining their original positions, the helicopters landed. The third, ninth, and tenth helicopters were missing. I had been standing at the head of the line to board the third helicopter, but it wasn't there. Unsure of what to do but anxious to get going, I told Spencer to follow me and went to the fourth helicopter, telling two riflemen there to get off.

As we crawled into the helicopter, I noticed bullet holes in its side. The pilots sat in front of the controls and looked forward, shaking with the vibration of the blades, their faces impassive behind their helmet visors.

When the helicopter lifted off the ground I got Woolley on the radio and reported what he already knew about the missing helicopters. A third of my platoon was still at the airstrip.

The helicopters stayed low. Some distance to the front we could see jets strafing the ground. Clouds of smoke drifted up from an area on the horizon and gnatlike gunships moved in and out of it. As we got closer we saw bombs falling from diving planes. The napalm tanks tumbled and exploded into fireballs when they hit the jungle.

As the large, open LZ finally came into view, the gunners on both sides of the slicks began firing into the jungle. I had the impulse to sit on my M-16 to give me an extra measure of protection from bullets that might come up through the floor.

In the field ahead I saw soldiers moving around. Several downed helicopters were lying on their side. Fires were burning in the nearby jungle. I felt myself breathing faster. I tightened my grip on my M-16, and retightened it.

Get on the ground. Get on the ground! Why are we moving so goddamned slow? I thought angrily.

The helicopter finally flared out to brake its forward speed and settled down in the field. Everyone in the platoon knew we would be landing south to north and that we had to move to secure an area along the wood line to the east. As the helicopter settled to the ground I was looking for a point of trees extending out in the field that was to be the platoon rallying point. I did not see the litter detail standing on the ground until the helicopter touched down. Adrenaline pumping, we barely avoided the soldiers carrying the stretchers as we jumped to the ground. Some of the men on the stretchers were dead.

With the wounded loaded quickly the helicopters took off behind us, and as the *bat-bat-bat* of their rotary blades began to fade we heard the popping of automatic fire to the north and to our front. Rounds zinged over our heads. Rockets landed among us.

High-stepping through the tall grass, we finally made it to the wood line and then to our rally point. Once established, I sat down behind a tree and contacted Woolley. Bratcher took a head count. Twenty-one men had made it. We had not seen anyone hit in the field. The missing men must have been left behind in the staging area. Woolley told me to hold my position until the remaining men arrived.

Taking a deep breath, I stood up to light a cigarette. Rome yelled at me as I had the match halfway to my cigarette. I dropped it and fell to the ground.

"Napalm! You're standing in some napalm that didn't ignite," he said. I looked down. Napalm jelly was on my fatigues and all around on the bushes. My match was still smoking on top of a glob and I quickly stepped on it.

By late afternoon all of my platoon had come in. Most of the fighting to secure the 1st/28th's part of the LZ had been done by Dunn's platoon north of the field. My platoon had no contact with Viet Cong ground forces that afternoon or that night.

At first light the next morning we moved into the jungle. Duckett's platoon, commanded by the platoon sergeant, was on my left. Woolley was with Arthur's platoon in the rear. We were heading toward our TAOR, a two-day movement through the jungle, and hoped to reach a midway point near a small village by nightfall.

Duckett's platoon began to receive sniper fire from its left front during the late morning. I yelled out to its platoon sergeant that I was maneuvering my men around to his front. We soon saw enemy small-arms fire coming from a clump of trees. Manuel fired a long burst into the trees and the enemy stopped firing. We slowly walked into the stand of trees as we reconned by fire.

No one was there. Strange. I had seen the firing. We would have noticed anyone leaving the thicket.

Beck found two spider holes close to the forward edge of the thicket, partially covered by debris. Each opening was smaller than a basketball rim, barely large enough for a man to squeeze out. A cool, earthy smell emanated from them.

"Are the VC at the bottom of these holes, or do these go back to some room or tunnel?" I asked Bratcher as Woolley came up.

I sent men out to the front as security and looked back at the spider holes. Spencer stuck a long bamboo pole down one. It hit bottom after about five feet and then, when Spencer pushed, it went down another four feet. We shined a flashlight down the holes. Both holes curved out of sight to our front.

Yelling "Fire in the hole," we threw in grenades and ducked behind trees. The explosions were muffled and only a small amount of dust came out and blew away. We walked carefully back to the holes and looked down. I said, "Damn. We either send someone down or we leave and keep on toward our TAOR."

Woolley told me to send someone down. I called one of the Puerto Ricans, PFC Fernandez-Lopez, the smallest man in the platoon, and told him to take off his web gear because he was going on a little trip. He looked around at us, shrugged, dropped his gear, and started walking toward the hole barehanded.

"Hold it," I said. I gave him my .45 and Woolley's radio operator gave him a flashlight. We told him to just go to the bottom of the first hole, see what was there, and come back. He said something in half-Spanish and half-English that I couldn't understand, but it was a question. He looked at me for an answer. I asked him to repeat it, but I still didn't understand. Finally he put his hands over his head like he was diving. "Yes," I said, "head first. We'll hold your feet."

Fernandez crawled on his stomach to the nearest hole and stuck the flashlight over the side. He looked down for what seemed like a long time. Then he turned around, said something to Castro in Spanish, crossed himself, and crawled over the edge. The .45 and the flashlight were in front of him. Bratcher grabbed his feet and began pushing him. Yelling "Slow, amigo," Bratcher gradually pushed him down until his feet were the only part of him out of the hole.

"What do you see?" Bratcher yelled. Fernandez's comments were muffled.

Woolley told Bratcher to pull him out.

When he came out and got to his feet, dirt was caked on his fatigue jacket and on his face where the sweat had run down. Someone gave him a cigarette and he talked quickly to Castro.

Turning to us, Castro said Fernandez didn't like going down the hole.

"Well, fuck him! What did he see?" Bratcher asked.

"A lot of hole. Just hole. Some spent casings, but just the hole going on out that way," Castro said, pointing to our front.

"They are ahead of us," I said. "Waiting."

"There're tunnels here. Maybe that's why they've been so successful in this area," Woolley said.

We ate lunch before moving out. A short time later we received sniper fire. At mid-afternoon one of Arthur's men, behind us, stepped on a mine and blew his foot off. He was evacuated, and we were on our way again within the hour.

For two days we patrolled west. We encountered more mines and snipers; sullen, menless villages; and more spider holes leading down into tunnel complexes. There was a different sense to the jungle here than we had experienced in other places. It was quieter, and seemed more deadly. When we stopped occasionally to get our bearings or to rest, we heard no sounds—no birds flying or chirping, no insects humming. We felt someone was watching us all the time.

As we moved into a company defensive perimeter around a small field the third night of the operation, Major Allee arrived on the supply helicopter with small revolvers, field telephones, and spools of wire. He told us what we had already realized—we were walking over an extensive network of tunnels. They were unexpected and had not been part of the intelligence package for this operation. The spider holes were openings to the tunnels, and Allee told us to investigate them wherever we found them. They were enemy sanctuaries. We were to send down a small man, a tunnel rat, with a pistol, flashlight, and telephone. Someone was to feed the wire down as the tunnel rat explored. The man in the hole should send back situation reports every five minutes or so. He could find his way back by following the wire.

Pete led his recon platoon by our area the next morning on their way to a village off to our south. He stopped for a cup of coffee and said that a group of men from the colonel's battalion headquarters group had gone down a hole the previous night. They had run into VC in the tunnels and had a running battle. They got back by following the telephone wire; however, one man had not returned. Pete had no idea what had happened to him.

"Tunnel ratting, is that infantry duty?" I asked.

Pete stood up after finishing his coffee and told his men to saddle up. I told him to be careful. He turned toward me and smiled.

"Your mother said that, be careful, I heard her," I said. "Me, I'd rather have it the other way. You die, I'm a rich man."

"There's something on that insurance I need to talk with you about, when we have a chance," Pete mumbled.

"What?" I asked, suddenly uncomfortable. I was the one who needed to talk about the insurance; I had yet to find the change of beneficiary form.

"I'll tell you later," he said, and then he was gone.

Company A continued sweep operations that morning. Snipers pinged at us, and we encountered mines and more tunnels. Cu Chi was not friendly.

The battalion came together at mid-afternoon with plans to dig in and spend a couple of days licking its wounds. We had been on the move almost constantly for three days and had slept very little. The men were grouchy with fatigue. We welcomed the opportunity to rest, receive mail, and eat hot food.

When my platoon tied up with Arthur's on the left, Spencer, Bratcher, and I sought a central position in the rear to drop our gear and dig a small hole. Woolley came up as we were removing our packs and asked me to take a few of my men and do a "cloverleaf" patrol—make a short circle out about five or six hundred meters from the perimeter—to ensure that we hadn't inadvertently camped next to a VC position.

The men grumbled as they dropped webbing not needed for the patrol. I left a few men behind to begin digging in and the rest fell in behind Lyons, who was followed by Beck and King. We moved out to a small clearing a hundred meters to our front. The setting sun cast long shadows and made it hard to see the opposite side clearly, so we skirted it.

The jungle woods were not thick and Lyons walked along

briskly but cautiously. We were all anxious to get back. Suddenly Lyons stopped and raised his hand. Because the area was so open, most of the men dropped to one knee. Beck, his M-79 at the ready, continued to walk forward beside Lyons. I remained standing with several men back in the patrol, but I could see the two point men squinting ahead in the jungle.

Finally, Beck turned around and said in a loud whisper. "Looks like a plane."

I scowled as I walked to the head of the column. However, I could see something metallic reflecting the setting sun in a bamboo thicket ahead. It was long and cylindrical and covered with vines. Incredibly, but clearly, it was a small plane, minus the wings.

Lyons, Beck, and I approached the thicket one slow step at a time. The plane could be the bait to a trap. When I could read the number on the tail, I called it out to Spencer and told him to report that we had found spotter aircraft apparently shot down some time ago, but we were moving on and would come back and check it in the morning.

We saw no sign of the wings, wheels, or propeller. Beck guessed that the plane had crashed somewhere else and been hidden in the thicket. I pointed out that the fuselage looked intact and there didn't appear to be any evidence of a crash landing.

Beck said he was going to look inside, but I told him no—too much of a chance that it was booby-trapped. Plus, we had only a few more minutes of daylight. If we didn't move on it would be dark before we got back to the perimeter. I motioned the patrol around to the right of the thicket. As King came by, Beck and Lyons fell back in at point.

A small clearing was behind the thicket, and a three-foot-high dirt berm ran out of the jungle along the east side of the field. Spencer was coming up the column to walk behind me. King was turning around as he walked and asked me what the hell a berm was doing coming out of the jungle like that, when an automatic weapon opened up from our right. Rounds zinged between King and me.

Everyone hit the ground. Manuel was carrying the machine gun, and I yelled at him to start shooting. Short bursts of fire continued to come at us from over the berm. We crawled forward.

Bratcher was at the end of the patrol. As I reached the berm I yelled for him to move out, flanking whoever was firing to the right; we'd cover him.

Bratcher yelled for Sgt. Ollie Taylor Jr. to follow him. I told Manuel to bring the machine gun to the top of the berm. He stood up and fired from the hip. The rest of us slung our guns over the top and fired.

Beck fired his M-79 grenade launcher. The round hit an overhanging tree limb, bounced back, and landed squarely in his lap. Beck screamed, expecting the grenade to go off.

Bratcher was maneuvering in from the right. He yelled for us to stop firing. He and Taylor advanced, firing as they went. Bratcher yelled, "We got him! I saw him go down."

As I was waving the men over the berm, King turned to look at Beck. His mouth open and eyes wide, Beck was staring at the grenade in his lap.

"You lucky motherfucker," King said scornfully. "The round has to travel fifteen yards to arm itself. It didn't go fifteen yards. It ain't armed. It ain't going off. Pick it up and put it on the ground beside you."

From the other side of the berm we could see that the firing had come from beneath a couple of shelters, each just four posts holding up palm-frond roofing and no sides. Bratcher and Taylor were moving in from our right, and the rest of us came straight in, with Manuel occasionally firing the machine gun.

We saw that the ground under the roof of the larger shelter had been excavated, leaving a pit perhaps five feet deep by fifteen feet wide by twenty feet long. A trench led from the main shelter to a similar pit under the smaller one.

Expecting to see the VC lying in the bottom of the hole, we covered the last few feet very slowly, guns at the ready.

Behind us, Beck still hadn't moved and was telling King, "Maybe, maybe, maybe the round's only gone fourteen yards and something. Maybe I pick it up and, and, and, that's enough." He was trying not to breathe hard for fear of disturbing the round lying on his stomach. He took short breaths and talked as he exhaled.

"Help me, Sergeant, help me move it." Beck looked up at King.

"Nope," King said, leaning against the berm. "You can do it as well as I can. You either slap it off and roll out of the way quick, or you reach down very carefully and lift it off."

"Tell the lieutenant to come here," Beck said.

King looked over the berm in my direction. I was easing up to the shelter. The sun was almost down, and it was hard to see into the hole. Bratcher and Taylor reached the edge first.

"He's gone, the son of a bitch, down a fucking hole," Bratcher said.

A pool of blood lay next to the forward edge of the hole under the main shelter. An AK-47 assault rifle was nearby amid some empty casings and dark green cotton pouches holding AK-47 magazines. A blood trail led over to a spider hole in the corner, like the drain in a sink. Taylor, standing by the smaller shelter, said he saw another spider hole there.

"He's down in that hole, probably down in a little room between these two shelters. Wounded. Without his gun," I said.

The radio on Spencer's back squawked as Woolley asked what all the firing was about. From the far side of the berm I heard King call out, "Lieutenant, you got a minute?"

I told Spencer to tell Woolley that we wounded a VC and that we were going to try and ferret him out of a hole. Didn't know how long it was going to take.

King called again, insistently, "Lieutenant."

I told Bratcher to see what King wanted and told De Leon and Ayers to move out to a guard position near the small field. After sending some other men to protect our other flank, I walked over to the smaller shelter, where Taylor was shining his flashlight down the spider hole. It led down and away. We tied a small piece of nylon cord to the flashlight and lowered it down the hole.

Meanwhile, Bratcher had walked back to the berm. King nodded toward Beck, who was sitting awkwardly with the M-79 grenade round in his lap and a sick look on his face.

"Lift it off, Beck," Bratcher said firmly. Like King, he saw no value in putting two men at risk.

Beck's hand shook slightly as it moved slowly to the round. When he lifted it with two fingers, the head of the round rotated downward. Beck opened his mouth as wide as he could, as though he were going to yell, but he didn't drop the round. Moving it slowly to his right and then toward the ground, he rolled out of the way as he set it down. Quickly he got to his feet and looked down at the small metal ball.

"You son of a bitch. You goddamned son of a bitch. You nasty little son of a bitch," he kept repeating as he climbed over the berm. Beck borrowed Patrick's M-16 and went back to the berm. He fired most of a clip of ammo at the M-79 round until he finally set it off.

Thinking we were being probed or attacked, I turtled my neck and started to jump into the pit when Bratcher said, "No problem. It's just 'Bad News' Beck."

Spencer had finished sending the radio message to Woolley and was looking down the spider hole under the main shelter. He mentioned that he could see the light from Taylor's flashlight shining at the bottom of the hole. Woolley came back on the radio and said that battalion wanted us to take the man alive. They wanted a prisoner. I told him we'd do what we could.

Convinced that a dying VC was beneath us, I told Fernandez that it was time for his starring role again, to get a pistol, and to get ready for a trip down the mine shaft.

Fernandez did not take it well. He was angry and mumbled in Spanish under his breath. I told him I was sorry, but he was the smallest and had to go. He pretended to not understand me.

By now the sunlight was almost completely gone. I told Bratcher to ensure that the men were set up in good guard positions all around the shelters. As I went under the small shelter, we started to receive small-arms fire from across the field.

We ducked down. Looking closely at the spider hole, Fernandez started saying, "No, no, no."

Sitting with my back against the side of the larger hole, I was suddenly very tired. I wanted to be back with the battalion, eating my C rations and maybe drinking a cup of coffee. I did not want to be beside the entrance to that hole that led to God knows where. We knew only that at least one wounded VC soldier was down there.

We received more probing rounds from the area near the plane and then some rounds to our front, from deep in the jungle. The VC were all around us.

I grabbed Fernandez by the collar of his fatigue jacket and told him not to get me angry. He kept saying, "No, no, no."

Finally I said, "Ah shit." I told Spencer to throw a grenade down the hole under the large shelter, and I took a grenade off my web gear, pulled the pin, and dropped it down the other hole where I was standing. It wasn't necessarily going to give us a live prisoner, like battalion wanted, but my reluctant Puerto Rican tunnel rat wasn't going down the hole until we did something.

The grenades went off with muffled thuds. We lowered Taylor's flashlight down the hole again, and Spencer said he could see the light shining dimly from the other area.

I looked at Fernandez and said, "Okay, friend. Time to go to work. Go down the hole."

He gave me a long, angry look. Then he took off his web gear, retrieved Taylor's flashlight, checked the magazine in his pistol, crossed himself, and crawled over to the spider hole. After looking inside it for several moments, he went over the edge and was quickly gone, head first.

Almost immediately Spencer said that he could see the tunnel rat's light. I kept expecting to hear a shot.

Fernandez popped back up near me. He said something I couldn't understand and then disappeared down the hole again. Within a minute he appeared in the spider hole under the large shelter where Bratcher and Spencer were sitting.

Occasionally bullets whistled through the shelters from all sides. They made startlingly loud sounds when they crashed through the palm fronds.

I crawled over to Spencer, who was holding a flashlight as Fernandez began drawing a diagram in the dirt of what he had seen underground. The spider hole under the small shelter was connected to the spider hole in the large area, and from there the tunnel led away to the west. The blood trail led down this tunnel. Fernandez said the tunnel curved and he had not been able to see how far it went, but there was a lot of blood in there.

The VC probably had sat near the spider hole, perhaps to bandage his wound. He had probably been there when we were talking with Woolley. Maybe he had stayed until we first dropped the flashlight down the hole. Even now he could be right around the edge of the bend.

I told Bratcher that I was going down. About then Beck came

crawling up to the shelter and asked if we had gotten the VC in the hole. I told Bratcher that Beck would go with me. Beck said okay.

Taking off my web gear and steel pot, I took the flashlight and pistol from Fernandez. I crawled to the spider hole and shined the flashlight down. It was about four or five feet to the floor of the tunnel. I could see the opening on one side back to the small shelter and, on the other side, the opening as it went down and away.

I went over the side head first and caught myself with my hands on the bottom. Shining the flashlight down the tunnel, I could see the blood trailing out of sight around the bend. I came back out of the hole and went in feet first. Going down to my knees, with my feet back inside the tunnel toward the small shelter, I bent down and into the tunnel. I was suddenly enclosed in a solid earthen tomb. Sounds from above were muted. I felt as though I were in another dimension. Everything was quiet, cool, and very confined. With the blood trail and bend ahead, I faced the real prospect of a deadly, subterranean confrontation at any moment. Holding my finger on the trigger of the pistol in one hand and the flashlight in the other, I crawled slowly forward. Beck landed with a thud behind me and clawed ahead quickly until one of his hands grabbed one of my feet.

When I came to the bend I inched around it, pistol first. I expected to see the wounded VC at any moment, but about thirty feet ahead the tunnel came to an abrupt end.

There was no VC in sight.

I lay down and looked at the end of the tunnel. It looked as if people had maneuvered around the area often, coming and going, their bodies wearing off the loose dirt and rounding out the sides. My first thought was that a hole at the end led up and out—the tunnel must be an escape route away from the shelters. Once I reached the end, I might find myself coming out of the tunnel into a nest of VC, or coming out near one of our guard positions and being shot by my own men.

"Where da' fuck did he go?" Beck said behind me.

"I think up and away," I said as I got back to my hands and knees and inched farther down the tunnel.

The air was stuffy. I could smell my own body odor and Beck's. I did not like the confinement and wished as I inched along that I had not invited Beck. He blocked any escape and seemed to close off the tunnel behind me. As I moved along my world became smaller and smaller.

Every few feet, I stopped crawling and lay down to study the tunnel end. As I came closer I saw that there was no hole going up. The end was a round circle, with no opening at the top. On the floor I saw what looked like a toilet seat, but it proved to be a hinged door.

"No," I said to Beck, "I don't think he went up and away, I think he went down."

I continued to look at the trapdoor, in the hope of divining a course of action that was safe. Why a door? What was underneath? Was it filled with VC? Was it booby-trapped? In the flashlight beam it looked liked the gate to hell. I wished I had more air to breathe.

"What are we going to do?" Beck asked.

The trapdoor was covered with bloody fingerprints, and smeared blood was on the front of the wooden base. Our wounded VC had indeed gone through. The blood was not dry, he was only minutes ahead of us. I felt very close to my prey.

"Beck," I said, turning to look at the burly soldier behind me, "I'm going to turn on my side, and you're going to crawl by me. There's a trapdoor in front, at the end of this tunnel. I think you can stand over it. You're going to take the pistol and the flashlight and I'm going to open that door. You shine that light in and be prepared to shoot."

"Okay," Beck said with his usual cheerful willingness.

I turned on my side and Beck squeezed by on his hands and knees. When he got close to my outstretched hands, I handed him the flashlight, but I said I'd hold the pistol to cover him until he was in place. It was a well-intended idea; however, when Beck passed by me, all I could see was his butt. I would have little chance to fire around him if any VC suddenly appeared out of the hole.

When Beck reached the end of the tunnel, he came slowly to his feet. His back was against the top of the rounded-out area overhead, he was standing with his feet on either side of the door. There was a small handle on the top of it.

"You want me to pull it open?" Beck asked.

For a fleeting second I thought about telling Beck to come on, we were going back up. We were still alive, but we might die if we opened that door. My face was only inches from the wet blood.

"No," I said. "Here, you hold the pistol. I'm going to open the door with my bayonet. You keep that flashlight and gun pointed inside."

Lying on my stomach, I got the bayonet off my belt and extended the blade forward. On second thought, I turned the bayonet so I was holding the blade and tapped the handle on the door to see if the tapping in the eerie quiet would draw fire. Nothing. Nobody home. Sweat dropped from Beck's face. Above us, we heard more small-arms fire, a few single rounds as the VC probed and then the return fire from the platoon.

I turned the bayonet around and stuck the point between the trapdoor and the base. Stooping over the hole, Beck had the flashlight and pistol inches above the knife. I lifted the door slightly and Beck moved the flashlight forward to shine in the crack. Lifting the door wider, I rose up on my elbows to look down inside.

The room below was narrow and long, three times the size of the tunnel and filled with olive drab boxes. I saw a pool of blood on some clothes at the end of the flashlight beam.

There was no VC. I was suddenly angry. Relieved, but angry.

"Lieutenant, my back is killing me. Let's do something," Beck said.

Taking the flashlight from him, I lifted the door all the way and bent down into the room. The blood trail went to the end of the room. Bloody handprints were on the rear wall. I figured the VC had made his way up the wall to the hold above.

I dropped into the room and could almost stand up. Old carbines and mortar tubes were stacked in one corner. I told Beck to go back and get Fernandez and a couple more men because we were going to clear all the stuff out of the room. When Beck dropped the door, I suddenly realized that I didn't have a weapon. I opened the door and told him to leave the pistol. I left the door open and went back to the other end of the room. As I suspected, there was a trapdoor in the ceiling above the bloodstains. Aiming the flashlight at the door, I eased it open with the barrel of my pistol.

There was nothing but more tunnel on the other side. I opened the door completely and stood up. With my head up through the door opening, I shined the light down the tunnel. It went to a dead end, but I thought I could see openings off to each side.

Fernandez soon appeared, and I sent him down the tunnel after the VC. He went reluctantly.

Beck joined me in the lower room, and we began to hand out items to Lyons, who was waiting in the tunnel above. They included medical supplies, textbooks, mine parts, clothing—civilian and military—ammo, weapons, maps, letters, pots, and pans. The room was the supply cache for a VC cell. On the side of one wall in the dirt was a square area that had been hardened with water and some cementlike agent and contained several lines of Vietnamese writing and a small American flag. I had Beck write the Vietnamese as best he could.

When the tunnel rat returned, he said he had gone down the tunnel to the dead end, taken a right, and followed the blood trail until the tunnel got so small he couldn't go any farther. The tunnel that led off to the left continued to what appeared to be a cave-in.

Still no VC.

Back aboveground, I leaned against the wall of the hole under the shelter and breathed deeply. The moon was full and the night was surprisingly bright. Bratcher and Spencer were nearby. Spencer handed me a cup of coffee, and, hiding the match in my cupped hands, I lit a cigarette. The pile of material from the underground room lay in the middle of the hole. Occasional rounds whistled overhead.

I called Woolley to report that we had lost the VC down a tunnel but, in chasing him, had come across a small VC supply cache. We were being probed, but I thought we could hold our own until sunrise. No casualties—we were hungry and tired, but okay.

When I finished my report, I leaned back against the dirt pit wall.

Bratcher pointed at the spider hole in the corner and asked, "Do you want us to wake you up if any VC come out of that hole tonight, or do you just want to sleep through it?"

More rounds zinged overhead.

Kiss my bejesus, I thought. Will this ever end? I was so tired that it was difficult to focus on the problem with the hole, but it was clear, once Bratcher mentioned it, that the tunnel was unprotected and the VC could come in during the night and attack us from the inside out. It would be hard to find all the men and move away from the shelter in the dark. The easiest thing would be to protect the hole.

I looked at it in the corner and thought that, at any second, a VC could jump out like a jack-in-the-box and start shooting. I noticed that Spencer and Bratcher held their weapons pointed toward the hole.

More rounds zinged overhead. I borrowed Spencer's bayonet, took a couple of grenades off my web gear, picked up some tape and a trip-flare kit, and went down the hole feet first. After crawling to the trapdoor at the end of the tunnel, I banged on the door with the handle of the bayonet before opening it, but I saw no signs that anyone had been there since we had left. I shut the door again and drove one bayonet into the ground on one side of the door. Repeated attempts to get the other bayonet into the ground on the other side failed, so I impaled the blade on the bottom of the doorframe. I taped the grenades to the bayonets, attached the wire from the trip-flare kit in the ring of one grenade, and ran it across the trapdoor to the ring of the other grenade. My shoulders were tired when I finished. I laid my arms on the tunnel floor and then brought them back to cushion my head. I closed my eyes and was drifting off to sleep when I heard more gunfire above.

I looked at my booby trap, knowing that I hadn't straightened out the safety pins. If I hit that wire after I straightened the pins, I was dead, because I couldn't back out of this tunnel in time. Carefully thinking through every movement before I made it, I straightened the two pins and moved my hands back in front of me. Slowly I backed out of the tunnel and joined Bratcher and Spencer.

We were probed for the next few hours. Sometime after midnight the firing stopped. Then, about 0200, VC opened up from all sides. I thought they were attacking and called in mortar flares. A tracer round hit the straw roof of the smaller shelter and it started to burn.

The mortar flares went off. Woolley asked if I wanted mortar rounds fired around my position. I said yes, but I wondered if he and the mortar crew had our exact position plotted. Within minutes mortar rounds began crashing around us. We stopped firing and hugged the ground.

When the mortars stopped, there was no more fire from the VC. I called the company commander and thanked him. He said a relief column would be out to us at first light. Around 0500 the first rays of the morning sun began to seep into the jungle, and it was light by 0530. From across the hole under the shelter, Spencer said, "Hell of a night."

I told Bratcher that I wanted us up and moving soon. If each man carried some items, we could take everything we had brought out of the underground room.

I looked at the spider hole in the corner and thought about the two-grenade booby trap over the door. I could leave them there, but the VC would certainly get the grenades when they came back and eventually use them against us.

I told Bratcher and Spencer that I was going to get the grenades and picked up a pistol and flashlight. Down in the tunnel, I saw that the wire between the two safety pins had been bent upward. During the night someone from below had pushed the door up but stopped before the wire across the top pulled out either of the pins.

I smiled to myself, but I was suddenly unsure how to bend the safety pins back. One of the safety pins was slightly out of the detonator. I backed out of the tunnel and asked Bratcher for the pliers he carried to crimp claymore detonators. They had wire cutters on one end.

Back in the tunnel, I crawled to the trapdoor and caught my breath before reaching up and cutting the wire between the safety pins. Then, one at a time, I bent the pins back. I was backing down the tunnel when I heard small-arms fire from above. It started slowly, then a full battle erupted. I backed out furiously and was almost to the spider hole when I heard Bratcher yelling for everyone to hold their fire.

Coming out of the hole, I saw Bratcher running off to the side with Spencer on his heels. I heard loud, frenzied talking in the bush ahead of them.

Castro was yelling, "Ah shit, man! Shit! Shit!"

I recognized Peterson's voice yelling for the medic and telling his men to spread out. Wondering why Peterson was there, I rushed forward.

Ten or fifteen feet from the shelters, Castro was holding Private Patrick in his arms. Patrick had been shot in the chest and shoulder. The medic was on his knees. Patrick's arms were lying loosely at his sides, his eyes roaming around the faces of the men standing above him. Castro helped open his fatigue jacket. Blood was gushing from a number of holes, and his eyes started to lose their focus. Castro yelled for him to hold on and told the medic to hurry. Patrick coughed, and blood came out of his mouth. I dropped to my knees beside him.

"Goddammit, don't you die, Patrick! Don't you die! Don't give up!" I said, helping to rip open his shirt.

Blood was everywhere. Patrick closed his eyes and his head rolled to the side, and he died.

We stopped what we were doing. The medic shook his head, took a deep breath, and stood up.

Castro was still holding Patrick and rocking back and forth on his heels. Then Castro laid him down on the ground. I stood up and looked at Pete. His eyes were moist. He had his hands out with the palms up.

"I left as soon as I could this morning to get here and help you," Pete said. "Colonel wouldn't let me come last night." He paused. "Patrick must have fallen asleep, lying here in these bushes. He fired at my point man. Just jerked up and started firing. He and my point man just fired at each other. I'm sorry."

I looked down at Patrick, then at each man who stood around him in slight shock—Castro, Bratcher, Spencer, Beck, Pete's point man, and Pete. I was tired; it took a while for me to understand what happened. Then, more quickly, I sought some meaning. I couldn't yell at Pete or his point man. It certainly wasn't their fault, nor was it Patrick's. I felt a mindless rage, like I wanted to cry and scream at the same time.

"Goddammit," I heard myself say as random thoughts drifted through the fog of my mind. Death is so ugly. War is so unfair.

Why Patrick? What's the use? Who's to blame? No answers. My mind turned numb.

Without comment, we built a stretcher out of ponchos and bamboo and gently rolled Patrick's body onto it.

Pete's platoon would stay in the area and try to pin down the VC who had attacked us during the night. As I began to walk away with my platoon, Pete fell in beside me and we walked along together for a short distance. We didn't look at each other or talk. I was exhausted. Pete didn't know what to say. He stopped and I walked on.

— NINE —

Phoenix and Fate

We delivered Patrick's body to Spec-5 Heyekiah Goss Jr., the company medic, and then slept most of the day under shady makeshift shelters. Soon after I awoke, Pete's recon platoon returned to the battalion perimeter with the bodies of two of his men killed during the day.

A hot meal, cold beer, and mail came in by helicopter late in the afternoon and the platoon slept through the night. The following morning, 15 January, the battalion swept toward a village west of our bivouac site that was suspected of harboring VC. Alpha Company's route was just inside a wood line by a large open rice field. The company would follow a small trail, with Duckett's former platoon on the left and mine on the right. Ernst's platoon, commanded by Arthur, would ride on armored personnel carriers and bring up the rear in reserve.

To contain the VC, several units were moving on the village from different directions. As we were getting on line that morning and preparing to move out, Pete's platoon moved by on my right to reconnoiter ahead of our advancing line. When Pete and I saw each other, we smiled and nodded our heads. Pete looked tired. He raised his M-16 up in the air and then went out of sight.

As Alpha Company moved out, gunships passed overhead and buzzed the tree line by the rice field. Random artillery rounds landed across the field. We heard occasional bursts of gunfire around us as the men fired into suspicious bushes and tufts of bamboo. In my platoon, Ayers was at the front of one file, Beck led another, and Sergeant Rome was off on the right.

Far to our left across the field, Charlie Company was pinned down by fire from a VC machine gun bunker. Arthur was ordered over to help. The VC gun crew retreated when they heard his

APC tracks coming through the jungle. After sweeping the area, Arthur was ordered back behind us again as reserve and he fell in somewhere to our rear. We overheard Woolley talking with him by radio. According to the coordinates that Arthur gave, he should have been directly behind us, but no one could hear any noise from the tracks. Woolley was walking down the path that separated Duckett's old platoon from mine. His point man spotted a trip wire running across the trail. We slowed down while the company first sergeant cleared the brush around the wire. When he found it led to a flare, we moved out again. Woolley went back to the radio and began talking with Arthur again. Duckett's platoon encountered some heavy brushes, and Beck yelled for us to slow down so we would stay on line.

Suddenly an automatic weapon opened up on the company to our left front. Everyone dropped to the ground. I looked at Spencer and lit a cigarette. It was 0915, and I noted from my map that we were at the coordinates XT 637177. For no particular reason I made a dot at that location on my map.

To our front, perhaps five hundred meters away, we heard a couple of shots fired, then a pause before a tremendous blast. The violent sound of a dozen automatic weapons followed the blast. Grenades went off, followed by sustained bursts of fire.

Peterson's platoon!

Breathlessly I scrambled back to Spencer's radio and tuned it to the battalion frequency.

Up ahead the grenades went off one after another—boom, boom, boom, boom—amid the continuing small-arms fire.

I recognized Pete's platoon sergeant talking on the radio, "They're on both sides, all around us, no place to go."

He went off the air. I started to get up. The battle continued in front with no letup.

Why wasn't Peterson on the radio?

The platoon sergeant came back on. "Almost every man's hit. I ain't got no one. Give us some fire. Help us! Give us some fire! Give us . . ."

I stood up. Pete was in trouble. His platoon was pinned down.

Someone came back on the radio. "This is the 1st Squad leader. We're almost wiped out. The radio operator's dead, the platoon sergeant's been shot in the head, the lieutenant's dead. Help us! God give us some help!"

Yelling for the men to get ready to move out, I crashed through the bushes to the trail where Woolley was listening to the radio. I told him I had to go help Pete.

"Okay," Woolley said. "Let me coordinate with Battalion."

I had taken the captain's arm as I talked and was pushing him along the trail. We had passed other men in his company head-quarters group and were now well ahead of even the two platoons on either side. He and I were leading the company down the trail. I kept looking off to the right front, where the firing was still heavy. There had been no letup since the first blast. Hand grenades, M-79s, automatic rifles, machine guns.

With one hand still on Woolley's elbow I turned around to his radio operator and yelled angrily for him to catch up. "Come on, goddammit, I got to go!"

Then the whole world exploded.

A mine went off beside the trail, midway back in the company headquarters group. Shrapnel flew by my head.

"Goddammit to hell, goddammit!" I dropped to one knee and was still looking back at the blast as dirt and debris fell around me. I was intent on getting to Peterson—all this struck me as just another delay.

The firing was still intense in front. Dust continued to settle as I looked back and tried to spot the radio operator. I thought it might have been a mortar round, short.

Then, out of the dust, Beck walked up with blood streaming from his ears. Bratcher, who had blood oozing out of his fatigue jacket near his shoulder, was behind him. They had followed me over to talk with Woolley and been caught in the blast.

I turned and saw several other soldiers, dead or wounded, lying along the trail. A round zinged down the trail over our heads. Bratcher and Beck, both in slight shock, quickly regained their wits and dived to the side of the trail.

Some men from Duckett's platoon started firing.

Goss, the company medic, was still on the trail lying on his back, his fatigue jacket shredded from shrapnel. He was laboring for breath, his eyes open wide as if in surprise.

I knelt beside him and yelled for another medic. I took a bandage off my belt, opened it, and tried to remember what to do with a chest wound. Put the plastic from the packing next to the wound, I thought, when Bratcher yelled from the bushes, "The man's dead, Lieutenant! Get off the fucking trail!"

"He ain't dead!" I yelled as I placed the bandage on his chest.

"He ain't breathing no more," Bratcher said right above me.

Dirt and dust were settling on Goss's eyes, but he was not blinking. He stared vacantly off in the distance, his mouth open. I knew by the smell that his bowels had emptied as his body relaxed in death.

"Get off the trail, Lieutenant," Bratcher insisted.

I stood up and turned to look at the radio operator, who was lying half on and half off the trail. A bullet zipped by in front of me. Out of the corner of my eye, up the trail, I saw a VC rise up out of a hole.

I had reached a point where nothing was making much sense. I had been absorbed in moving out to help Pete—and then the mine blast and Goss dying and the radio operator lying dead and rounds coming down the trail. Everything seemed to be happening in slow motion as adrenaline surges overloaded my mind. Trying to focus on each separate event, I saw things in flashes, as if my surroundings were illuminated by a strobe light. The VC was still coming out of the hole. I started to turn and look at him, but then I thought about Pete and getting to him and I looked down at Goss and I turned back to see the radio operator's feet lying out on the trail and I started yelling at myself: Think! Think! Think!

Another round whizzed by in front of me. I turned back around so that, for a fleeting moment, I was looking up the trail. Then I clearly saw the VC standing up in the hole near a ditch and aiming his rifle at me. Bratcher was in the bushes beside the trail, and I dived toward him. I saw the muzzle flash from the VC's gun.

A searing pain in my buttocks brought me to my senses. In mid-dive, I knew that I had been shot. Bratcher grabbed me by my fatigue jacket and pulled me into the bushes while Duckett's men opened fire down the trail.

A medic crawled up. Bratcher said he was okay; the medic should look after me. Lying on my stomach I took some deep breaths, pulled off my web gear, and undid my belt. When I pushed my pants down I felt blood collecting between my legs.

Woolley knelt down beside me. "We're going to move out, Jimmy, and try to get to Pete's platoon. I've called a medevac. You're going to be all right. Sergeant Rome will take your platoon." There were heavier mortar explosions now, in the distance to the front of us.

"Get to Pete. Hurry," I said as I looked up.

The medic worked on my buttocks. I could not see what he was doing, but he moved off soon without a word and started treating other wounded, including Bratcher and Beck. I felt weak as the adrenaline faded. My butt felt like a knife had been plunged into it.

Later, the less badly wounded in my ragged group carried the more seriously wounded to the edge of the field and went back for the dead. Beck carried Goss in his arms.

In time a medevac helicopter landed near our purple smoke. It was almost completely loaded with other casualties when it landed and could only take the two most seriously wounded from our group. Bratcher and I were the last to leave, with the dead, a couple of hours later. As we lifted off, we saw rows of men in body bags by the edge of the field, close to where Peterson's platoon had been hit. I knew that Peterson was in one and I felt like crying.

At a medevac clearing station, Maj. Gen. Jonathan O. Seaman, commander of the 1st Division, came through and passed out Purple Hearts to us. Later, at what must have been the most impersonal, the most insensitive aid station in Vietnam, I had my wound cleaned and stitched. Beck and Bratcher had their wounds treated and were discharged to return to the battalion base camp. I was admitted to the convalescent tent next to the operating room.

The next morning I was aware of the trucks before I opened my eyes. Air brakes hissed as the tractor trailers came to a stop. When the trucks started out again, they whined in first gear and then, after a pause, more whining as the driver shifted into second.

I shared the tent with six men who were talking amongst

themselves, undisturbed by the trucks. The sides to the tent were raised and only the mosquito netting was between me, lying on a cot in the corner, and a busy intersection of two dirt roads. Heavy olive-drab transfer trucks were passing, one after another, throwing up billowing clouds of dust. It was barely past sunrise and I was already covered by a thin layer of dirt.

"Get used to it, man," said one of the soldiers from the other end. "It goes with the territory here. But look on the bright side, it's better than the fucking field, right?"

I lay on my stomach most of the day and thought about Peterson. I remembered when we first met in OCS, Pete's exhausted face during the eleventh-week run when he kept saying, "We're going to make it, we're going to make it, we're going to make it," and then a few days later when Pete's friend scared us into thinking Pete was going to be paneled. I could see Pete's shock as the man came to our door and just stood there. For days thereafter we said, "Oh no, Mr. Death, get away from our door. Get away!" Other memories flashed through my mind—our nights drinking in that honky-tonk bar in Junction City, laughing together, racing our sports cars over the prairies of Nebraska, sitting on the top deck of the USNS *Mann* on the way to Vietnam, talking about the past, wondering about the future. Ours had been a rich, robust, and trusting bond. He was my best friend, ever. Now he was dead.

Then I thought about the insurance policy, and not sending in my change-of-beneficiary form. I felt tremendous guilt. Pete had been so trusting and I had been such a heel. "Pete," I said under my breath, "I promise to you, wherever you are, that when I get that check, that I'm sending it to your Momma. Please forgive me."

More trucks hissed and whined outside and dust continued to settle on my bed. The men joked and talked loudly among themselves at the other end of the tent.

I felt so terribly lonely.

I recalled how Pete and I had silently shared the sorrow of Patrick's death a few days before, how we had walked alongside each other as my platoon headed back toward the perimeter, and the pain in his face later that same day when he came back in with his dead. The last time I saw him he was lifting his M-16 in the air as his platoon went out of sight to recon in front.

Every word I had heard over the radio when I switched it to the battalion frequency came back to me. Pete's platoon was wiped out. "The lieutenant's dead," the platoon sergeant had said. The platoon sergeant, himself to die within minutes, had eulogized my best friend with the noise of battle in the background: "The lieutenant's dead." Pete was so proud of his commission. Maybe it was the way he would have wanted to go, but for me, I had never felt such sorrow.

I tried to write a letter to his parents that day, but it was blubbering nonsense. I crumpled it up and threw it toward the trucks outside.

That night after supper the medic came down the aisle of cots. He was humming and had a gigantic needle in his hand. "Needle time, Parker, show me your fanny."

I reacted angrily, without thinking, telling the medic to stick the needle up his own ass.

The man walked away but soon returned with a medical corps major.

"Specialist Wallace says that you are very uncooperative," the major said with a frown, "that you refused to let him give you your tetracycline shot. It is not helpful if you act like a child. You can understand that, can't you? We won't stand for any more outbursts. We have too much to do to hold the hands of everyone here."

He was right, of course. After he left the medic jabbed me with the needle and I yelled.

About midmorning the next day Terry Mulcay, the battalion headquarters company commander, walked in. I yelled out a greeting, happy to see a familiar face.

He sat on a nearby cot and handed me some mail. He told me the battalion had secured the area around Cu Chi before being replaced at night by the 25th Division. Some VC had popped up in the middle of the substitution of forces and fired off a couple of rounds. The 25th Division, new to Nam, returned fire with everything they had. It was a helluva show outside Cu Chi that night, he said.

Our battalion was now located in a defensive position near the Cambodian border. It had taken heavy casualties, and he named some of the men killed. I waited for Peterson's name but sensed that Mulcay would name Peterson last, out of respect for our friendship, or so he could offer his personal condolences.

He didn't mention Pete.

"Pete? Pete wasn't killed?" I asked incredulously.

"Nope," he said.

I knew before the word was completely out of his mouth that Pete was alive. Happiness surged through me—incredible joy. Peterson, that son of a bitch, wasn't dead. He was alive. That son of a bitch!

"He was one of the first ones hit in his platoon," Mulcay said. "Took a round in his right shoulder. It knocked him back, and as he was spinning around, he took another round in the same shoulder from behind. The first one took out most of his shoulder bone, and the one in the back took out a lot of meat and muscle, but he's okay. He's going to live. I just saw him in the 93d Field Hospital. He's heading back to the States tomorrow or the next day. No more war for him."

Peterson was alive. That son of a bitch.

Later that morning on the way back from the latrine, I shuffled down to a Jeep ambulance parked in the shade at the rear of the tent. Behind the wheel, Private First Class "Richardson" [alias] was reading a *Playboy* magazine.

"Howyoudoing?" I said in my best "good ol' boy" tone.

The driver looked first at my face and then down at my gown. "Okay," he said.

"Where's the 93d Field Hospital?"

"It's about twenty-five miles from here. Nice, very nice-looking nurses there. Round-eyed beauties. Got me some lady friends over there. Why?"

I said, "I got a friend there, too, who's heading back to the States tomorrow. We've gone through a lot together."

Richardson continued to look at me.

"No problem in driving over? You can just get on the road and go? Can you go there, Mr. Richardson?" I asked.

"Well, you're supposed to have an armed escort. When we're carrying people back and forth, we get an MP (military police) detail to come along, but it's no problem. Only once in a blue moon does anyone ever get shot at."

"What do you think about us going, you and I, over to the 93d? Who you got to ask? You got to ask anybody, Private Richardson?"

"You got any war souvenirs? VC flags, guns, that kind of thing?"

"Nope," I said, but I had hope. This guy had a price. This guy would go.

Suddenly I had a thought and left without a word. In the ward I bent over awkwardly, pulled my fatigues from under the bed, and took the Purple Heart medal General Seaman had given me out of my pants pocket—dried blood was on the box—and carried it outside to Richardson.

"General Seaman gave me this Purple Heart," I said, opening the box as if it were very special, "and I'll give it to you if you take me to the 93d today. Twenty-five miles there, I'll spend an hour with my buddy, and twenty-five miles back. No problem. You'll have an interesting day, I'll have an interesting day, and you'll get a real trophy for the rest of your life. What do you say?"

Richardson examined the medal closely. He finally looked up and around to see if anyone was looking.

"Okay, go get dressed, we'll go."

"Get dressed?" I asked.

"You ain't going like that, with your ass sticking out of that gown, are you?"

"No, I reckon I'm not," I said, knowing that the only clothes I had were the bloody fatigues I was wearing when I was wounded.

Specialist Wallace, the needle man, watched me as I came back in and shuffled to my cot. I smiled at him, the fatigues at my feet. He must have noticed a change in my attitude and thought something was up. He started toward my cot.

"I wonder," I asked in a friendly tone, "if there is a shuttle that runs from this aid station to the 93d Field Hospital? You know, a bus or something?"

"You can't just check into any hospital you want to, you know. You're here, you belong to me, I'm going to make you whole again. You can't make no reservations at the 93d."

"No, you don't understand. A friend of mine is there, leaving tomorrow for the States. Got shot up pretty bad. Need to see him. Just over and back, that's all. Shuttle?"

"No shuttle. The doctor has ordered bed rest for you until your wound has healed. Even if there was a shuttle, you couldn't go. You can't even sit down."

"What if I were to catch a ride? Say, a helicopter ride over and back? What do you think? Would the major go along with it?"

"No," he said, crossing his arms over his chest.

"Would you please go ask him? Just ask him if I could get a pass to go to the 93d. That's all."

"He's going to say no," Wallace assured me, but he turned and walked out of the tent.

After dressing in the latrine and slipping on my boots—the laces had been sliced by the hospital staff when I arrived—I shuffled down to the ambulance. The stitching hurt when it caught in my pants. Richardson started his Jeep and I walked around to the passenger side. Suddenly I realized that the corpsman was right—I couldn't sit down. I went to the back and painfully climbed up. Some of the stitches came loose and blood ran down my leg. As I crawled onto a stretcher behind the passenger seat, the bleeding stopped.

Richardson jerked the Jeep into gear and I grabbed the stretcher like a rodeo rider. On the open dirt road he floored the accelerator and whipped around the first turn without braking. My legs flew off the stretcher and I ended up half on it and half off. Screaming in pain, I yelled for Richardson to stop while I got back on the stretcher.

"Personally, my friend, I'm not that interested in getting there, you know, real, *real* fast. Fast is good enough. So you don't need to speed just for me, and the VC weren't that good a shot anyway, they only got me in the ass," I told him as I crawled back up on the stretcher.

Back moving again, we did not go slower, however, and we hit bumps with jarring thuds. Passing a slow-moving truck, Richardson whipped out to the left and I was slung off the stretcher again. Finally he stopped and tied a strap around my legs. Back on the road, he went as fast as he could, playing chicken with oncoming traffic all the way to the 93d Field Hospital. He parked, asked for my friend's name, and went into the administration building.

When Richardson was gone, I tried to reach down and undo

the broad strap holding my legs, but as I turned around and stretched out my right arm, a stitch popped. I yelled from the pain, jerked my arm back, and threw the stretcher off balance. My upper torso fell to the floor and the stretcher turned on its side, although the foot end stayed on the bracket because of the strap around my legs. I was trapped, tied upside down in the ambulance.

"Aaaaaauuuuuuuggggggg," I was moaning when Richardson returned.

"You're dangerous, you know that?" he said quietly. "You sure you didn't shoot yourself?"

He helped me out and gave me the number of Pete's ward. He said he would meet me in Pete's Quonset hut in a couple of hours.

I found the right building and straightened my bloody, dirty fatigue uniform as best I could. Smiling, I walked in.

Classical music was coming from speakers on the wall. Concrete floors. Bright lights. Clean sheets. Metal bed frames with thick mattresses. Pretty nurses. Air-conditioning. Smiling people.

Pete was halfway down the aisle on the right. A nurse was sitting on the edge of his bed writing a letter for him. His right shoulder was covered with thick bandages. Sitting propped up, he was watching the nurse as she wrote. His hair was wet and combed.

"You son of a bitch," I said softly.

He looked up, his face expressionless, and then he smiled.

"Well, goddamn," he said after a moment. "You look like hell."

"I'm alive, though," I said and shuffled around the bed to grab his left hand.

"This guy is a good friend of mine," Pete said to the nurse as he continued to look at me. "Can you look after him?"

They brought in a rolling dolly and squeezed it alongside Pete's bed. When the nurse noticed my fresh blood, she insisted on looking at the wound and had my pants down to my knees in a matter of seconds. I said that I thought she had undressed men before.

While I lay there talking and laughing with Pete, she called for a couple of corpsmen and they restitched my wound.

Pete showed me the bullet taken out of his shoulder, which he kept on a bedside table. Someone produced some champagne, and we drank it from bedpans, even though glasses were available.

A doctor came in and wanted to know if I was registered in that ward. I explained that I had just come over for the day from Division, which he took in stride and then he left.

Pete and I talked without stopping.

Finally I said, "Pete, I have something to say about that insurance, something that I'm terribly, terribly embarrassed about—sorry about."

"What?" Pete asked.

"I, ah, I, ah . . ." I couldn't get it out.

"What the hell is it? I know it's something 'cause every time that insurance came up, you'd look away or change the topic. What is it?"

"I never sent in my change-of-beneficiary form. If I died, Mother would get the money."

Pete looked at me without expression.

"But I want you to know, Pete, I want you to believe me on this, that when I thought you were dead, I made a solemn oath to send the insurance money to your mom. I swear. And I am so glad that I won't have to do that." I looked away. "I am so glad you're alive."

Pete smiled and looked away. Finally he said, "I got a letter from the insurance agent right before we left base camp. Our policies were canceled. War zone clause or something. His company doesn't write policies on people who swallow swords or go fight wars."

"Why didn't you tell me?" I asked.

"Never had a chance."

Richardson came back late in the afternoon. He said we had to be leaving so we could get back before dark. By then, most of the people in the ward were around Pete's bed—telling stories, laughing with the nurses, drinking champagne.

I told Richardson it'd only be a few more minutes and invited him to have some champagne.

We continued with the bedside fellowship until Richardson said the "Richardson freight" left in five minutes.

I bounced my eyebrows, Pete smiled, and I crawled off the dolly.

As I started shuffling down the aisle Pete said, "Be careful. Your mother told me to tell you. Be careful."

"Thanks," I said. "Take care. See you in the States."

"Hey, by the way," Pete said suddenly, and I turned around. He reached under his bed, "Take this back with you."

He pulled out a box and put it on the part of his chest that wasn't covered with bandages. I returned to his bedside, and he extracted a bathroom scale.

"Momma sent this. Maybe she was thinking I was getting out of shape." Pete handed me the scale with his good hand. "Put it by the bar."

"Yes, sir," I said, trying to think of something silly to add, but nothing came to mind.

Outside, Richardson strapped me in and I grabbed the stretcher. Racing the setting sun, we took off for Di An.

We arrived as the MPs were putting barricades across the road at the perimeter's main entrance. Specialist Wallace and the doctor were standing in front of the tent when we approached. Both men walked toward us while Richardson unstrapped and helped me to the ground.

"There are several things here," the major said, "that we need to talk about. Like AWOL. You were ordered to bed. No one authorized the dispatch of that ambulance. You've been nothing but a problem since you arrived."

"Sorry," I said, but my tone and the set of my jaw probably indicated that I didn't care.

"I am going to discuss your case with the adjutant general. You can't just take a vehicle like that and go out on unsecured roads. You are in my hospital ward and you answer to me. You understand?"

As I walked by them with Pete's scale in my hands, I said, "Yes, sir."

I put on the fresh gown lying by my bed. One of the men from the other end of the tent said in the half light, "Man, you are in some heavy shit. These people are mad."

I didn't respond as I awkwardly crawled onto my cot and went to sleep.

When I woke up the next morning I put on my fatigues and

jungle boots with the cut laces, picked up Pete's scale, and shuffled out the rear door of the tent. Ignoring the looks from other people, I crossed the busy intersection near the hospital tent and shuffled to the division helipad. I located the dispatcher and told him I was looking for a ride to the 1st Battalion 28th Infantry base camp.

At midday I was back in the company and ate lunch standing by a table in the back of the mess hall.

For the next ten days, as my wound healed, I worked at battalion operations. Standing by a battery of radios, I followed the movement of the battalion as it completed its sweep of the area near Cu Chi. On the night of 27 January, the VC attacked my platoon as it lay at rest in a defensive perimeter. Sergeant Rome was killed, blown apart by shrapnel.

Two days later the battalion returned by truck from Cu Chi. Woolley was the first off. I thanked him for getting to Peterson as fast as he did, but he said that Colonel Haldane and Sergeant Major Bainbridge were the first to get there. Pete was in the hospital at the 93d within an hour after he was shot.

"Pretty fast," Woolley said, and then added with some suspicion, "like your return to battalion."

"Sir, on that, ah, there may be some paperwork on the way," I told him.

He shook his head. "I'm not surprised."

My platoon clambered off another truck and walked by me, making comments about my wound. Spencer came by with the radio. "We been talking. That toilet seat you are so famous for, I think that VC knew about that toilet seat. Pissed him off. Someone carrying a toilet seat around ought to be shot in the ass. You know what I mean?"

Bratcher came over to me. The hospital staff had told him to go back to the base camp, but instead he had rejoined the platoon in the field. He was the acting platoon leader the night Rome was killed.

"What happened?" I asked.

"I don't know, a round came in on top of us, could have been ours, could have been theirs. Landed by Rome. He never heard nothing."

That night when McCoy and Dunn came by the tent, we talked about the randomness of war.

"It is altogether a proposition of chance," McCoy said. "Remember when we were talking on the USNS *Mann* about courage and presence of mind and that kind of shit. War for us grunts is none of that so much as it's just pure luck. War—this war—has no heart, no rhyme or reason." We got drunk that night, toasting our men who died at Cu Chi and to Pete's safe exit to the States.

During the next few weeks, as my wound continued to heal, I stayed in the base camp and occasionally helped at the battalion S-3 (operations section) manning the radios. Someone had bought a chess set and McCoy I would play a game most evenings when he was in the base camp.

After Operation Crimp, my platoon was down to twenty-one men. Some of the wounded had been sent to the States, other men had left because their enlistments were up. We got few replacements because the limited reserve of infantrymen in the United States was used to fill out new units for deployment to Vietnam.

We collected Rome's personal effects and sent them to Division so they could be forwarded to his next of kin. In preparing Patrick's effects, however, Bratcher and I realized that his billfold and some other personal items must be with his body, which we assumed was in the morgue at Bien Hoa. I took a day trip down there to pick them up. Starting out by the brigade helipad at sunrise, I caught an early flight for Bien Hoa and was standing in front of the MACV (Military Assistance Command, Vietnam) field morgue later that morning. There was an unusual smell about the place—antiseptic and forbidding. When I walked into the reception area, I told a young corporal that I had come for the personal effects of one of my soldiers killed in mid-January and gave him Patrick's name and service number. The corporal looked off into the distance for a moment and then reached for a field telephone on his desk. He was soon in lengthy conversation about what was Patrick's and what wasn't. He hung up and suggested that we go in the back.

We walked into the working area of the morgue. Six dead, nude GIs were laid out on marbletop tables. Other, unprocessed body bags lay in the rear. The concrete floor around some of the tables was covered with blood. A man was calmly hosing down the area. The morgue operators, wearing rubber boots, were talking among themselves as I walked through. One or two apparently noted that I was trying not to lose my breakfast. My muscles froze and I walked awkwardly.

The smell in the midday Vietnam sun was putrid: excrement, alcohol, and another atrocious odor akin to rotten oranges. Trudging along behind my escort and stepping through water, blood, and slime, I felt the stark image of the room etch itself into my brain. Dark blood dripped from the cold marble tables. Some of the men had lost limbs; the mouths of some were open, as if gasping for breath. Some stared wide-eyed, vacantly at the ceiling. The black men so colorless, the white men so chalky. All quietly, patiently waiting to be processed.

The scene assaulted my senses. Time stood still as my mind involuntarily examined every detail. It was too ghoulish, too sudden, too unexpected, too macabre—the most horrible sight I had ever encountered.

When we arrived in the supply room, the receptionist asked whose effects I had come for, but I could not speak. Patrick's name was finally mentioned, and some personal items were put on a table in front of me. I went through them as though I were hypnotized—taking this, discarding that, not sure why. When I finished, I looked at the supply sergeant and said, "That's it."

He put the items in a plastic bag. I signed for them and walked out without a word, away from the working bay, around the building, and out to the road in front. I jogged to get away from the place. Finally, a quarter of a mile away, I stopped and looked back, still afraid. What a godless, deadly place. The gateway to hell.

We heard that General Seaman was being replaced by Maj. Gen. William E. DePuy, called "Peppy" by some of the men who had served under him. He did not like sedentary troops and immediately began launching extended field operations: "Rolling Stone," "Lavender Hill," "Quick Kick II," and "Silver City" came one right after the other.

I went on the first operation, but because of my healing wound Woolley was easy on my platoon and we were held in reserve. Just a casual "walk in the woods," said Spencer. He suggested that I get wounded more often.

Between operations we received replacements. The base camp had a rough-hewn battalion officers club, and when we came back for refitting between operations Dunn used it as his private venue to instruct new officer replacements on the history of the 1st Battalion, 28th Infantry Regiment, 1st Infantry Division, United States Army. The history was his lead-in to a welcoming toast that had a typical Dunn ending.

He'd get to the end of the bar and say something like this: "Okay there, you clean-smelling, unscratched, undented newcomers, come over here. Come here, come on."

I used to marvel at how he took command like that, how those replacements responded to him.

"You have been assigned to the 1st Battalion 28th Infantry Regiment in III Corps, Vietnam," he continued, "though by the looks of you, you're hardly deserving, because this unit, youngsters, is one of the finest fighting units in the world—we have fought and died for our great country since 1813. Our colors have flown wherever America has needed strong, courageous men, willing to die. That's what we do; we fight, we die. We are called the Lions of Cantigny 'cause in World War I, after we took the town of Cantigny, we held off five German counterattacks. This unit, this one you're assigned, took more 'an five thousand casualties in World War I. In World War II this regiment landed at Utah Beach in Normandy and fought its way across Europe. We never, never, never backed up. We don't do dat. We fight, we die. We are, you are, the Lions of Cantigny. You are the newest in a proud tradition of officers in a storied battalion. Gentlemen, you need to buy some drinks here. Champagne. We're going to make some toasts."

With glasses charged, he'd say, "Here's to the President of the United States—the Commander in Chief." He downed his drink and insisted that the replacements do the same. When the glasses were refilled, Dunn said, "Gentlemen, here's to the Chairman of the Joint Chiefs of Staff," and everyone downed their drinks. He went all the way down the chain of command until he got to the battalion commander, Haldane. The bartender, who had one champagne bottle filled with gin, poured gin into the replacements' glasses.

Bob then said, "And here's to the best damn battalion commander of the best damn battalion in the whole history of the United States Army," and he downed his champagne. The replacements downed their drinks, not knowing that it was gin.

The reaction was always the same—the replacements' eyes bulged, they opened their mouths, slammed their glasses down on the bar, and gurgled, *"Aaaaaaauuuuuuuggggggg!"*

"Replacements are so dumb," Dunn always said as he walked away from the bar, leaving the replacements gasping for air.

Because we had been wounded and returned to duty, Dunn and I were among the first two officers in the battalion to be selected for a week of out-of-country rest and recreation (R&R). Bob arranged to meet his bride Linda in Hawaii, and I picked Hong Kong.

The day I left I was surprised to see Moubry, the supply officer, dressed in his best, also on the way out for R&R. "Extra billet," he said, "came in at the last moment."

Yeah, right, Moubry, was all that came to mind. A celebrated incident had occurred several weeks before when Moubry had flown into the battalion forward base on a resupply helicopter that took enemy small-arms fire when it made its landing approach. An enemy round came up through the fuselage and hit Moubry in his seat; the spent bullet lodged in his wallet. On the ground he rushed up to Colonel Haldane, dropped his pants to show how he was bruised from the round, and asked about getting a Purple Heart. Haldane eventually said no, but everyone remembered Moubry running after the battalion commander with his pants down to his knees as he pleaded for a medal. He was hard to like, and I had to share my R&R with him. Didn't seem fair.

On my first night in Hong Kong, I took the Star Ferry from Kowloon to Hong Kong island. I paid something like ten cents for the ride in passenger class. It was a superb voyage—Chinese junks sailing by, a huge freighter sitting at anchor, barges being moved around, and the lights of Hong Kong going up the side of the mountains on both sides—how majestic and grand. Getting on and off were thousands of people, young and old, stooped and tall, beautiful and ugly, exotic and dour, richly dressed and in rags.

I stayed on board when we reached the island and sailed back to Kowloon, then to the island and back again for a total of five round-trips. No one could have been more enthralled, more captivated, with Hong Kong, and I vowed to come back.

In a small bar, I spent hours talking with a bar girl who had a Dutch-boy haircut. She did her job well and kept me entertained. Her English was perfect. How strange, I thought, for an Oriental to speak the Queen's English.

I had suits, sport coats, and silk shirts made to order. After living in holes and eating out of cans for six months, I had never been so fit and trim. The clothes looked smashing.

On the third day of my R&R, Moubry ambushed me in the lobby of my hotel. He said he was running short of money and wondered if he could stay in my room with me. He'd share the cost of the single.

I could have said, "No, Moubry, I don't like you," but I didn't. I said okay and went out and rode the Star Ferry.

Over breakfast the next morning, Moubry wondered aloud what was happening back at the battalion. He said he had a feeling in his bones that something tragic had occurred. We were having a grand time, and those poor slobs back there were facing danger every minute. He hoped he was wrong and said he was going to pray for the men in the battalion.

Two days later, Moubry and I walked into the battalion perimeter. I had the tailor-made clothes in bags under my arms. R&R had been altogether too short, but it was good to get back to the unit.

The battalion was in camp, getting ready for an operation scheduled to kick off in the next couple of days.

I waved to Woolley, who was down the company street, as I ducked into my tent to drop off my new clothes. I was on the way out to tell Woolley about my R&R when he came in.

"Jimmy," he said, "I've got some bad news." He paused. "McCoy was killed by a mine two days ago."

I stood perfectly still. "No, he wasn't."

"George was here at the base camp. He went out to do some maintenance in his minefield and something happened and a mine went off. He was dead before he hit the ground. There was nothing the medics could do."

I was stunned. McCoy. Dead. Gone. I stood absolutely still—

only my eyes blinked—sinking into shock, thinking about nothing at all.

Woolley left, and Dunn soon arrived. He sat down at the chessboard where George and I had played so many games. He didn't say anything.

I lit a cigarette and sat down in a chair by him.

"What happened?" I asked, my voice breaking.

"Well, one of those things. The trip lines to the mines around the perimeter have got tangled in undergrowth and a couple of days ago one of the mines went off in front of George's positions. Someone said a dog had gotten into the minefield, someone else said they saw some villagers near the concertina. George went out to check. He was walking down the safe lane and he took a little half-step off to one side and a mine went off. He never knew what hit him. No reason. There is no great combat story here. Our friend was just walking along and he took a misstep and he died. No moral. Nothing gained. Just one of those things."

George's death was on my mind for days. I could not shake the sense of loss. The only consolation was George's contention that if we die in combat, we're at peace. If others get upset, it's their problem. Even so, my attitudes changed. I did not make friends with the replacements but kept to myself, relaxing only with Dunn, Woolley, and the men in the platoon.

── TEN ──

Lavender Hill

The operations around Phuoc Vinh continued. Dunn was wounded again when a bullet grazed one of his legs. He was not medevacked and was out of action for only a few days.

During "Operation Lavender Hill" we were searching for VC supply caches in an area near the Song Be (Be River). On point in my platoon was a young soldier who had recently arrived as a replacement. He came to a clearing, took a couple of steps out, and dropped to one knee. Beck, coming up behind him but staying inside the wood line, said, "Get your ass back here. You goin' to get shot."

I was walking forward up the platoon file as the new man stood up to move back. Suddenly a VC automatic weapon opened up from across the clearing. The point man yelled out, grabbed his stomach, and lunged forward and to his right behind an anthill out in the clearing. Other VC began firing at us from around the field. The point man was hit again in the leg and screamed. He pulled his legs up as far as he could behind the anthill and continued to yell.

I called Manuel to come up with the M-60 machine gun and told the rest of the platoon to get on line and put some fire on the enemy positions. As our counterfire increased, the VC sought cover and their fire died down. The point man was still yelling, and I went to the edge of the clearing and looked out at him. He appeared lightly wounded in a couple of places but seemed to be in fair shape otherwise.

"Hey, shut up," I said over the din of the firing. "You're all right. Just keep your head down. You'll be okay."

He continued to yell, and I dived out beside him.

That encouraged the VC, and they began firing again—at me.

There wasn't enough room behind the anthill for both of us, so I rolled to my left behind another anthill. I brought my knees up to my chest as rounds began to hit the ground on either side. Then fire from an automatic rifle began to saw down the anthill gradually. As chunks of the rocklike structure were shot off, pieces fell on my helmet. When I looked up I saw the top of the anthill coming down.

"Shoot that son of a bitch with the machine gun! Shoot him!" I yelled to my men.

More VC rounds came in and hit the ground on either side of me. The top of the anthill was getting lower and lower. Trying to roll myself into a smaller ball, I looked back at the wood line where my men were firing past me.

I had a clear thought: if I were to get out of that alive, I'd never worry about the small stuff of life again. Then I had another clear thought: I hope no one in my platoon shoots me.

Firing continued back and forth, but we were gaining the edge in volume. Finally, the gun that was cutting down my anthill stopped as the VC pulled back and disengaged. I slowly got to my feet. The medic was treating the point man as other members of the platoon moved around the clearing to chase the VC.

Later I told Bratcher about my promise to myself not to worry about the small stuff if I survived the anthill attack. "Naw," he said, "you'll forget about it."

Back in the battalion area after the operation, Sp4. Burke, Colonel Haldane's radio operator, sought me out and told me the colonel wanted to see me. Strange—this had never happened before. Maybe, I thought, a court-martial order had come through from the division aid station. I could take the heat, I thought, because I had no guilt about the aid-station problems.

Dunn also had been summoned and was waiting outside the colonel's tent for me. We went in together and saluted the battalion commander, who was sitting behind his desk. He told us we were good officers, good platoon leaders, and that we were lucky. Of the twelve line platoon leaders in the battalion who had arrived in-country, only five remained. New replacements were coming in, and the colonel had decided to rotate some of the staff officers at battalion headquarters into platoon slots. He asked if

Dunn and I would like to leave our platoons and join Major Panton in battalion operations.

Without hesitation, Dunn and I said together, "Yes, sir."

I would be replacing 1st Lt. Paul Trost in operations. Dunn was replacing a man who had left because he had finished his commission commitment.

Smiling, I asked Haldane if he thought he could live with Dunn and me underfoot all the time.

He did not smile. "Yes. Can you live with me?" he asked.

Colonel Haldane was best known for his quiet confidence— he always seemed to know what to do. Even if he didn't, he never showed indecision. He was the boss and he was right; Dunn and I were going to have to mind our manners in our new jobs. The relationship between the colonel and us would be straightforward—friendly but professional.

I found Trost packing his things inside the operations tent. A serious, studious man, he said that our exchange of duties was fair although he had mixed feelings about taking my platoon.

"Bratcher is a well-known, popular personality in the battalion. He's used to working with you," he said as we walked toward his tent, which he shared with Moubry. "Will he turn surly if I do things differently? Plus it's going to be hard to replace someone who is still on the scene."

"Don't worry. Just don't feel the need to assert yourself," I suggested. "Things will take care of themselves."

After Trost gathered up his few things, we walked to Alpha Company. On the way, he said, "Okay, I'll not try to get out ahead of Bratcher, and you resist the temptation to judge how I'm doing with your old platoon. It's mine now."

"Deal," I said.

I went down to the platoon area and gathered together Bratcher, Spencer, and the squad leaders to tell them I was changing places with Trost. For the most part they shrugged, but their faces indicated to me that they were wondering how this change would affect them. I said I appreciated working with them. They were the best men in the world. I walked through the platoon and shook hands—Ayers, Castro, Beck, King, Lyons, De Leon, Manuel, Taylor, Spencer, Bratcher. They were tough combat veterans. We had been together for less than a year, but it was as if I had known them all my life. They were so familiar, so dependable. If, instead of saying good-bye, I had told them that we were going on a dangerous patrol, they would have turned to their equipment and put it on without question. Spencer would have bitched, Beck would have told him to shut up, and Ayers would have been first out the tent. No one would have wanted to be left behind.

Outside, I told Bratcher to work with Trost, bring him along.

"Ain't no sweat, Lieutenant," Bratcher said as the muscles in his neck tightened. "You always thought overly highly of yourself. Trost'll do all right."

"Don't be a wise-ass, Bratcher," I said. "I'm telling you, Sergeant—listen to me, look at me—don't let that man get blown away or get someone else blown away. You hear me?"

Bratcher was a born leader. All through his Army career his biggest problem was serving under less talented, less experienced officers, especially young lieutenants. Actually, the best situation was to let Bratcher handle the platoon by himself—he didn't need Lieutenant Trost or any lieutenant, for that matter. But that's the way that war was managed; there was a constant rotation of the chain of command in the field, and the combat efficiency of the U.S. Army suffered.

I said good-bye to Woolley, packed my personal equipment, and walked back to Moubry's tent. Dunn, already there, was surveying the accommodations. Moubry had built up one end of the medium-size tent with sandbags. He had a metal hospital bed and a thick mattress; a desk with a Bible open in the center; a wall locker; and three lights—one over the desk, one over the bed, and one over the middle of his area. Moubry's area was neater and more comfortable than a dorm room at UNC. Behind it, a step below Moubry's lovely sandbag floor, was the area for Dunn and myself. It was marshy, with a layer of mud from side to side. A shipping pallet was near the cot where Trost had slept so that he wouldn't have to step out of bed directly into the mud. A duffel bag suspended from one of the inside guy wires served as a dresser.

"Now, what's wrong with this picture?" Dunn asked as he motioned first to our muddy end and then to Moubry's neat, dry end.

Moubry came in about that time and said gaily, "Hi, guys."

"Moubry," I said, "I don't like my accommodations here. I had a bar in the other area and the same sleeping stuff that everyone else had. I want a metal bed and a wall locker and a desk, and I want lights and a sandbag floor."

"But you people are out on operations all the time. What's the use?"

"The use, Moubry, is that you'll be our friend. And if you don't, we'll kill you. We want a nice bed and a nice desk just like yours. We don't want a packing crate and a duffel bag and a cot on a muddy floor. You're the supply officer. And our friend."

"Well, put in a requisition. I'll do everything I can. I promise."

When Moubry left, Bob turned to me and expressed his doubts about the man's sincerity and general character.

Sp4. Burke came in through the back door. "Welcome to Headquarters Company. Nice place you've got here. You guys like it muddy? I am, as you know, Sp4. Burke, and you will be seeing me off and on. You will not see me when you are looking for someone to help you clean this mud up or, say, when you need money or when there is make-work to do. You will see me, you lucky devils, when Colonel Haldane or the sergeant major ask you to do something and you don't know what they're talking about. Because I do. And I will tell you, but I remember, and after a while you owe me. Big time."

"Okay, Burke," Bob said with a big smile. "Tell me how we get some equipment here, a bed and a wall locker and a desk."

"You go downtown and you buy it or you get someone in one of the other battalions who knows the supply officer to get some stuff for you."

"But we live with the supply officer here."

"Right," he said.

"So?" Dunn asked.

"As far as anyone knows, he hasn't done anything for anyone since he's been here. Except the colonel. And the sergeant major. You have to respect him for that. You can't threaten him or coerce him, or intimidate him, or blackmail him, and it's very difficult to steal from him. He thinks if you don't get it, the world's a better place. It's part of his religion, I think. You can't beat him. Hell, even I can't beat him, and I am good. He is the quintessential support officer."

"I'll break his scrawny neck," Dunn said.

"Not bad thinking, Lieutenant. I think I am going to enjoy working with you," Burke said. "Good to have you aboard."

"Right, Burke," Dunn said. "You got a first name?"

"Nope, not in this job. I'm Burke, or as the colonel likes to call me, 'Hey you,' or when he's in a hurry it's 'You.' And that ain't bad. Makes me everyman. I'm 'You.' "

Two days later, Dunn and I accompanied Colonel Haldane to division headquarters, where we received orders for "Operation Birmingham." Like Operation Crimp to clear Cu Chi, the next field exercise was a heliborne assault into a VC area close to the Cambodian border. Also, like Crimp, we were going in force.

Preparing for our first operation as liaison officers, Dunn and I studied all of the maps for the battalion and memorized the radio frequencies for medevacs, artillery, Air Force, division, brigade. (We didn't have to, we learned later—this was the battalion RTOs' responsibility.) We plotted objectives and routes of advance, known enemy locations, villages, and depths of rivers. The comedian Burke helped tremendously, as he had said he would. He knew everything. He also carried the colonel's radio.

The battalion was airlifted to an air base west of Saigon by C-130 transports. On the day of the operation we were standing by the airstrip there in groups of eight. I was to travel in the helicopter with Colonel Haldane, and Dunn would be with Major Panton in the helicopter behind us.

The helicopters arrived in flights of ten, a swarm of giant mosquitoes. As we boarded, I saw two choppers behind us descend toward the airstrip. Still twenty or thirty feet off the ground, they were swaying as the pilots brought them down and then they came too close to each other. Their rotor blades collided first and the impact jerked the helicopters around in strange new directions. One chopper dropped out of the sky straight down. The other, with the pilot fighting to gain control, veered off to the side and then began to pinwheel toward the ground. It landed with a thud near some men who were running to get out of the way.

The incident occurred within the few seconds that it took our chopper to gain altitude. We changed directions and the scene was lost from view.

I was watching the dozens of helicopters flying around us and thinking how much they reminded me of pictures I had seen of Allied planes on bombing missions during World War II when Burke hit me on the shoulder and handed me a radio handset. He said the colonel wanted me to monitor the Air Force net.

Over the *battey-de-battey* of our helicopter, I heard the cryptic conversations of the Air Force jet pilots who were prepping the LZ. This wasn't so bad—I felt like a spectator. I looked out to our front and tried to see the jets working the area, but it was hard to associate what I was hearing with the streaking planes ahead.

One pilot said he was receiving small-arms fire, and I asked Burke to relay that information to the colonel. "Yep," he said, "it's a hot LZ."

We landed in waist-high grass. After helping to off-load the chopper, I picked up the maps and fell in behind the colonel. We made our way to a line of trees extending out into the field, and Panton said we would set up headquarters there. Dunn was on duty first to monitor the radios and plot the maps. I went out to ensure that the men with the heavy mortars knew where we were and that the Headquarters Company guard element was in place to protect our western flank.

Later, I was sitting on commo equipment near Dunn when reports started to come in about contact with the VC, who were all around us and staying to fight. A couple of times Dunn was reminded to get the "body count."

The heavy 4.2-inch mortars came on line and began firing over us in support of a unit across the field. Nearby, to the west, a machine gun began firing, then two, then three or more. They were so close that we all ducked. The guns did not sound like our M-60s; their sound was deeper, more throaty.

Panton yelled at Dunn, "What unit is that? Who's over there?"

Burke, leaning over a map, yelled back, "Alpha Company."

My old unit.

The firing increased. Some rounds zinged over our heads. The colonel asked Dunn to find out what was happening. Panton got on another radio and told the mortars to support Alpha.

Dunn got Woolley on the radio, while Burke turned to a frequency that brought up the platoon in contact with the VC. Bratcher was talking. He said that the platoon was ambushed. They had taken casualties, both killed and wounded.

"Press on," Haldane said in an even voice. Then louder, "Tell Woolley to have his men press on. Attack. We'll get someone out to look after his wounded. We're close by."

Picking up my M-16, I trotted by the heavy mortars that were being moved around 180 degrees to support the A Company engagement. I came up beside the guard unit digging in and told the sergeant in charge to come with me. We moved through the trees to the back edge of the field. Down the tree line I saw Beck leading a party of men in my direction. At the end of the field behind him, tracers were coming from the jungle. There was some return fire from the field, but not much. Then the mortars behind me began firing and rounds *swooshed* overhead, followed by the *poof* from the tubes, and then the *crash* in front as the round exploded in the trees. Ahead, small-arms firing continued.

Beck was followed by Ayers and Castro, both of whom were carrying men in a fireman's carry. Behind them were other 3d Platoon stragglers. I motioned for everyone to get into the woods. A medic came up and we made our way down to the group. Beck, Ayers, and Castro all had flesh wounds. PFC James A. Livingston and Staff Sgt. Julian Willoughby, both recent replacements, were dead.

Castro said that when they came to the edge of the field, Ayers started to go around it inside the wood line. The lieutenant told him no, to go straight ahead, that they had to get to a rally point. They were caught in the middle of the field with no place to hide. Everyone in the front was killed or wounded.

Goddamned Bratcher, I thought angrily, why did he let the new man send the platoon out into the field? Trying to get to a rally point? What was that, hurrying to a rally point?

More men came from the guard unit. Some body bags appeared, and I helped put Livingston and Willoughby away.

When I got back to battalion headquarters area the colonel was at the center of activity. To his right Dunn and Burke were busy taking his orders and relaying them on the radio. Panton, on his left, was plotting a map. I was sitting on the commo box when the wounded men from my old platoon came in with the two body bags. I told Bob that we needed a dust-off. Burke looked over and gave me a thumbs-up. Soon Bob told me to take some purple smoke and go out into the field near where we had landed. A medevac helicopter was on the way.

I led the group out, threw smoke, and stood aside as the chopper landed and the men boarded. Castro and Beck waved from the helicopter as it lifted off, bent its nose down, and gained altitude. Both would be back in a couple of days.

Ayers's wounds were light, and he stayed. I sent him to join the battalion guard unit until we linked up with Alpha Company again. I slapped him on his broad back as he walked away.

The various units of the attacking force maneuvered in the area for three days and then moved out into separate tactical areas. The division killed 119 VC and wounded many more, in addition to capturing five hundred tons of rice, one hundred tons of salt, mortars, bombs, and mines. We were becoming better at our jobs, but at a price. Even very good units have casualties in war.

On the fourth day my old platoon came by the battalion area. Trost stopped in to see Panton. Ayers was leading the column and I nodded to him as he passed. Bratcher was midway down the column. I made eye contact but did not smile. I blamed him for letting the platoon walk out into that field. He dropped out and came to stand in front of me, his neck tightening occasionally.

"Goddammit, you told me to let the man alone."

"You dumb fucking asshole. Don't come over here with any fucking excuses. You don't let people walk out in an open field like that."

"We were told the other side was secure."

"Who said that, Sergeant? Goddammit, all the time we were together, we didn't trust anyone else. We took nothing for granted. Someone says the other side's secure? Fucking show me." I paused. "You don't go putting your people at risk trying to get to some fucking staff officer's rally point on time."

Trost walked by and I looked away. Bratcher turned and followed him.

That afternoon we received mail, cold beer, and hot food. I had a letter from Pete, who was convalescing in a hospital near his home of Lincoln. He was in the same ward with Ray Ernst and they both sent their regards. Pete said being wounded wasn't all bad. Some of the nurses loved wounded GIs.

As usual, that evening a duty roster was drawn up to monitor the battalion's radios throughout the night. Each man had two hours. I had 0200 to 0400. Dunn had 0400 to 0600.

At 2300 the mortar platoon fired a short round that landed in the area where Company B was dug in. Several men were wounded. The battalion surgeon, another of the staff officers ordered into the field that day, worked to keep them alive. He said they had to get to a hospital soon or they would not make the night.

We got the men in Company B on their feet and moved them to a clearing a half mile away. After they secured the tree line, we stood in the field, with the monsoon rain falling, and shined flashlights at the sky to guide in the medevac helicopter. We put the three wounded men aboard and retraced our steps to the battalion perimeter. By then it was almost 0200.

I fell on my mattress but had not slept for more than fifteen minutes when I was awakened for radio duty. I went over to the radios and made a note in the journal that I had taken over radio duty. There were sitreps every half hour from the various companies in the battalion. The mortars continued to fire H&I periodically. I labored to stay awake. At 0400 I went over to Dunn and told him he had duty.

After fourteen days in the field, we were heli-lifted to Tay Ninh for a C-130 flight back to Phuoc Vinh.

Dunn and I were the last to leave the LZ. We had to coordinate on the heli-lift out and make sure the men were lined up in the right numbers and that no one was left behind. The sergeant major had found several sets of tanker goggles to keep debris out of our eyes. They were perfect in the turbulence of the helicopters.

As we trudged up the road from the airfield at Phuoc Vinh, our goggles pulled down to our necks, we looked like raccoons, with clean rings around our eyes. Our fatigues were dirty and sweaty from the two-week operation, plus from all the debris they had collected from the dozens of helicopters in the lift. Our hair was matted with dirt and grime. We were tired to the bone and we trudged along with our heads down.

When we arrived at our tent we found devastation. A river from the monsoon rains had run through our section of the tent. Bob's cot had been swept to my side. Our clothes, hanging on the mosquito netting of the tent, were mildewed. A package of cookies from home that had been ripped opened and destroyed by rats was lying on top of my cot. Mud was six inches deep across the floor to Moubry's elevated section.

Moubry had added an easy chair and a rug. The light over his desk was shining down on his open Bible.

Still carrying our guns, we walked around our area of the tent in mud up to our ankles and tracked it across Moubry's new rug, out into the company street, over to the supply tent, and behind the counter. Moubry saw us and went out the back. Going down the line of supplies, we pulled out new fatigues, new skivvies, new socks, new sheets, and new pillows. We went back to our tent and put our supplies on Moubry's bed. On a revisit to the supply tent we picked up shipping pallets to put on the floor of our tent section.

After showering, shaving, and dressing in our new fatigues, we went to the mess hall and persuaded Cookie to make us some sandwiches, even though he had long since closed the line for supper.

Later at the officers club, Dunn and I were joined by 1st Lt. Frank Bradley, who had taken the recon platoon from Pete. We sat by ourselves and stacked beer cans five levels high until Dunn knocked them over. Then I went to my old tent in the Alpha Company area and retrieved the picture of the nude from behind the bar.

Back at the battalion officers club, I put the painting of the nude in a position of honor behind the bar and proposed a welcoming toast to her. Bradley, drunk, stood up, staggered to get his balance, saluted the lady, and left. He stumbled down the battalion street as he tried to light a cigarette. He was so intent on lighting his cigarette that he lost his way and weaved off between two tents. Finally getting the cigarette lit, he found the tent that he shared with the communication officer, 1st Lt. Larry Lingel, who was in bed but not yet asleep. With the cigarette still in his mouth, Bradley stumbled to his cot and pulled up the mosquito netting. He turned around, sat down heavily, and reached forward to undo his shoes. He couldn't. He came halfway back up and fell back on the cot, his legs still off the side.

Lingel had seen the cigarette in Bradley's mouth, but he didn't know what happened to it, so he turned on a small bed light over his head.

Bradley started to breathe deeply. A couple of seconds later the cigarette rolled off his chin and landed on his neck.

A few more seconds went by.

Suddenly he jerked forward and became entangled in the netting. He swung his arms around and became more ensnared—fighting, twisting, kicking. The cot turned over and he fell over backward with his upper body completely wrapped in the mosquito netting. He thrashed around on the floor for a few more seconds and then lay still.

Lingel, propped up on one elbow, looked down without expression.

The cigarette began to smolder inside the mosquito netting at Bradley's back. He lashed out again, jerking and struggling, and rolled across the floor away from the overturned cot. Coming to rest in a ball in the middle of the tent, he lay silently.

Finally, from inside the netting, came a faint voice. "Lingel, Lingel, save yourself, I'm done for. Can't get away."

── ELEVEN ──

War Is War

Within a couple of days we received orders for "Operation Adelaide," a search and destroy mission in the VC-held Ong Dong jungle. The operation began with an overland move down the road south of Phuoc Vinh with armor from the 1st/4th Cavalry attached. 1st/4th, always referred to as the "Quarterhorse," employed medium-size M-48 A3 tanks and armored cavalry assault vehicles (ACAV) outfitted with a .50-caliber machine gun in the commander's cupola and two lighter 7.62mm machine guns at the top rear. Additionally, M-113 armored personnel carriers modified as flamethrowers, referred to affectionately as "Zippos," were included in most cav formations. A Quarterhorse unit of tanks, ACAVs, and Zippos was an awesome fire and maneuver force, unlike anything ever deployed in war before.

Because we were moving to a forward position on all-weather roads, the battalion would use the command van for the first time in Vietnam. Mounted on a standard deuce-and-a-half chassis, the van itself looked like a refrigerator container. The only door let out to the back. Inside on the right was a console for eight or nine radios, with two tables beneath the radios. A walkway on the left led to a large map board fastened against the front wall and an area large enough for a half dozen men to stand before the map.

Burke drove the van. Dunn and I were in accompanying Jeeps behind the colonel. Halfway to our objective we drove by Alpha Company, which had moved south the previous afternoon to help secure a bridge. Bratcher was sitting on a berm with Castro. I gave them a thumbs-up as we passed. Bratcher smiled back and gave me the finger. Infantrymen did that to staff officers in Jeeps.

We turned off the main road and traveled down a smaller dirt road past several clusters of huts where stone-faced villagers stared at us. Ten miles down the secondary road we arrived at a large field that had been secured by advance elements of the battalion. We drove across the field with Panton, who was responsible for locating and setting up the battalion CP (command post). Dunn and I were drawn to a large tree with low, sprawling branches inside the far tree line, and we convinced Panton to set up the command van nearby. We dropped our web gear and went back to the edge of the field. Dunn motioned with a big wave of his arm for Burke to drive the van over to the tree.

Because Burke was not large, he was flung around behind the wheel of the van as it bounced across the field. He looked out of place, overmatched, and the van was traveling too fast. Dunn and I jumped out of the way as Burke passed us heading into the woods.

"Hey!" we yelled. "Hey, slow down!"

Burke stopped the van near the large tree, but not before it had rolled over our gear and mashed most of it into the ground. It almost seemed as if running over our stuff was the reason for his haste.

"Sorry," he said when we came up beside him, "couldn't stop."

Other members of the command staff, seeing the van stopped inside the wood line, figured that's where the CP would be set up. They began to unload nearby trucks parked in a semicircle in the field.

Dunn told Burke that he almost killed us. Besides, he was in backward. We wanted him to back in so the entrance to the van would be under the tree.

Burke said, "Okeydokey," and tried to find reverse. He finally popped the clutch, and the van jerked quickly backward. Dunn and I jumped out of the way as it ran over our gear again. Burke looked somewhat confused. He almost impaled himself on the steering wheel when the van hit a tree. We saw him grab his chest and shake his head. Suddenly the van lurched toward us again and ran over our gear for the third time.

"Hey!" we yelled.

Burke was crashing through the jungle when the colonel came up. Like a rampaging rhinoceros, the van rumbled through the trees and passed us as it went out into the field. It almost ran over some men getting out of their vehicles.

"Why is Burke in that van?" the colonel asked. "He's from New York City. I don't think he can drive. He's going to crash."

Burke did a turn in the field and the van headed back toward us.

"Holy shit," I said, "he's coming back."

The men trying to form the battalion perimeter looked up and scattered. Burke ran over some commo gear and finally stopped, well out in the field. I climbed up on the running board.

Burke looked at me calmly and said, "Is this okay?"

"Crash Burke, you are a piece of work," I replied.

The squadron of cavalry that had provided security for our move appeared across the field. Several tanks and accompanying ACAVs spread out and raced in our direction. The lead tank came to a stop near the wood line, and a short, square-jawed tank NCO jumped out. Pulling down his goggles and smiling, he said that he was "Slippery Clunker Six," and his Slippery Clunker boys would be with us through the night. The name tag on his fatigue jacket read Bretschneider. Despite his friendly, cavalier manner, he looked rock solid. His diction was crisp and precise, and his eyes—prominent in the clean circles where his goggles had been—were bright and intelligent.

Panton pointed out where the cav commander could put his tracks and asked if he could dig a hole for our command vehicle. Slippery Clunker Six said, "Certainly, it would be our pleasure," and ordered one of his tanks with a dozer blade on the front to dig a wide trench.

When the job was finished, I told "Crash" Burke—a name that seemed to fit him—that I had better back up the truck, to prevent more damage, plus we didn't want the infantry to look bad in front of the Quarterhorse.

By dusk all of the battalion units were in place and the command van was in operation. A mess hall with lights powered by a small generator had been set up. Dunn and I built a small rain shelter under the large tree. Sitting on our air mattresses after supper, we looked around at our surroundings and decided that that was the way to go to war—you got your mess tent, your shade, your rain-proof, bug-free, air-conditioned office. It was almost civilized.

"But I don't know," I said. "Over there, that tank looks like a big metal building, looks like it would draw fire. And it's loud. You hear that thing today? How you going to sneak up on VC in a tank?" From our position on the ground the tank appeared monstrously large.

Dunn said, "Ah, the American man and his fighting machines. One good thing, though, Crash Burke wasn't assigned to armor."

Slippery Clunker Six walked purposefully over to us and asked if we'd like something to eat. He had a little cooler in his tank where he kept some very good sausage and pâté and wondered if we wanted any. I said we'd just taken supper in the local diner, but added quickly that, of course, we would like some sausage and pâté; we hadn't been asked things like that nearly enough since we'd been in Nam.

"You got any wine?" I asked.

"Of course," he said.

We walked over to his tank. He had a folding table set up, and we sat on boxes and ate exotic food out of several containers. Dunn compared it to what he thought it must be like going on a safari, certainly not what we were used to as grunts in Vietnam.

As we ate and drank, the cavalry NCO said that he and his men had it a little easier and were a little more distant from this jungle war than the infantry—maybe it was the noise or the tracks they left.

"You guys aren't in harmony with the jungle," I suggested.

"There you go," he said. "But you know, the VC stay away in droves. 'Course there are those damn mines which take all the fun out of it. But it is not supposed to be fun, is it?" He paused a moment to give us a chance to respond. Dunn shrugged, and he continued, "Ours is a noble endeavor here. We are crusaders, the fortunate ones in our generation. 'Far better it is to dare mighty things, to win glorious triumphs, even though checkered by failure, than to take rank with those poor spirits who neither enjoy much nor suffer much, because they live in the gray twilight that knows not victory nor defeat.' That's from the late great Teddy Roosevelt, who knew about war and noble causes."

Eloquent quotes from former statesmen were seldom heard on the battlefields of Vietnam, but they did not seem out of place coming from Sergeant First Class (SFC) Hans Karl Bretschneider.

Maybe that was because he was so self-assured. Confidence writes its own rules.

"Ah," he continued, "but I'm afraid Kipling also knew about fighting, especially war in this part of the world. He said:

" 'At the end of the fight is a tombstone white
With the name of the late deceased.
And the epitaph drear:
"A fool lies here
Who tried to hustle the East." '

"Something which we fools might be trying to do here in Vietnam, don't you think? Aren't we trying to hustle 'em? I think if we are, there is a tombstone out there with our names on it."

Dunn laughed. "You think so?"

"Yeah, I think so," the tank commander said, "but, you know, for us that shouldn't matter. We're soldiers. 'Ours is not to question why, ours is to do and die.' "

"Now there you've almost got it," Dunn said. "We fight, we die, but damned if we don't kill a bunch of them son'bitches, too."

Slippery Clunker Six smiled slowly and said, "There you go."

The cavalry left the next morning to provide security for elements of the 1st Engineer Battalion, which was improving the road to Phuoc Vinh, but we saw Slippery Clunker Six occasionally throughout the operation. For several days, small elements patrolled around the battalion CP and then company-size forces moved out to protect engineer work parties that were cutting pioneer roads through the jungle. There were occasional firefights, but the VC avoided contact. Then, on 2 June, Alpha company stumbled on a VC base camp and a fierce firefight ensued. Trost and the 3d Platoon handled themselves very well, and I noted with pride the competent way RTO Spencer handled Trost's tactical communications—calling for supporting artillery fire and bringing in reinforcements—and the way he handled the medevacs. Trost was in command, there was no question, but Spencer made things work and made Trost look good. In the heat of the battle, Spencer's thick urban brogue had a soothing effect. The tone said, everything's going to be okay.

We had been in the position with the command van under that beautiful tree for five days. Dunn and Crash had the 0700-to-1500 shift in the van. I had the 1500-to-2300 shift that day with another NCO. Colonel Haldane left by Jeep for an early briefing at brigade headquarters. At noon, I was sitting on the step of the van. Inside, Dunn and Crash were taking down radio messages on a clipboard. When the messages were about firefights, enemy sightings, or movements of friendly units, they plotted the positions on the map board. With the colonel out of the area, Dunn was singing as he worked the map board.

I left for lunch and a short nap and returned around 1430. Dunn was sitting on the top step of the van. Crash, on the ground in front of the van, was talking about all the great Fred Astaire movies he had seen. Settling on the step below Bob, I asked him what was happening, referring to the battalion patrols, and he said everything was quiet.

Crash was absolutely grand entertainment. He had energy, enthusiasm, and the ability to tell a good story. Skinny in his big combat boots and T-shirt, he reminded me of Bugs Bunny as he danced around, held an imaginary Ginger Rogers, did a softshoe, handled an invisible top hat and cane, and swayed back and forth. He talked about one scene where Fred Astaire did a softshoe number with two other men. He said he knew the whole routine—it was marvelous and simple. He invited us down to the ground and said he'd show us.

"Not on your life, my friend," I said.

"In the van," Dunn said.

Crash climbed up the steps around me. I looked both ways. There was nobody around, and I followed them inside. Crash had his arm over Dunn's shoulder near the map board.

"Okay," he said, "we got on spats, straw hats, and black canes with solid gold caps on the top. The music is 'Dun de dun, de doddle de doddle do.' Got it? It's that simple, Dun de dun, de doddle de doddle do,' over and over again. Two steps and then three steps. We go left—come on, Lieutenant," he said to me, "join us, we go left two steps. 'Dun de dun,' then we shuffle three times, 'de doddle de doddle do,' then go back to the right. Okay, now bounce your canes in step. Here we go. 'Dun de dun, de doddle de doddle do.' "

We practiced until we had it down—Crash on one end, Dunn in the middle, and I on the other end. We were working on the finish, in which the two of them would spin me off to the right. I would do a pirouette and land on one knee as I raised my hand, holding an imaginary hat, into the air and say "Ta-daa!" Mine was the showcase move, the grand finale. At first, I had trouble facing in the same direction as the others when I came out of the spin onto one knee, but we practiced the whole set several times and I was getting it down. I came out of one spin—the whole routine had been perfect, our best performance—and I put gusto into my "Ta-daa."

Colonel Haldane was standing in the door of the van, looking at me.

Dunn and Crash were standing at attention.

"Who's on duty?" he asked quietly and slowly.

I got to my feet and turned toward the clock on the wall. It was 1520. Theoretically, I had been on duty for twenty minutes.

Dunn and Crash both said, "He is," and pointed at me.

The colonel took a step in and put his map case on one of the tables below the radios. He continued to look at me very seriously.

Dunn and Crash said, "Excuse us," and walked out. Standing behind the colonel, Dunn had an exaggerated smile on his face, his eyes wide and twinkling, as he closed the door to the van.

Inside, the air conditioner and the lights came on. I stood at attention. There were only two people in the whole world—me and the colonel.

"What's happening?" he asked, seeking a briefing on the movement of the various units in the battalion. His battalion.

The clipboard was beside him on the table. Sweating, I figured if I could get to the clipboard and read the messages maybe I could get through this.

I got the clipboard, walked to the map, and read the last entry on the clipboard about an enemy sighting. It wasn't plotted on the map. I read the next entry. It wasn't plotted either. Nothing on the clipboard had been plotted since 1400. And it was past 1520.

The colonel cleared his throat, and there was a pause—like

those last few seconds before an incoming rocket explodes. Then he began talking to me in a low, even voice, his eyes hard.

When he finished, I wanted just to be by myself, to walk alone down a quiet country road.

He said he would be back in fifteen minutes and he wanted a complete briefing. He opened the door and left.

Dunn and Fred Astaire Crash Burke were standing in the distance. They waved and did a soft-shoe to the right. It wasn't funny.

The colonel had received orders from General DePuy, the division commander, to bring in the battalion and prepare the men for a heliborne move to the Michelin rubber plantation, near the Cambodian border. We would support the brigade's attack on a suspected VC command center. Thankfully, for the rest of the afternoon and evening I was busy calling in the companies and coordinating how they would tie in around the battalion CP.

A lone helicopter brought in replacements the next morning. Jumping off the helicopter in their new uniforms, some held their rifles by the handles and bent over more than necessary to get away from the blades. When the chopper lifted off, I noticed a black man who had gotten off on the other side. Standing erect, taller than the rest, he started walking toward us behind the other replacements who were jogging our way.

Duckett.

Smiling, I stood up and met him halfway. We hugged. I asked how he was doing and pointed at his bad ear. He said, "Say what?"

"How's the ear?" I asked. "How you doing?"

"Say what?" he said again, then he smiled. "It's okay."

I told him that it was good having him back, and we went to find the colonel. Although I was still in trouble from the previous day and the colonel ignored me, he smiled broadly at Duckett and welcomed him back. Haldane told Joe that he would like to put him in a staff job, but we were low on platoon leaders. We were losing one a month. Only two officers, Woolley and Trost, were left in Alpha Company. Arthur had been wounded and evacuated to the States. Duckett said he wanted to work with Woolley again, wanted his own platoon back.

As we walked away I told Duckett not to be surprised if he didn't see too many of the old guys around.

The next day the entire battalion was heli-lifted in one flight of helicopters. Dunn and I were on the last chopper. All of our trucks, including the van, had already moved out for the battalion rear camp. I looked down at that very good hole under the old tree as we gained altitude and headed west, leaving the Fred Astaire stage behind.

Our battalion landed at an old airstrip near the Michelin plantation. We established a battalion CP just inside a forest of rubber trees near the airstrip. The four companies in the battalion, Alpha, Bravo, Charlie, and Delta, were deployed to secure individual TAORs.

Alpha Company broke down into small units. My old platoon, on a patrol the third night of the operation, walked into a North Vietnamese position and Ayers and Castro were killed.

Bratcher led the party that brought their bodies back to the battalion CP. Covered by ponchos, they lay at the edge of the CP in the shade by the runway for a long time. Sticking out from the ponchos, tags on their boots identified them and their unit.

I tried to go about my work that morning, but, from deep inside, thoughts of the two soldiers kept interrupting. A picture of Ayers would come to mind, and I would remember that he was an eighteen-year-old boy from the midwest. Strong as an ox, he stayed on point until he dropped. Never complained. Bad teeth. No one wrote to him much. Quiet most of the time. No rough edges. Responded to praise. Did everything asked of him. Dead now—over there under the trees.

I would shake my head and try to focus on the staff work. Then I would see Castro, laughing, getting to the train at the last moment and once aboard, stomping his feet in a circle like he was doing a Mexican hat dance. He was in his late thirties, twice the age of some of the other men. He made good hot stew out of C rations. Friendly, humble. A sergeant E-5 from the old Army. Over there under a poncho, with his boots sticking out, tagged with his name and his unit. Dead.

Suddenly I had trouble breathing. I took a deep breath every few minutes, and I finally had to get away from my work. I

Elmer Lee Van Pelt, III, basic training buddy extraordinaire.

Lieutenant Taylor, the Officer Candidate School tactical officer who was determined to run me off. I always felt better when I knew exactly where he was.

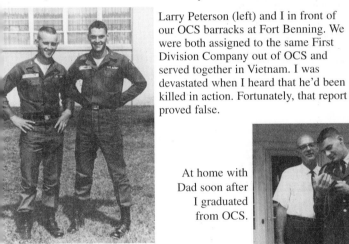

Larry Peterson (left) and I in front of our OCS barracks at Fort Benning. We were both assigned to the same First Division Company out of OCS and served together in Vietnam. I was devastated when I heard that he'd been killed in action. Fortunately, that report proved false.

At home with Dad soon after I graduated from OCS.

S.Sgt. Donald "Cottonpicker" Lawrence, my hero and best friend in the 1950s.

Larry Peterson and I with his parents in Fort Riley, Kansas, shortly before we left for Vietnam. The Petersons always looked after me as if I were a son.

One of my rare moments of solitude aboard the USNS *Mann* as we crossed the Pacific.

Preparing for patrol. I'm on the far left; PFC Ayers is the big soldier at right front.

Pvt. Jack Lyons shortly after coming in from a platoon sweep around the battalion base camp. Note that he is wearing regular fatigues and leather boots. Our battalion did not receive jungle boots and camouflage fatigues until several months later.

Battalion-level memorial service.
We had a service after every operation
in which we suffered casualties.

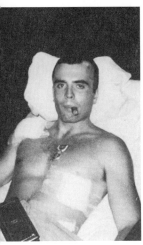

Bob Dunn in the aid tent
after being wounded the
first of three times.

A First Division soldier inside
a VC tunnel near Cu Chi.

Point man fording a
creek. He is carrying
an M-14 while the
others have M-16s.
As point man, he
probably wanted the
more dependable
weapon.

First Division soldiers
waiting to move out.

First Division soldiers waiting for a
helicopter pickup. This was a typical
scene as we prepared for the Battle
of Min Thanh Road.

A VC flag found in the village where
PFC Cipriano was wounded. After we
found the flag, we considered blowing
the village up but decided against it.

A rocket-launcher gunner
and his ammo bearer.
Carrying the ammo was hard
work, and during a sweep
operation, it was divided
among several men.

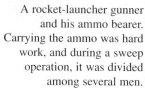

Armored personnel carrier
destroyed in the Battle of Min
Thanh Road. A dead VC is in
the foreground.

Faculty from the Fort Ord Drill Sergeant School. I'm at the far left, the officer in charge.

On May 25, Brenda and I were married at the Cool Springs Baptist Church in Sanford, North Carolina, only five months after we'd met.

Brenda and I just weeks after we'd adopted Joe and Mim.

The airfield in the Long Tieng valley. The CIA compound was to the right of the large rock formation.

Hmong troops on a CH-53 helicopter. In the 1960s, these men were some of the best fighters in the world.

I am sitting with men from my GM on a position northeast of Long Tieng shortly after the cease-fire in 1973.

My bodyguard, Loi, standing by the gifts for the orphans at the 1974 Christmas party. He desperately wanted to leave with me when the war ended but, in the confusion, was left behind.

Tom F. (left) and Mac (bending over, right) on a boat outing with the staff and families from the CIA office in Can Tho in early 1975.

South Vietnamese refugees aboard the *Pioneer Contender* en route to Phu Quoc Island from Cam Ranh Bay. I boarded the same ship days later and bid farewell to Vietnam.

Capt. Edward C. Flink, master of the *Pioneer Contender*. He evacuated tens of thousands from Vietnam.

Barge similar to the one used to transport refugees from the pier at Vung Tau to the *Pioneer Contender*.

Hmong recruits receiving military training.

Hmong recruits receiving marksmanship training in the mountains of Laos.

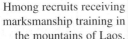

Three members of my rifle platoon during a break from field operations.

Terry Barker and I at the 1974 Christmas party for the orphanage at Vi Thanh.

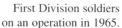

First Division tunnel rat entering a Cu Chi tunnel.

First Division soldiers on an operation in 1965.

walked across the airstrip and sat down. Looking back at the CP, I tried to think about nothing. Don't moralize, I said to myself, my lips moving. Nothing to do, nothing to say. Just sit here quietly, everything will be okay.

Then clearly, in my mind's eye, I saw Ayers and Castro moving quietly through the jungle that night. The sudden, deadly firefight. I saw Ayers fall. His finger still on the trigger of his M-16, he fell backward without expression, his M-16 firing into the night. Then Castro, moving forward, caught in a deadly hail of fire with bullets, one after the other, going through his chest, getting knocked around by the impact, coming to rest finally on top of Ayers. The sound of battle fading as they died.

I could no longer keep from looking at the two lumps lying under the ponchos, and I stared, transfixed, running the imagined nighttime engagement over and over again in my mind. Finally I focused on the peacefulness that was surely on their faces. I remembered McCoy saying on the boat over that we either live, get wounded, or die. No matter the way, it's no problem. If we die, maybe others have a problem with that, but, for us, we're dead and at peace. It isn't bad. It's simply the way things worked out.

Sadly, I constructed a compartment for Ayers and Castro in the back of my mind and I put their memories in a basket there.

A medevac helicopter came in sometime later that morning and took away their bodies. Emotionally paralyzed, I watched from a distance.

I would never be the same again.

Occasionally their memories would escape their compartment and leap out at me in my mind, along with others, but I would put them away and go on. In time, with practice, I kept them securely in their baskets in the back compartment, under control.

Several days later, Bravo Company engaged an enemy unit. The battle raged throughout most of the morning in an area that the VC had not previously controlled. It was possible that a new North Vietnamese outfit had moved in, which would affect the security of Saigon. Because the enemy troops were staying and fighting, Haldane guessed that they were not guerrillas but were, in fact, from a mainline North Vietnamese unit. We could hear the firing from the CP.

At midday, a Bravo Company platoon leader reported that he had a prisoner. Haldane told the Bravo Company commander to bring the prisoner out. We searched on a map for a clearing near the company's location where we could get in a helicopter, and I notified the air controller in the area that we would soon have a priority requirement for a slick and a gunship or two. The company commander came back on the radio and said it was useless, the man was shot up too badly. He wouldn't live another ten minutes.

We could not find a clearing large enough to get in a helicopter close to the fighting, so Haldane told the commander to start moving overland toward our location. If the prisoner died en route, then it was too bad, but he wanted to talk to the man if possible.

Less than an hour later, a group carrying several stretchers broke through the tree line across the airstrip. I called for Colonel Haldane, the medics, the battalion intelligence officer, and the Vietnamese interpreter, "Jose," assigned to our unit. Dunn walked up and I asked him to call in a dust-off for the Company B soldiers who were wounded. He picked up a radio and jogged onto the airfield toward the group coming our way. A couple of medics slung bags over their shoulders and joined him.

Dunn pulled on the PRC-25 radio and talked into the handset. Looking up, he yelled at me to get some purple smoke for the medevac.

By then the colonel was at the CP. He picked up a smoke canister and headed toward Dunn and the medics. When they reached the group in the middle of the airfield, the medics began frantically working on the men on the stretchers. Finally two men picked up one stretcher and started walking toward the aid tent beside the CP. Haldane fell into step beside them. I told Crash to look after the radios, and I followed the interpreter and the colonel inside the small tent. The soldiers had just lifted the Vietnamese prisoner onto the operating table. They moved away and began unwrapping their ponchos from the two bamboo poles used to make a stretcher.

The Vietnamese prisoner had one arm blown off above the elbow. His right leg was cantilevered at a crazy angle, and his left leg was torn open at the thigh, with a jagged piece of bone sticking out. His olive-green uniform was matted with blood, dirt, and slime, and the jacket had several bullet holes in it. Half of his face had been blown away. Some of his teeth and lower jawbone were exposed. Most of his left cheekbone was missing, and his left eye was dangling by a few strands of muscle and tissue.

But he was breathing—deep heavy breaths. His good eye was moving and making contact with us as we looked down at him.

Haldane told the interpreter to ask the man what unit he was from. Jose leaned close to the man's ear and said a long sentence in Vietnamese. The prisoner's one dancing eye continued to scan us. Jose raised his voice and repeated the sentence. The prisoner turned his head and looked at Jose. As the prisoner tried to talk, he spit blood on Jose and on Haldane's hand, but he managed to say something in Vietnamese. Jose leaned forward quickly as he listened. He said something in Vietnamese. The prisoner responded with a few fractured words.

"What did he say? What did he say?" Haldane asked. "What's his unit?"

The man on the table continued to mumble.

"Don't know," Jose said, shaking his head. "He calls his mother, father. He says Vietnamese names."

"Ask him, please, what is his unit?" Haldane, a good and moral man, was having trouble keeping his focus on the job at hand without lapsing into pity for that mangled boy, still alive, calling out the names of loved ones.

Jose repeated his question, but the prisoner was losing ground. His eye stopped roaming and he looked straight up at the top of the tent. I noticed that blood had stopped seeping from the wound on his leg. His breathing became weaker.

One of the medics came in hurriedly and broke through the crowd of men around the table. He looked at us with some disgust because no one appeared to be helping the man. The medic had been opening a bandage package as he moved, but when he looked down at the mess lying on the table, his hands dropped to his sides. He said, "Ah, shit."

Dunn, apparently finished with medevacking the wounded soldiers from Bravo Company, came in and stood beside me. Two more medics walked in.

The man on the table was barely breathing. Then he gathered some energy from somewhere and started to babble. He blinked his good eye. His raised his arm slightly. Jose repeated his sentence. A medic reached down and put the man's whole arm on his stomach and wiped his forehead. His breathing became slower again, irregular.

One of the medics said, "The man is dead, he just doesn't know it yet. His whole body's in shock. He can't think. He doesn't know who he is."

I remembered when Goss died. It wasn't sudden. Most of him was dead while his heart was still beating.

But this boy—any one of his wounds should have killed him. Tough son of a bitch, I thought, but give it up. Go on. Give it up. You're blown apart. You'll never be whole again. There is no hope.

Most of the men around the table began to slip away. Dunn and I remained at the end of the table. Bob's platoon had suffered as many casualties as had mine. He had held some of his men as they died. We hated the VC for causing so much pain, for killing so many good men. This one, in fact, might have killed Castro and Ayers, and here he lay. The enemy. Castro and Ayers had been avenged. This enemy was dying in front of us.

But I kept saying to myself, give up, please give up. You must hurt. Die and it will all end. You'll be okay. Your mother will be sad and those other people you called out to. Your father, if he knew, would be proud. You are so strong. You must have stayed to fight when the others pulled back, and now you still won't give up. Give up and there's peace.

Bob and I were alone in the room with the man when he stopped breathing.

You were a good soldier, I thought. You did your duty. How noble to have lived and died doing something as well as you did. You should have been in my platoon. You have my respect. You, Castro, Ayers. I shall always remember your sacrifices, one against the other.

Then we heard a loud gasp. The prisoner suddenly bent forward at the waist and sat up straight, reaching out his arm toward us. He looked at us with his good eye, his other eye bobbling around like a bloody ball on a string. His mouth was open. He was gargling, and blood splattered over us, but his eye remained focused on us, on both of us at once. Then, Mother of Jesus, one leg moved off the operating table. He garbled again, louder. His weight followed the leg that was draped over the side of the table. His whole arm moved across the front of us when he turned—as though he wanted to get off the table.

His body twisted around and he fell to the floor. There, thankfully, he died.

Dunn and I had jumped back to the far side of the tent. We were holding each other's arms, our eyes and mouths wide open. Maybe we yelled. One of the medics came running in and around the table to the man on the floor. Bob and I walked out.

"Goddammit, that was a tough son of a bitch," I said.

"I think I poop-pooped in my pants," Bob said.

Two days later we received word that Gen. William C. Westmoreland, commander of MACV, would visit our unit for an awards ceremony. To Haldane's credit, he didn't break a sweat over receiving the highest-ranking American general in Vietnam. Instructions about security, timing, and ceremony arrangements came in gradually. Throughout the day before Westmoreland's arrival, Haldane said that we were not going to stop the war or fall down dead because one man was coming for a thirty-minute visit. He was upset, however, when he received word that Westmoreland would be handing out Silver Stars.

"Well, just who do we give them to? Sorta getting the horse in front of the cart, isn't it?" he asked no one in particular when he received the message. "I don't remember recommending anyone for Silver Stars."

Major Allee thought that perhaps Westmoreland was upgrading the level of decorations for combat bravery. He remembered that we had about eight recommendations in the works for lesser medals and suggested that we line up the people who had been recommended for awards and think of the general's visit as a dry-run ceremony.

Westmoreland's party arrived exactly on time, as if the U.S. Army and the whole Vietnam War were running on his schedule. We saw the covey of helicopters coming in long before they landed. Gunships making passes along the tree lines looked like advance bodyguards, eventually landing at both ends of the runway. Westmoreland's command helicopter arrived near our CP right on the smoke that Crash threw. Photographers jumped off a following helicopter and focused their cameras on the general as he stepped to the ground. They swarmed around him like gnats and took pictures of his every move.

The general had a regal manner. With silver-gray hair and a square jaw, he stood taller than those around him. I noticed that he had his arm in a sling. Assuming that he had been wounded, I asked one of his aides about it but his answer made no sense. The aide wasn't very friendly, in fact. I had shaken his hand when we first met. He had small, dainty hands and manicured fingernails.

The visit turned out to be pure public relations for General Westmoreland. We were props. He trooped the line and, smiling warmly, presented medals to the assembled men. And then he was gone, back on his clean helicopter, with the escort gunships lifting off first. The newsmen hurried to get on a trailing slick.

Panton went along the line of men as the helicopters lifted off and took back the medals, an awards ceremony in reverse.

Within hours, Crash learned that Westmoreland had fallen on his elbow while playing tennis in Saigon and had suffered a sprain.

I told Dunn and Crash later, "I'm a little sick of this war. There isn't much to make me proud. Platoon leader, at least I had the men and it was us against them. Being a staff officer—I don't know—Ayers and Castro dying. This is one useless fucking war. Westmoreland handing out medals. Show time. We got all this stuff, helicopters, medals, hot meals. What's Charlie got? He ain't got shit. Death's a blessing. What's the use of it all? Nothing, one big fucking waste." I was not making sense, nor was I trying to. I was just mouthing thoughts coming into my head. My voice trailed off.

"What exactly are you talking about, Parker?" said Dunn, never a sentimentalist. "There ain't no great truth here. This ain't the first war man's ever fought. This is all you have to remember: 'Ours is not to question why, ours is to do and die.' It's just w-a-r, as simple as a three-letter word. Some people die, some people live. That's it. Some people win and some people lose. Winners are right and losers are wrong. It's no more difficult than that, so don't agonize over it."

"Screw you, Dunn."

"If you ever did, you'd never go back to girls." Dunn refused to be drawn into my despair. "Don't go around moralizing, Parker. Forget about it. Kill them before they kill us, and fuck the reasons why. Win. Survive."

— TWELVE —

Minh Thanh Road

We returned to the base camp later that week. Bob had a calendar above his cot. In seventy-six days we would be eligible for rotation, after being in-country for one full year. That night in the makeshift battalion officers club, I sat with Dunn, Duckett, and Bradley at a rear table. Bradley, a replacement, would be around for several more months. Duckett's convalescence time counted toward his year, and he would rotate home with Bob and me.

We were talking about what we would do when we got back to the States when Dunn mentioned that Colonel Haldane was returning to the States through Europe.

Bradley said we all could. Any active-duty person could book passage on a scheduled round-the-world U.S. Air Force charter called the Embassy Flight. It was used primarily by Defense Department attachés, diplomatic personnel, and couriers, but seats were available for military personnel with legitimate reasons for travel, like us. He suggested that the three of us try to go home on Air Force One, like Haldane.

In our typical, grateful fashion, we told him he was full of shit: Haldane's a colonel. We're second lieutenants. There's a little difference there.

"Fine," he said, "don't believe me. But the next time you're in Saigon, go to the Travel Section at the U.S. Embassy, and ask about seats on Air Force One."

Dunn, intent on getting back to Linda in California on the fastest plane going, had no interest in traveling through Europe. But Duckett and I liked the idea, we just didn't think it was available.

Later that week, Haldane authorized in-country R&R and Duckett and I took off for Saigon.

We stopped off at division headquarters on the way down and I sought out a friend of Crash's at the Administration Section, and we asked him about our exact departure-from-Vietnam date and orders.

"Ah," he said, "the magic ticket. DEROS orders. The Date of Estimated Return from OverSeas orders. Very, very valuable. The keys to heaven. You don't leave Nam without it. I have yours here. Burke told me you were on the way and to look after you, so I have taken the liberty of running off a couple of extra copies for both of you."

I was authorized to leave 13 September 1966. Joe was authorized to leave on the fourteenth. Signed, stamped, mimeographed, in duplicate, everything. Legal. Some people didn't get their orders until the day they left, and we had ours two months early. Crash Burke, I thought, you and your friend are very good people.

On the afternoon of 2 July, we were standing in front of the Marine guard post by the main entrance to the U.S. Embassy in Saigon. Throngs of people were coming and going. We felt out of place. We looked out of place. Our uniforms, though clean, were not starched and tailored like others that we saw, and we were leaner than most military personnel on the streets of Saigon. I had a funny steel-pot tan—my forehead white and my cheeks tanned. And we must have looked unsure of ourselves.

The Marine said that the Travel Section was in a Quonset hut to the side of the embassy building. Walking along tentatively, we stepped out of the way when busy embassy people hurried by us. A Vietnamese receptionist in the front of the Quonset hut did not act surprised when we asked about signing up for the Air Force One flight on 14 September. She gave us some forms to fill out and a mimeographed sheet explaining what was required— DEROS orders, passport, military ID, uniform while traveling. Although I was authorized to leave 13 September, we decided that I would stay over in Saigon until the fourteenth so we could leave together. We finished filling out the forms and were directed to an Air Force sergeant in a rear room. He said everything looked in order. We nodded.

"What's this going to cost?" I asked.

"Nothing," the sergeant said.

"That's it, then?" I said, still not sure that this was for real.

The sergeant looked at me hard, curious about my hesitation. "Let me see your DEROS orders again," he said.

He examined the one I offered for a moment, shrugged, and said, "Everything's all right. You two are the first signing up for the fourteenth, and unless something extraordinary happens and you get bumped a day, that is when you'll be on your way to Europe."

We left the embassy in a more confident manner.

We went to Tu Do Street in downtown Saigon and had some photos taken for our passport applications. That night we practiced our international barroom skills. We liked the feel of being out together. Duckett was six-feet-four and I was six-feet-two. Maybe it was the look in our eyes from our experiences in the field, maybe it was our size and our smiles, but people treated us with deference. When we walked into bars, people noticed us. And we had Europe right down the road. Hold on continent, here we come.

In the coffee shop of our hotel the next morning we heard that Tan Son Nhut airfield had been bombed during the night. Rockets had landed in the departure area and killed several 1st Cav soldiers who were due to leave country that day. After surviving a year of combat, they were killed in their sleep in the departure area in Saigon, the night before they left country.

"Fortunes of war," Duckett said.

"Yeah, and I ain't staying one more night here than I have to, my friend. I'm leaving on the thirteenth. I'll meet you in Bangkok or Europe or Philly, but I ain't staying here one extra night."

We went back to the Air Force sergeant and I made the change without a problem. Duckett and I would meet in Bangkok, Thailand, 14 September; depart on Air Force One on the fifteenth for New Delhi, India, where we would overnight; and then go on to Afghanistan, Athens, and Madrid. We were on our own there to rent a car for a drive up to Germany, where we could get a military hop to the east coast of the U.S.A.

On our return from Saigon we found the battalion going through familiar preparations for another field operation. Two days later, Haldane asked the entire battalion staff to division headquarters for a briefing. Representatives from every battalion in the three brigades were on hand.

Dunn and I stood at the rear of the room before the briefing and greeted other staff officers whom we had met previously. Colonel Haldane was talking with the cavalry commander, Col. Leonard L. Lewane. When Haldane went to the front of the room, Dunn and I asked Lewane about Slippery Clunker Six. The colonel said that call signs had been changed, but the man whom we knew as Clunker Six had volunteered to lead this new operation.

After Col. Sidney B. Berry Jr., the 1st Brigade commander, took the stage, an officer called us to attention as General DePuy walked in through a side entrance and up the stairs to the stage. Speaking in a surprisingly strong voice, his comments went something like this: "In this war, we have to kill more of the enemy than they kill of us in order to win. It's that simple. It is a war of attrition. They try to get us; we try to get them. They have advantages we don't have; we have things they don't have. The monsoon weather has been on their side for the last three months, and they have operated in some of our area with impunity. We haven't been able to use our Air Force, our cavalry gets stuck, rivers are swollen, men get foot rot. But the rains are almost over, replacements are in, we know where the enemy is, we know his weaknesses, and we are going on the offense. We are going to use our advantages, and we are going to kill a lot of the enemy. And we are going to win. I have worked on this next operation with Colonel Berry, and it is good. We have borrowed from the Air Force, the Navy, and the Marines, and all the U.S. Army units around us, and we have all we need." He paused. "Now it's up to you. Be tough. Be aggressive. Do your job. This is the 1st Infantry Division. We have a reputation to live up to." He paused again. "I'll turn the briefing over to Colonel Berry. I want all battalion commanders to remain after the briefing and join me for lunch."

General DePuy left the stage. Colonel Berry pulled aside a curtain behind him to show a map blowup of the area along the Cambodian border north of Parrot's Beak. The following is a paraphrase of what the colonel told us that day:

"Because we are not allowed to attack the Vietnamese inside

Laos and Cambodia, they have developed, as you know, a highway that originates in North Vietnam and comes all the way down, inside first Laos and then Cambodia, to this area, north of the Parrot's Beak, here [pointing to map] northwest of Saigon. At the terminus is their forward field headquarters, called COSVN.

"The VC unit that operates between COSVN and Saigon is the 272d Regiment of the 9th Division. Because of our operations in January near Cu Chi, 272d Regiment forces do not stay inside South Vietnam for very long now. They move across the border, attack a target, and move back to their base sanctuaries in Cambodia.

"During the recent monsoon rains, elements of the 272d Regiment came into South Vietnam to attack American and ARVN positions in the following locations." He used his pointer to indicate a dozen points on the map.

"I now call your attention to this area." Berry replaced the first map with a map showing the South Vietnam/Cambodia border to the left and Highway 13 dissecting the center. On Highway 13, at the top of the map, was the town of Loc Ninh; farther down was the town of An Loc. Near An Loc was a spur road running west toward the South Vietnam/Cambodia border and ending at the Minh Thanh rubber plantation. At the bottom of the map was the Ho Bo woods and the town of Cu Chi. "During the rains, the Viet Cong attacked Loc Ninh three or four days a week. It was difficult to give the Special Forces unit there fire support, and it was difficult to airlift in supplies. We dropped ammunition and food when we could, but the enemy located rockets in close and our resupply planes had to fly high when they dropped. Fifty percent of our supplies landed outside of the wire and were recovered by the enemy.

"These two engagements," he pointed to two marks along the road, "were the result of Quarterhorse efforts to open the road into Loc Ninh. On 8 June, Troop A of the 1st/4th Cavalry was ambushed by elements of the 272d here south of An Loc, and, on 30 June, Troop C with the 1st of the 2d Infantry conducted a reconnaissance in force and engaged elements of the 271st Regiment here south of Loc Ninh. The Quarterhorse, as some of you know who participated, took heavy casualties but killed close to four hundred VC.

"The VC 272d Regiment has been hurt but not destroyed, and we think it will engage our units operating in this area again, if it has a chance. We want to give them that chance. We have told local Army of South Vietnam forces—for the sake of the known VC agents in their ranks—that, on 9 July, we are going to send a convoy composed of an engineer bulldozer and several supply trucks from An Loc to Minh Thanh. We expect word to reach the VC 272d Regiment and we expect they will ambush this convoy for its supplies. They think it will be lightly guarded, and it will be traveling down a road only ten miles from their sanctuaries in Cambodia.

"What we will send down the Minh Thanh road on 9 July will be Task Force Dragoon, commanded by Colonel Lewane. It will be composed of Troops B, C, and D of the 1st/4th Cav, augmented with Company B, 1st/2nd Infantry Battalion. Plus, on standby, we are going to have three heliborne battalions of infantry and all available artillery and Air Force/Marine fast movers waiting to spring a counterambush—a vertical counterambush.

"This is Operation El Paso II. We're going to have a deception move on D day minus 1 to put the standby infantry and the artillery in position at LZs near the road. ARVN units will be told this deployment is for a sweep south toward Cu Chi, a goodly distance away from Minh Thanh. Artillery will be deployed at the same time to colocate with the infantry in the staging areas.

"At 0530 on D day, the three battalions with artillery will move from their deception ops staging areas to launch positions. These launch positions, which are within artillery range, are located here, here, and here." He pointed to three points on the map in the vicinity of the Minh Thanh road.

"At 0700 D day, Task Force Dragoon will depart An Loc. There will be radio silence except necessary communications between Colonel Lewane in the command and control [C&C] helicopter and the lead elements of the task force. We have established checkpoints on the road; please mark them on your maps. The first, at the intersection of the spur road and Route 13, is Checkpoint John. Approximately four miles farther is Checkpoint Gordon. Four miles farther is Hank, then Dick, and finally Tom, four miles from the Minh Thanh plantation.

"If—when—the VC 272d Regiment takes the bait, the artillery will begin immediate fire. They will be tracking the movement of the convoy—turning their tubes as they get location reports—and when the VC bite, they will lay down a blanket of fire on the south side of the road. The fast movers will be on station. They will drop napalm and high-explosive ordnance on the north side of the road. Artillery has the south. Task Force Dragoon has the inside. The cavalry will sustain a high volume of fire during the counterambush; they will not split up; they will use flamethrowers—their Zippos—as offensive weapons. We will have the first flight of infantry counterambush forces on the ground within ten minutes to relieve pressure on Task Force Dragoon and to mop up along the sides of the road. We will put one battalion of infantry in blocking positions near the Cambodian border.

"If the VC 272d takes the bait, we will destroy them."

In outlining the responsibilities of the various units, Colonel Berry said that the 1st/28th Infantry Battalion would be the first to respond if the ambush was sprung at checkpoint Dick or Tom, near the Minh Thanh rubber plantation.

There was a flurry of movement by groups of officers as each unit's responsibilities were announced. Many had questions.

"Before I take your questions," Berry said, "the deputy division commander has something to say. Sir," he nodded to a one-star general at the side of the stage.

Gen. James F. Hollingsworth rose and picked up a pointer from the map board.

"We are going to kill gooks in this operation," he promised us. "We're going to take some casualties. Goddammit, it's a war. But I don't want the war to stop when we take casualties. We don't have time." He said each word in the last sentence slowly, loudly. "We gotta keep going, like a good fighter, we keep going. These son'bitches are going to be surprised all to hell. We don't get 'em like that often. We will be in control, and goddammit I want to think we're pushing a mean pointed stick out there against those son'bitches. Get your men ready, get 'em mean. There are times to go slowly, and there are times to lock and load—kick ass. This is that time, won't be a long period. Gotta get in there fast and move fast. Kill fast. The ambush could take place less than ten miles from a line we cannot cross. That doesn't give us much time to muck around. Don't stop because one of your men gets hurt. Press on. Leave a medic behind or a guard and push on. Those son'bitches aren't going to stay around long."

Hollingsworth stopped and walked to the front of the stage. "You're good soldiers, in the finest tradition of the 1st Infantry Division. Good luck. Remember: Kill 'em, kill 'em fast." He paused. "Kill 'em," he added for good measure, then turned and left the stage.

"Damned fine plan, Bobby," I said to Dunn as we left the briefing and started back to the battalion. "Damned fine."

"You know," he answered, "the cav commander said ol' Slippery Clunker Six's leading this thing. I bet this isn't the last month of Slippery Clunker Six's tour here. He wouldn't be doing something like this if it were."

I said, "Maybe this is his last month here—on this earth. He must feel invincible. He volunteered, too, you heard that. Volunteered? Can't imagine that from someone who appeared so—so balanced. So perceptive. Seemed like such a smart fellow. Why you reckon he volunteered, Bob?"

"I don't know. Maybe it's the fumes inside those tanks. I wish him luck. He's the best we got, and as a poet he's going to be stage center here pretty soon."

Dunn and I were busy fourteen hours a day as Haldane and Panton directed our battalion's coordination with artillery, Air Force, the division G-3, the other battalions, and the helicopter units. Every new unit we had to liaise with was a problem multiplier.

I sought out Duckett and told him to keep his head down. "Europe is right out there, right where I can see it, at the tip of our fingers, Joe. Don't get yourself blown up. This is important. Stay low, you big black lug. You hear me, you half-deaf son'bitch?" I went by his platoon sergeant and told him to protect Duckett with his life.

On D day minus two, we moved by C-130 to Quan Loi and were deployed to a rubber plantation off the runway where we would bivouac for the night. As we were walking along the road to the plantation, a cavalry troop came up behind us and, with their tracks clanking and clamoring, slowly passed. Slippery Clunker Six was in the lead tank. He touched his hand to his tanker's helmet as if to tip it when he passed Haldane and the command group. He recognized Dunn and me and gave a "V" sign with his right hand. He did look invincible—bigger than life.

Behind him were several ACAVs filled with cavalry troops. Our two groups exchanged taunts, probably the same barbs traded between the cavalry and foot soldiers since wars began.

I had the feeling that after a year in Vietnam, we were all coming together somewhere out there, going full speed: us, the cavalry, the artillery, the Air Force, the enemy.

We carried mountains of material in the command group and had extra radiomen assigned. Crash, loaded with gear, looked like a mountain guide from Kathmandu.

The following day, D day minus one, we were to be heli-lifted to the staging area to the south as part of the diversion operation. Except for those we put out on guards, the men stayed in their groupings for the heli-lift to the launch site at first light.

I woke up about 0430 the next morning. It was 9 July 1966. Crash was already up. He had made coffee and was looking over the colonel's map, which he carried. Talking to the colonel as he gave him a cup of coffee, he said he thought the North Vietnamese would attack in our area. It was the closest point to the Cambodian border, and there were river valleys between the road and the border for the VC to use. Also, according to intelligence, elements of the VC 272d Regiment were reported near Minh Thanh as recently as the previous day. "It's going to be our nickel, Colonel," Crash said.

The transport helicopters and their gunships came in low over the trees at first light and were on the ground at the staging area by 0530. The men were onboard within minutes, and the helicopters lifted off for the forward launch site, ten minutes' flying time from Checkpoint Tom.

Dunn went in the first chopper. I went in the last, after ensuring that no one had been left behind.

When I arrived at the forward launch site about 0630, Panton had already set up the battalion CP near a tree on a berm at the side of the field. The field itself was a half-mile square. In one corner, two artillery batteries, a 105mm and a 155mm, had arrived, and the artillerymen were running around in organized chaos as they uncrated ammunition and prepared the guns for action. The thirty-one helicopters that had moved our battalion were in two files down the center of the field. The gunships, looking like a group of thugs, were off to the rear. All of the aircraft were in the process of shutting down. Most of the men from the battalion had disembarked and were lying around. Some of the pilots were walking around and talking to each other, while others remained sitting in their seats. The doors to the choppers were open.

Panton had laid out a map on the ground under the tree. A round rock, representing the convoy, lay on top of An Loc. Clearly marked along the road to Minh Thanh were the checkpoints: John, Gordon, Hank, Dick, and Tom. If Crash was right, the attack would come near Checkpoint Tom. We had six radios set up around the map on the ground. Haldane stayed close to the division command net radio, but we were most interested in the radio monitoring the cavalry's frequency.

D hour of 0700 came and went. Finally, at 0710, Slippery Clunker Six broke static on the cav frequency and reported that the convoy was on its way—he was moving out. We recognized Slippery Clunker Six's voice, which had the casual, reassuring tone of a friendly airline pilot.

Colonel Lewane in the C&C confirmed. We knew from the briefing that Slippery Clunker Six would be leading the task force in his tank, followed by another tank, then two ACAVs filled with troops, and then another tank. The remaining elements of Troop C would be dispersed within the convoy. Troop B would bring up the rear behind a wrecker. Colonel Lewane soon reported that the entire convoy was on the road and moving.

Shortly before Checkpoint Gordon, Slippery Clunker Six said he would begin to recon by fire as he went along. As he passed Gordon, he called out his position. We could hear the booming of a .50-caliber machine gun in the background.

Panton moved his rock. We drank coffee and smoked—waiting and listening. Birds sang in the distance. Flies buzzed around. Time dragged. I reread letters from my parents and from some children at a Nebraska public school.

Between Checkpoint Gordon and Hank was the first of the three areas from which Colonel Berry thought the Vietnamese might attack. Lewane reported that he saw people moving across the road around the bend from the lead tank. On the cavalry net we heard Slippery Clunker Six alert his troops and tell them to tighten their chin straps. Their Great Adventure might be coming up soon. He said he was going to recon ahead and told the ACAV behind him to follow. Everyone else was to hold back. Over the radio, we could still hear his .50-caliber machine gun firing. Then there was silence on the radios. All U.S. forces involved in the operation stood by and waited.

Finally the Quarterhorse colonel came back on and said that the people he had seen must have been hunters or farmers. He found no one in the area. The convoy moved on.

On the other side of Checkpoint Hank the road left the sparse prairie grass and entered a dense jungle forest. The convoy would travel under the canopy of the forest for more than two miles. It was the most dangerous area of the operation. If the convoy were attacked here, the closest place where reinforcements could land would be on either side of the forest.

Slippery Clunker Six said, on the cavalry net, that he was going into the Enchanted Forest and God be with anyone who tried to stop him before he came out. Lewane told him to be careful, he'd see him on the other side.

Ten minutes into the forest, Slippery Clunker Six reported, "There are some logs across the road three hundred meters to my front. Hold the convoy."

Panton asked Colonel Haldane if we should alert the men and possibly start the helicopters. The colonel said no, not yet.

On the Quarterhorse radio frequency the cavalry platoon leader—several vehicles back from Slippery Clunker Six—said, "This could be a VC tax point. If it's an ambush it's not very subtle. I'm going to send a tank down with a blade on the front to act as a battering ram." He told Slippery Clunker Six to move ahead and clear the road. He told one of the ACAVs to follow shooting.

We waited, looking around at each other.

Slippery Clunker Six came back on the radio and said, "We're moving out again, the road's clear. No Charlie, but we sure scared the hell out of some trees."

The sun was climbing in the morning sky and it began to get hot. Down by the artillery we could hear one of the NCOs in the fire direction center of the 155 battery yell an alert to the gunner. Apparently the convoy was coming into range of its guns. We saw a man climb over one of the traces to the gun and put his eye into a sight.

Colonel Lewane said that the fast movers orbiting on standby were running out of fuel and would be replaced by new jets.

Panton pointed out that the convoy had not received any sniper fire, which proved to him that something was planned. The VC operated all along the road. Unless they were told to keep down because a big attack was planned, they would have been sniping.

The convoy approached Checkpoint Dick and the 105 battery in our area went on alert. The gunners turned the tube slowly as their fire direction center plotted the movement of the convoy.

Haldane sent Dunn and me to tell all the company commanders to have their men take a piss and get ready. We walked down the line and spoke to each commander. Woolley was, as usual, full of good cheer. Our relationship had not changed since I had moved to battalion. He was a fine officer and a gentleman, and I did not try to become familiar. I would have followed him to hell.

Dunn started back to the battalion group and I told him I'd be along soon. I walked over to my old platoon. Bratcher was sitting in a helicopter with his feet dangling over the side. Propped up on his radio, Spencer was lying on the ground close by. Lieutenant Trost had contracted dengue fever during the previous operation and was back at the division aid station. Bratcher was acting platoon leader.

Beck came out of the crowd of men and stood beside me. I sat down next to Bratcher, who offered me a cigarette. Spencer stood up, and Manuel, Lyons, and King walked up to join Beck in a semicircle around us. Bratcher asked if I knew anything they didn't about this upcoming operation. "Nope," I said, "you know about as much as I do. But I know this—we got less than a couple of months to go in-country. You don't have to be a hero to catch that plane out, just alive."

"Yeah," Bratcher said, "we'll be okay."

Returning to the battalion CP, I noticed on the map that Panton's rock was near Checkpoint Tom. I looked back at the helicopters and saw that most of the pilots were in their seats. The gunships started up with their individual swooshes and whines.

Slippery Clunker Six came on the air and said that across the field ahead was Tom, the intersection of the road, and a tree line. He was moving out front as point.

Trees came down close to the road for about a half mile and then the road went through a marshy area and up a short incline. The road had been built up in the swampy area and had steep banks. Crash had a stick in his hand and tapped the map just beyond Tom.

Slippery Clunker Six said that he was approaching Tom and was going to move ahead through the woods at a good pace.

After telling Panton to motion for the helicopters to crank, Haldane stood on the berm and raised his hand—his signal to the company commanders to load.

I picked up the satchel I was to carry for the colonel, then helped Crash put on his radio. The entire command group packed up and started moving toward two helicopters near the front of the column. Haldane had insisted that he get on the ground as soon as possible to coordinate the counterambush. If an attack occurred now, we would be the first in. We would be going in on both sides of the incline near the marsh.

Crash had the division radio. The RTO behind him had a radio on the Quarterhorse frequency, and as we walked to the helicopter we heard the Quarterhorse commander in the C&C saying that he spotted some people ahead of the convoy.

Slippery Clunker Six, on his net, reported the same thing and said he was taking the people under fire.

Then, suddenly from Capt. Steve Slottery, commander of Troop C in Task Force Dragoon, "We're under attack! All around us! My lead tank's hit. They're all over us. . . ." In the background we heard catastrophic, violent firing and explosions.

On the Air Force spotter aircraft frequency, a calmer, businesslike pilot's voice said, "Bingo, Bingo, Lead 42 come down on my smoke."

The artillery at the end of the field began firing before we reached our helicopter. As I jumped on, it began to lift off. The gunships were already in the air and heading toward the convoy.

The artillery behind us began to fire at a steady, deafening rate, the concussions pounding off our chests one after another. All around us helicopters were gaining altitude and heading toward the road. I was sitting beside the Air Force radio and tried to make out the indistinct messages between the spotter aircraft and the jets. From the radio to my left I could hear the sounds of battle on the Quarterhorse frequency above the noises of the helicopters, and the frantic messages among the cavalry leaders as they fought for their lives in the middle of the ambush.

In the distance ahead of us, a jet streaked down from the heavens and, after it pulled up, a giant ball of fire flashed. Nearby, within seconds, another ball of fire appeared from an unseen jet.

I caught myself whistling, looking ahead, tense. Faintly, from the distance, we began to hear explosions on the ground. The helicopters moved off the treetops and gained altitude so they could get a diving run down into the LZ. The higher they lifted, the more fires we saw in front of us. Off to the southeast I could barely make out the end of the convoy still out in the field. Some vehicles were ablaze.

The road through the woods was clearly marked by the Air Force and artillery fire. Some gunships already on the scene came into sharp contrast as they streaked past burning napalm.

Ahead, I saw the incline and the marshy area as the lead chopper landed in the clearing by the marsh. The lead vehicles of Task Force Dragoon were on the road to our left. Some were on fire. In the distance I could see flames from the snout of a Zippo spray the roadside with a hellish flame. In the jungle, napalm had burned long black splotches along the north side of the road. Some trees stood naked.

Amid more explosions and more fireballs we began to hear the clatter and heavy thumping of machine guns. Tracers from some of the tanks were still streaking into the woods.

Men from the lead choppers raced for the wood line. Several fell. People were moving about hurriedly on the road. It was hard to tell whose side they were on. For a fleeting second it appeared that most of them were Vietnamese running across the road from the south. We were landing in the middle of the battlefield.

On the ground seconds later, I lay down until the helicopter lifted off, then moved under its skids to join the command group running through the waist-high grass for the trees. I could see the turret to the lead tank off to the side, near the marsh. It was at a crazy angle. The tracks on the tank were blown askew.

Panton had a simple map of the area between Checkpoints Tom and Dick in his hand and was plotting the locations of the companies with a grease pencil. I walked past him and joined Dunn, who was staring into the woods.

The area smelled like spent gunpowder and burnt wet weeds. Bushes were burning everywhere. Suddenly to our right, a Vietnamese got up and started running through the woods. By the time Bob and I got our rifles up, other men in the battalion had cut him down. He was dressed in olive-green fatigues but did not appear to have a weapon.

Haldane came up behind us and told us to move out. Most of the battalion was on the ground. I took the point for the command group as we moved cautiously by the burned-out area on the tree line into dark jungle. We could see sunlight ahead where napalm had burned through the foliage, and I headed in that direction.

Firing continued all around us. Occasionally a round zinged overhead. Slow-moving, heavily armed, prop-driven Skyraider aircraft came on station, and Haldane asked the company commanders to have each platoon throw smoke to identify their forward positions. He told them to hold up until we got a fix from the forward air controller (FAC).

Company C was beside the road, Company B was beside them to our left, and Company A was to our right. The lead elements of Company B suddenly began firing. Grenades went off. The commander came on the radio and said they had run into Vietnamese.

Some walking wounded from Company A had approached our group and were being treated by the head corpsman when the FAC came on the air and said that he had our smoke. We were even with the cav unit at the head of the convoy, more or less on line. He told us to hold up for five minutes while the Skyraiders worked the area in front of us. General DePuy came on and said four minutes—we had to move on.

The ponderous Skyraiders came from behind us. Suddenly

their firing drowned out everything else around us. Then, off in the distance, we heard other explosions and the ground shook.

The Skyraiders' fire cut down whole trees. One wave of two planes was followed by another wave and another.

General DePuy was on the radio yelling for us to move out, mop up.

Haldane passed the order.

Another bomb went off somewhere in the distance and the ground shook again.

Company B sent a gravely wounded man on a poncho stretcher to our area. Haldane told the two soldiers carrying the stretcher to stay with us, take point for the command group, and move out. We left the wounded man behind with the head medic. Haldane told the corpsman to make it to the road with his wounded when he got him patched up.

Company C called in to report they were stepping over Vietnamese dead. Did Haldane want a body count? Haldane said he wanted the company to move ahead.

About this time the two soldiers leading our group stopped in their tracks. Haldane asked loudly, over the din of noise around us, what the delay was about. I told him I'd check and I moved up by the men. They were looking down at a ravine that went straight across our front. It looked like a dried-up river. Beside us, Alpha Company came on the radio to report the ravine.

Down in the bottom was a trail—a "superhighway" through the forest that the ambushers were certainly planning to use as an escape route away from the road. I sent the two men across. As they reached the bottom, an automatic weapon opened up from the left and the lead man recoiled from a hit, but he gathered himself, dived to the side, and hid behind a log.

Company B soldiers were behind the Vietnamese gun. They threw grenades into the position and two Vietnamese soldiers were blown partially out. The other Bravo Company soldier in the ravine got across and up the other side. The command group followed. The remaining medic helped the first man up and treated his wound. Down the ravine, some of our soldiers were investigating the Vietnamese blown out of the machine gun position and yelled up to us that one of them was still alive. Haldane told them to take him to the road.

Charlie Company continued to report that it was coming across a lot of bodies and taking some prisoners. Haldane told them also to move the POWs to the road.

Firing picked up as we approached the heart of the ambush, where the bulk of the Vietnamese had been hiding as they waited to be used as porters to carry the supplies back to Cambodia. Rounds continued to zing over our heads.

Alpha Company reported that it was wading through the carnage left by one of the Skyraiders that had hit a Vietnamese group broadside with its .50-caliber machine guns. I heard Duckett say that it was a Philadelphia mess. Spencer was on the air and said that Bratcher and my old platoon were coming across individuals and pairs of VC trying to make their way north away from the ambush.

The small-arms fire subsided and two more men from Company B came our way with a soldier on a stretcher. Their charge— only a boy, a small, youngish eighteen—looked up at me and said he didn't want to die.

"Hell, man, I can't see where you're wounded," I said.

He pulled up his fatigue jacket, and I could see a small bullet hole near his navel. There wasn't much blood outside, but it was clear that he had extensive internal bleeding. His skin was bloated around the bullet wound.

Haldane walked up. The boy continued to say over and over again that he didn't want to die. He was going into shock.

"Gut shot," I said to Haldane. "He'll die unless we get him to a medic soon."

"We don't have any," Haldane said.

I suggested that we could send the litter detail to the road, but Haldane said the men with the stretcher were needed where they were. He told me to get the man to the road, find a radio, and tell him what was happening out there.

"Rog," I said.

Haldane directed the two Bravo Company men to return to their unit and told Dunn to move out on point. I stood beside the boy on the stretcher and watched the battalion group follow Dunn.

Firing was picking up, some of it coming from our rear.

At the end of the battalion group, an Air Force forward observer came along with his radio operator and another soldier who had fallen in with us. I reached out and grabbed the soldier as he walked by and called out to the Air Force officer.

"Hey, I've got a man here that has to get to the road. I got me a man here to take one end of the stretcher. Can I borrow your radio operator for the other end?"

The Air Force officer, who had not been in Vietnam very long, looked confused. "What about the radio?" he asked.

"You carry it," I said flatly.

"Okay," he said.

I helped the radio operator take off the PRC-25 and put it on the back of the officer. The battalion group had moved ahead, and, still adjusting the radio, the officer quickly followed.

Too soon, we were alone. Motioning the soldier to the front of the stretcher and the radio operator to the rear, I began moving toward the road with my M-16 at port arms.

The boy on the stretcher continued to cry out. After a half-dozen steps I went back to the stretcher, bent down on one knee, grabbed the boy by the chin, and said, "Shut the fuck up. Moaning don't help. It gets on my nerves. And it gives our position away. We're all alone, fellow. Shut up, and I'll get you out of here." I twisted his chin back and forth and smiled.

We went on, but had to stop every few feet to listen. We were standing still at one point when I saw someone dart between some bushes to my right front. I extended a hand back and motioned for the litter detail to drop to the ground. Putting the gun to my shoulder, I aimed at the bushes. A Vietnamese with an AK-47 in his hand came from behind a tree. He was looking away from me and heading toward the ravine. As he started to break into a trot, I had a clear shot and fired a short burst of rounds. The Vietnamese fell backward and disappeared into the undergrowth.

I suspected that there would be other Vietnamese ahead, so I turned and started toward the ravine. The two men with the stretcher followed me.

Nearing the ravine, I saw where the battalion CP group had climbed up the side. I knew that off to my right would be the machine gun position destroyed by Company B. Small-arms fire zipped over our heads from below.

"Ah, shit," I said as I dived for the ground. Vietnamese were in the ravine, but they did not attack. They had probably fired and run, I thought as I lay there. After a few minutes I got up in a crouch, came back around the stretcher, and started off again straight toward the road.

Near where I had shot the Vietnamese, I saw movement in the bushes ahead. Whoever was there was moving awkwardly. Far to my front, a Vietnamese moved out into a small clearing. He was carrying another man on his back. Although I could barely make out the pair, I knew that both men were Vietnamese and the shirt of the one being carried was bloody. As they went out of sight, I could see his head roll around as if he were dead or unconscious.

More Vietnamese appeared to the right. Three or four, I couldn't tell. Jesus, I thought as I dropped to the ground again, I'm making my way across the migration route of the whole North Vietnamese nation.

Do I stand up and shoot or let them pass?

The boy behind me moaned. I began to sweat. I listened. There was firing in the distance. I strained to hear what was happening in front of me. Two or three minutes went by. The boy moaned again.

I got to my knees. There was no one around. Where the fuck had they gone? The men behind me picked up the stretcher and waited in a crouch. Walking along, I looked quickly from one side to another. Where were they?

Suddenly, through a bamboo thicket ahead, I could see a Vietnamese standing, as if he were waiting for us. I stopped and went to one knee. Then, off to my left, the three men whom I had seen earlier bolted for the ravine. We had been hiding from each other. None of us had fired out of separate fear of not knowing exactly what we were up against—two opposing three-man groups, avoiding each other on a spent battlefield.

Except that the man ahead had not moved. I waited for him to turn and join the others, but he stayed his ground. Finally I was afraid of waiting any longer. With sweat dropping in my eyes, I fired toward him and fell forward. Lying on the ground, I wiped my face with my sleeve and waited. There were sounds all around me, but I could not identify any as belonging to the man ahead. I came back up to my knee and stared straight ahead. The man was still there. He was dead, I realized, hung up on some vines. He had been dead before I fired.

We moved by the thicket, past the dead man, then through a burned-out area, through more jungle, and finally onto the edge of the road. At a distance of about two city blocks down the road I saw the lead cavalry elements of the convoy. In front of me were trucks. Some of them were burning.

Men were standing around near the cav vehicles. Wounded and dead littered the shoulders of the road. We climbed up to the road and walked toward the cav vehicles. We passed a truck with the driver hanging out of the half-open door. The next truck was untouched. Off to the side, a patch of woods had been burned by napalm and a cluster of burnt Vietnamese corpses lay in a ditch. A truck was half in and half out of a crater near the first Quarterhorse vehicle, an ACAV. Quarterhorse troopers were in the process of removing some of their dead still draped over the top of it. Many had tanker goggles pulled down to their necks, their bulletproof vests hanging open. Two tanks at the lead were maneuvering in the road. As we approached someone yelled for them to stop because there could be more mines.

I could see a medevac helicopter taking off from the road near the incline past the marsh, and we walked in that direction. Black smoke, with the putrid smell of burning flesh, swirled from some of the burning vehicles.

The lead tank, off to the side of the road, was out of commission. Smoke was coming from an open turret near the front.

A Quarterhorse trooper with a radio was at the very head of the column. Some helicopters were landing in the field where we had first come in. I told the man with the radio that I needed to call for a dust-off. Without waiting for an answer, I reached down and turned to the right frequency, gave my position, and requested a medevac. A medevac chopper came on the air. He was in the area and coming down. I threw smoke and within a matter of minutes the helicopter was on the ground. We put the young boy aboard.

I went back to the radio and called the colonel to tell him that the action was in front of him. The battle back here was over. As I was talking, photographers were coming up the bank from helicopters in the landing zone. They were taking pictures of everything. I moved off to the side as they clustered around the lead Quarterhorse vehicles. When they moved on, I walked over to the lead tank to look for Slippery Clunker Six.

I turned a complete circle as I looked at everyone standing around. There was no one familiar. A tanker walked by.

"Where's Sergeant Bretschneider?" I asked.

He nodded toward a body bag lying on the bank. A short distance away were five more bags. Some cavalry soldiers brought over another body bag and laid it beside the rest.

Shit, I said under my breath. Don't think about it. I sat down, suddenly realizing how tired I was. The adrenaline was draining away. I lit a cigarette and looked at my hands. No shake. I looked back at Slippery Clunker Six's body bag. Don't agonize, I said again to myself, and I stared at the body bag without reflection. I noticed all of its lumps and its smell and I remembered Slippery Clunker Six eating pâté and reciting poetry. I had heard his voice just within the past hour on the radio. I put all those thoughts together, slowly, and put them in a basket at the back of my mind.

More wounded were coming along the road. I got up and started to walk down the line. The photographers were ahead of me. Up ahead, a soldier was bringing a Vietnamese prisoner in our direction. As they came by one of the burning tanks, a photographer moved around for a good angle. The soldier was Moubry.

I avoided the supply officer as he posed for the photographers, and continued down the line past the burned-out trucks, trying to get even with my battalion in the woods.

By nightfall the 1st of the 28th had swept the wood line along the north side of the road. It pulled back to the road and then down near the area where we had come in on the helicopters. The 1st/16th and the 1st/18th Infantry Battalions had been put in blocking positions near the Cambodian border. They continued to report that Vietnamese mainline forces were straggling toward them all afternoon and night.

The next day we watched minesweeping teams clear the road above the incline. Tank recovery vehicles were still hauling out the tracks damaged or destroyed by the ambush.

"Peppy" visited the troops and congratulated everyone for a damn good operation. A total of 240 Vietnamese had been killed. Our casualties had been light, twenty-four killed in action. We got 'em ten to one. Slippery Clunker Six would have been proud.

I could almost see him smile and say, "There you go."

By nightfall of the second day the road had been cleared and the convoy headed on toward Minh Thanh.

We were lifted out the next morning. As usual, Dunn and I were to be the last ones out. The battalion had the same helicopters assigned to it that had been used in the heli-assault, but some had mechanical problems and others had suffered battle damage. Fewer than thirty helicopters showed up for the move.

When they left, Dunn and I had an oddball collection of fifty men around the LZ. The road was deserted. Although the 1st/16th, augmented with cav, was going to stay around and help bury the dead Vietnamese, they were on the other side of the forest. Enemy soldiers—some wounded and some looking for wounded—were still around us.

Two helicopters that had just dropped off supplies to the 1st/16th arrived and took out twenty men. We were down to thirty men scattered around the LZ and we pulled them in close. It was quiet. Alert, Dunn and I sat by our radios in the shade near the edge of the field. We strained to see into the forest.

Three partially filled helicopters came in about thirty minutes later and we began moving out the last of the men. Two loaded and left. As the last helicopter was loading, Bob and I were standing by the radio. We indicated that we were the last two by holding up two fingers and pointing to one another. The kicker shook his head and waved the palm of his hand back and forth to say, "No more."

I picked up the radio and talked with the pilot. "We're the last two people here," I said.

"Sorry," he said, his voice shaking from the vibration of the helicopter. "Maxed out. Other helicopters in the area. We'll get you soon."

"Shit," I said to Dunn and turned back to look into the woods. I tried to focus on the shadows inside but, for some reason, the noise of the helicopter behind me made it more difficult. I told

Dunn that it was coming down to this. I had been alone in this "enchanted forest," as the late great Slippery Clunker Six had called it, once before, and here we were again. Dunn didn't respond. I continued to squint into the woods.

When I gradually turned my head in Dunn's direction, he wasn't there. He was high-stepping toward the helicopter in an exaggerated effort to move quietly. The kicker was holding up one finger, as if they could take one more.

"Jesus Christ!" I said. I picked up the PRC-25, sprinted by Dunn, and dived into the helicopter. He was laughing so hard he couldn't keep up. When he got to the helicopter he climbed aboard, even though the kicker was telling him he couldn't get on. Sitting on the floor beside me, he was still laughing as we took off.

—— THIRTEEN ——

Heading Home

We were back in the base camp for only two days before deploying to Bear Cat, southeast of Saigon near the Mekong Delta.

Duckett was able to get to Saigon once. He learned that our seats had been confirmed on Air Force One on 13 and 14 September.

We received a letter from Pete. His convalescence was continuing successfully, and he had orders to Fort Ord. He said that he had had indirect contact with an old OCS buddy who was working in the Pentagon. He had asked his buddy to try to get Dunn and me assigned to Ord as well, but he added that it was a very long shot. Fort Ord on the Monterey Peninsula of California was one of the U.S. Army's most sought after posts.

I was promoted to first lieutenant. The same day, I received orders for my next assignment, Fort Ord, California. Dunn also received orders to Fort Ord.

Colonel Haldane's replacement arrived. Two first lieutenants, who had arrived in the battalion as replacement platoon leaders several weeks earlier, were assigned to take Dunn's position and mine. We had a two-week overlap. Seemed awfully easy, they said about our jobs.

The new battalion commander was an uncommunicative, sullen man. After Haldane left, Panton was offering advice on means of reacting to a VC contact when the commander became angry. He told Panton that it was his battalion, and he would decide what needed to be done.

On 1 September 1966, I asked the angry colonel if Dunn and I could go back to the base camp at Phuoc Vinh to tie up some loose ends before we left. "Yeah," he said, without further comment.

I went by to see Woolley, who had been transferred recently to brigade headquarters. He showed me his recommendation to battalion that I receive the Bronze Star with V award. He said that I had set the standard in the company. After our first contact on the perimeter at the base camp, he knew that I was a first-rate soldier, he said. He thought that I was a natural and, under fire, I had a voice as calm and cool as lemonade on a hot summer day. I thanked him and said that his comments were a very high compliment to me because I respected his judgment. I saluted and we shook hands, but I didn't tell him that, during our first contact, I had been caught in my hammock like a monkey in a cage.

Bratcher, Spencer, King, Beck, and Manuel were still around, and each expected to receive DEROS orders any day. None of them wanted to go on operations.

"Beck," I said, smiling. "What'd you get? Three, four Purple Hearts? You have a death wish here or something?"

Beck stood as tall as he could, raising his head high on his shoulders. "I told you early on I'd make you proud. Plus you said one time that you could *will* victory. On the boat coming over, you said that. And that's what I've believed in. That's what I was doing. I weren't backing down from no little slant-eyed dink. Fuck 'em. Here I am, take your best shot."

Beck had wanted this war. He had bribed his way into the Big Red One when he was released from the brig at Fort Leavenworth. A lesser man would have accepted a dishonorable discharge and gone on with life. Beck, a throwback to proud gun-toting frontiersmen out of the Wild West, had set about to restore his honor. In doing that, he proved to be a helluva soldier. A helluva American. And I told him as much.

Leaving the platoon area after saying my good-byes, I had my arms around Bratcher and Spencer and we took a few steps together. As I took my arms down to walk away, Spencer reached up and ruffled my short hair. Smiling, he said, "The man."

Duckett said he was leaving for the base camp on 9 September. We confirmed where we would meet, either at the base camp or, if that didn't work out, at the BOQ in Bangkok. Get the women and children off the streets. Watch out Europe. Here we come.

Dunn and I went back to Phuoc Vinh on different helicopters. The one I was on skimmed the trees the whole way. I was looking out the front between the two pilots. Power lines appeared to come up across our front and head straight toward us. The pilot waited until the last moment, it seemed, to go over, and then we were back at treetop level. We almost skimmed the sides of large trees sticking up above the rest.

After landing at Phuoc Vinh, I leaned into the cockpit near the helmet of the pilot and asked him if Dunn had put them up to this wild trip.

"What?" he said. "Who?"

"Never mind," I said and walked to the base camp.

I wrote letters, separated my personal items into giveaways, throwaways, and take-aways, turned in my equipment, and hung around with Dunn for the next few days. On 8 September, I told Bob good-bye and said I'd see him at Fort Ord. Carrying my Hong Kong clothes in a Phuoc Vinh bag, I left the battalion for the last time. I took a scheduled flight to Saigon but then bummed helicopter rides out to Vung Tau, an in-country R&R site. I stayed in a cheap hotel away from other military people and spent most of my time lying on the beach, trying to get rid of my infantryman's tan, reading, or looking out across the South China Sea, with bottles of local beer buried in the sand beside me. For most of two days I didn't talk with anyone.

Occasionally I would think about the jungle sweeps, the fire-fights, the tunnels of Cu Chi, the dead and dying on the spent battlefield along the Minh Thanh road, and I would take a deep breath to relieve the tension in my stomach.

I remembered the bar with the nude painting and the toilet seat and Dunn's initiation and Crash Burke and Fred Astaire, and I would smile.

I thought about my deep devotion to the men with whom I had served and the circumstances that caused some of their deaths. Staring out across the water, I took the clear images of Patrick, McCoy, Ayers, and Castro out of the baskets where I had them stored in the back of my mind and I examined them. Not searching for answers why, because Dunn was right, there is imponderable morality to war. I just looked at the images calmly, detached. But I also felt a deep sense of loss, because I loved them in a way only soldiers at war can know. Going through the outer perimeter of our base camp on night combat patrol, as I chambered a round in my weapon, I knew that it was not me against the dangers out there in the dark jungle, it was the platoon against what lay ahead. A fraternal bonding, based on mission, fear, and survival, tied us together. My platoon—Patrick, Bratcher, Ayers, Lyons, Castro—was my only chance of survival. When I went to sleep in the jungle, I gave my life to Spencer to protect till I woke. And in firefights I faced live bullets, dodged grenades, moved ahead, because the platoon expected it. We had an obligation to one another. To fight. To die, even.

For a soldier, war is a proposition of doing your duty to your unit and surviving if you can. And winning.

I had won, I had survived.

That beach—Vung Tau—was where I had arrived a year earlier. To my right was the area where the band had been playing from the flatbed truck, where my platoon, confused, had collected around me in the surf. We had come there to fight and we did, out there, behind me in the jungle. And I was back, ready to go home. That's all there was to it.

On 11 September, I bummed a ride to Saigon. I checked into the Out-processing Administration Section on the following afternoon. I had dinner alone at the local officers club and was back in my assigned Quonset hut by early evening. A group of soldiers, who had just arrived in-country, had gathered in a corner. They were talking loudly while a tape recorder played at high volume. Two of them were playing cards and sharing a strange-looking and strange-smelling cigarette. After complaints about their noise, an officer asked them to turn down the tape recorder, but none of them looked up or moved. The officer was unable to determine who owned the recorder, and he left. The soldiers gleefully went through a hand-slapping, elbow-knocking, chest-thumping routine. Their raucous behavior continued until a group of MPs arrived and threatened them with the brig unless they knocked off the noise.

I watched it all, propped up on my elbow, and thought, Good I'm getting out now—different cast of characters coming in. Different standards and attitudes that I wasn't sure I knew how to deal with.

Around 0200 the next morning I was awakened by a familiar voice in the bunk below me. Bratcher. Drunk.

"1st Battalion of the fucking 28th Infantry Regiment is the

best fucking battalion in the whole fucking country. Last operation we killed them son'bitches by the hundreds. Hundreds, goddammit. Had 'em piled up. Crispy critters. You know how we did it? We did it because we had a goddamned good battalion, that's how. You talk to anyone, anyone, anyone, anywhere who served in the field in Vietnam and you goddammit won't find a better fucking battalion. Most of the shits in the battalion were wounded at least once. Every man I knew had killed a gook. Lions of Cantigny. Goddamned Lions of Cantigny. Lions of Cu Chi and Phuoc Vinh and Minh Thanh. Best fucking fighting unit in the whole fucking country, the whole fucking Army."

I jumped off the bunk and smiled at Bratcher. Unbelievably, he seemed lost for words, but just for a moment.

"I'll be a son'bitch," he said. "Where'd you come from?" He stood up and laughed.

From down the Quonset hut, one of the black replacements said, "Shut the fuck up."

Bratcher turned around quickly and swayed in place as he tried to locate the person in the half-light of the Quonset hut. He had a disbelieving look on his face, as if it was not possible that someone was talking to him that way. The old lanky sergeant from Tennessee stumbled down the line of bunks, came up to one bunk, and turned it over. He kicked the man inside as he fell to the floor. There was viciousness in Bratcher's actions that was unlike normal garrison scuffles, probably unlike anything that young man had ever experienced before.

"Don't you tell me to shut up, you chickenshit asshole. I'll break your skinny black ass."

Getting to his feet, the boy yelled, "It wasn't me, man, I didn't do nothing."

Bratcher pushed him in the chest. "Don't you fucking say anything to me, asshole." I came up beside him and grabbed his arm. "Let it go," I said. "I want a cigarette. Let's go outside."

The black boy said, "Hey man, you're crazy, you know that."

I turned to the black boy and took a step so that I was inches from his face. "Crazy? After a year in Vietnam? Crazy, yeah, crazy, so don't fuck with us 'cause we'll show you crazy," and I dragged out the words, "like . . . you . . . ain't . . . ever . . . seen. Want some? Say something."

We stared at each other in the half-light of the barracks. I felt unusually fearless and calm. Never before in my life and never since have I felt the way I did then. I was ready to kill him, anxious for the fight—adrenaline pumping, elbows protruding slightly from my sides, my weight moving forward toward the balls of my feet—angry, quick, and strong. Without looking away from his eyes, I took the measure of his neck and groin. I waited for something to trigger my reaction—a movement, or a word.

He did not move. After a moment, I relaxed. Only after Bratcher and I went outside did we hear his low mumbling.

Bratcher said, "Last night, shit, go out fighting, that's all right. Wanta go back in there and whip his black ass?"

"No," I said. "What do we have to prove? Time to go home. Plus, you got the wrong guy in the first place. I think that kid was just lying there, minding his own business. It was some other guy lipping off." And we laughed.

We talked about our first meeting in Fort Riley, about the different men in our platoon, Trost, Woolley, the last operation, small, recent stuff. People inside probably heard us. I suggested that it was all over for us, we'd done our duty, so we could sit back and smile.

"Naw," he said, "this war will be around for a long time. We'll be back."

"Not me," I said. "Back to school when my tour's up."

"You'll be back," he said. "You like the action."

He and I had sat side by side so often. The fact that it was our last night—that we had Vietnam almost behind us—didn't make much difference. I had been afraid of him early on—afraid that he would take the platoon from me—but it had worked out. Luck plays a big part in war. I had been very lucky that Staff Sergeant Cecil Bratcher had been assigned to my platoon, that we had gone to Vietnam together. I slapped him on the knee, got up, and went to bed.

He was still sleeping in the morning when I woke up to catch my flight to Thailand.

I was in Bangkok that night. Joe arrived the following night, and I showed him some of the places I had found. They compared with the Tu Do bars of Saigon and the harbor area of Hong Kong and Havana. For me, there was much to like about Bangkok.

The next morning we boarded Air Force One, a C-141, for New Delhi. Our overnight in the Indian capital was memorable for the filth, the cows, the people living on the streets, and the smells.

We stopped at Kabul, Afghanistan, and Athens, Greece, the next day, and landed finally at Torrejón Air Base near Madrid, Spain. We went to a BOQ when we arrived and slept for ten hours. The next morning we ordered a rental Volkswagen convertible from a base concessionaire for drop-off in Germany, picked up the car, and drove into Madrid. We got lost and ended up in the old town, where we rented a room in a hotel near several bars that featured flamenco dancers. The next day we went to the bullfights. Several horses were gored and several bulls were killed, but we missed the point. Too ethnic, we decided. We bought some playbill posters and called it a day.

The following morning we loaded our convertible and made Barcelona, Spain, by nightfall, then on to Nice, France, the following day. There, we checked into a pension and had a late sidewalk-cafe dinner with a couple of carafes of wine. Very continental. We felt conspicuous, however, often looking up to see French men and women looking at us.

"Salt and pepper," Joe said. "They're not used to us blacks and you whites being so—so familiar."

"Yes, they are," I disagreed. "They had colonies all over Africa. There shouldn't be anything strange about us sitting here. Maybe it's the way we're dressed? Or because we're so tall."

"Okay," he said, "if it isn't the black-white thing, then it's the eyes. They're looking at my eyes. You've never noticed them, have you?"

"No," I admitted. "I haven't ever really looked into your eyes, Joe. What about them?"

"The ladies," he said, "like them very much."

"How come so many men are looking at you, then?"

"Ah, the French. *Quiem sa ba?*"

"What the fuck is that?"

"French. Means 'Who knows?' "

"No, it don't. You don't know French. Sounds like Spanish anyway."

"The French would know it means 'Who knows.' "

Later, in a smoky bar not far from the beach, we were nursing beers when a group of locals came in. In the middle of the group was the most beautiful woman I had ever seen. She was tall and buxom, with blond hair and a deep tan. Her white blouse was tied under her bust to show off a flat, tan stomach above the red skintight toreador pants that encased sculptured legs. And her face—strong yet soft, exotic, sexy. In the half-light of the bar haze she appeared to be perfect. She looked at us as her group walked toward tables in the rear.

"Oh, my God, Joe, I'm in love," I said, my mouth agape.

The chattering from the group continued as they walked along, punctured occasionally by laughs. The woman held our gaze as she walked, quietly distant from her friends.

Turning on my stool, I saw her sit down so that she faced back toward us at the bar. The others fell into chairs around her. She lit a cigarette and when she inhaled the glow lit her face, her hair shining in the dark.

"She is absolutely the most gorgeous woman in the world. The sexiest. She is a goddess sitting over there. I have to meet her. I have to have her."

"Not your type," Joe said.

"I know what my type is, my friend. And that lady, that wench is what I've been looking for all my life. Oh, my God, she's coming this way."

She came up and slid between Joe and me on our bar stools and said something to the bartender in French. Her perfume was musky. She turned to look at me—her eyes wanton, smoldering, intense, like an animal's. Her breast rubbed against my arm.

"HellohowyoudoingWhatsyourname?" I mumbled as I slicked my short hair back with my hand.

She didn't respond but examined my face closely. Then suddenly, she looked into my eyes.

Those eyes! I could not get over them—they had no shame. They were predator's eyes.

Finished with me, she turned and looked at Joe.

"Bon jure, madomessel," Joe said in fractured French. I

couldn't see his face because the woman was between us. All I could see was the back of her beautiful head.

She put one arm around Joe's neck and turned his face and body toward her with the other hand. Then, with both arms around his neck, she leaned in and kissed him.

For "bon jure" he gets this?

Had to be something more than "bon jure."

Later, Joe said it was his eyes.

We went on to Monte Carlo. The first night there we put on our tailor-made clothes and went to the casino. Because we didn't have much money and didn't know how to play any of the games except blackjack (but we weren't so sure how to play it in French) we decided just to get some chips, say a hundred dollars' worth each, and walk around the gaming tables and look smart. After much dickering with the French bank teller, we managed to get the two $100 chips that he initially offered us broken down into ten $20 chips. We wanted something we could shuffle together as we walked about looking smart. It was such a simple transaction, we thought, and we became frustrated when the Frenchman didn't cooperate. Plus a long line collected behind us. Finally with our five chips each, we walked into the gaming room.

Jingling the chips in a way we hoped looked practiced, we walked over to a baccarat table where a guy had a paddle. We stood behind a velvet rope and watched, but we had no idea what was going on. When people looked at us, we smiled knowingly. The club was not unlike the Tropicana in Havana, but it was more reserved, cleaner, and quieter. The women were dressed the same, but the men were whiter, more haughty than I remembered from Havana. There were more sideways glances, more appraising looks.

We were having drinks at the bar and looking over the crowd when a woman at my left asked, "Are you a spy?"

"Pardon me?" I asked.

"I Spy," she said and smiled.

Duckett and I looked down at her. Maybe this is the way they talk in Monte Carlo—in catchphrases that everyone but us knew.

"You look like the characters in a U.S. television program," she explained, *"I Spy.* You are Americans, aren't you?"

"Yes, ma'am," I said.

"And you know about the program, *I Spy,* don't you? It began last fall."

"No ma'am. We're just coming back from Vietnam. We haven't watched much television lately."

"Oh, this is almost as good. We thought you were associated with the program *I Spy,* but Vietnam veterans, that is something. Will there be many of you coming back this way?"

"I don't know. What is the program *I Spy* about?"

"Two Americans, a black man and a white man, traveling around the continent, spying for the U.S. A very dashing pair. Like the two of you."

My first reaction was to say, "Ah, go on now," but then I thought that was not quite right for someone who had been taken for a movie star playing an international spy in the Monte Carlo Casino.

"Do say," I said.

We met the woman again the following morning while we were eating breakfast at a sidewalk cafe. In her early sixties, she was a well-to-do widow who spent half the year on the Riviera and the rest at her home in the United States.

She said that the French did not approve of our involvement in Vietnam, but in fact, the French did not approve of much that the Americans did. But she was curious about how it was over there. Joe and I told her it wasn't bad, we would prevail, we had more stuff. We were the U.S. of A.

Refusing to believe it was so simple, she said that more complex forces of good and evil were at work. The war, she said, will not be won on the battlefield. Attrition was an insignificant variable in the long run, and it was going to be a long war. She wished us well and thanked us for serving our country so well.

That afternoon we drove into Italy. Then we headed back into France and arrived in Paris three days later. We picked up college-age Americans when we saw them thumbing and learned that they were against the war in principle, although not against us personally. They expressed outrage easily and sometimes asked naive, leading questions in the hope of uncovering our involvement in mass murder. Joe especially enjoyed responding to their queries. He unashamedly altered his accounts from session to session to fit the audience. He told me that a black man can use his blackness sometimes if he wants to. Liberals will not challenge a black man on anything, especially an articulate black man. Plus, he reasoned, no matter what he said, these college kids would hear what they wanted. "That's the problem with the morally outraged youth of today," he said, "selective understanding."

Our money was running low when we reached Paris, so we looked at a tour map and decided on the one place, above all else, that we wanted to see there. Not the Arc de Triomphe or the Eiffel Tower, but the Crazy Horse Saloon with its topless chorus line. We went there, drove around town later, and headed for Germany.

The most pleasant part of our trip through Europe was just driving along with the top down, the two of us sometimes talking, sometimes with the radio on, one of us sometimes snoozing. We drove through clean and beautiful villages, along vineyards in the country, along the Mediterranean, in the mountains— sometimes with hitchhikers onboard. Laughing, lying, looking up at the sun and feeling its warmth. After the hardships of Vietnam, Europe was heaven. For some reason the words "Nothing could be finer than to be in Carolina, in the morn . . . ing" got caught on the end of my tongue and I sang the song off and on all across Europe. We talked about what awaited us in the States. Joe said we would not have had a chance of true friendship there.

"Why?" I asked.

"We come from two cultures. The American culture and the Negro culture. If you are a Negro, you can only play white. Black stands out on a white background."

"Get off that black-white shit, Joe."

"Hard to, Jimmy," he said. "I will always be a black man in a white man's society. We are friends here, but you're from North Carolina. You won't want me to date your sister, would you?"

"You know my sister?" I asked.

In Frankfurt we turned in the car and changed into our dress uniforms with our medals. We were more decorated than anyone else we saw. Singing "Nothing could be finer . . ." we marched into the terminal and got first priority standby tickets to the States. Within an hour we were on our way to McGuire Air Force Base, New Jersey.

There, on 30 September, Joe and I said good-bye. We didn't

have much money left. He took a bus to Philly, and I took a bus to New York City to see an old girlfriend.

No one noticed me in the bus terminal. Everyone seemed busy with their own lives. I took a seat toward the back of the bus and felt insignificant, lost.

The urban New Jersey countryside appeared dirty and in disrepair. The weather was chilly, especially to someone coming back from a year in the tropics. The bus rattled through the bumper-to-bumper traffic and crossed the George Washington Bridge into New York City, where I knew one person.

I took a taxi from the bus terminal in New York City to the apartment house of my friend. It was mid-afternoon of a weekday and she was working. I didn't have her office telephone number, so I stood on the sidewalk in front of the building and wondered what to do. When the bellman asked if I was waiting for someone, I told him that I was but had timed my arrival a couple hours too early.

"Lenore Mills [alias]," he said. "You're the soldier boy Lenore Mills talks about. I thought you were kilted once."

"Wounded maybe," I said, glad to find someone to talk to in this city of millions. "Is Lenore's roommate around or someone who can let me in?"

"I'll let you in. Lenore would want me to. Come on, follow me."

He showed me up to Lenore's door, opened it, and told me to relax. She should be in around six. I sat down on her couch and fell asleep. She was kneeling beside me and crying when I woke.

The next afternoon I left on the train for Southern Pines, North Carolina. When the train hissed to a stop at the train depot in downtown Southern Pines, I saw Mom, Dad, and my youngest sister Kathy and the Lylands, a couple from the church, waiting on the platform.

It is a special time for a young man when he comes home from war. The anticipation, the explosion of emotion, the touching, the feeling, the crying, the stories, the old news, the new news, and then the comfortable regular routine. My Bronze Star had arrived in the mail. After dinner, my mother pinned it on my tunic and then ran her trembling fingers across my lips. Daddy read the citation aloud. Kathy applauded. My other two sisters, Judy and Joan, came in the next day and we held hands as Daddy said grace at supper. He thanked the Lord for looking after me and returning me home.

I looked up old friends. The person I wanted to see most of all, Cottonpicker, was himself in Vietnam, assigned to the 173d Airborne Regiment. He had influenced much of what I had done in Vietnam, and I wanted to report to him, to get his approval.

Most of my other boyhood friends did not know what questions to ask about my experiences, and I did not volunteer much. Public energies during this war were spent on moral hand-wringing. There was little understanding about what was going on in the jungle of Indochina. American soldiers were not the war's heroes. Actually, they played a minor role in everyday reporting. The principal characters in this country were the politicians and media opinion-makers.

The media were a powerful influence in the war. Comments from everyday Americans tended to be reframed television and newspaper reports. Each day, the media people rearranged their words to deliver the same message: "bad war." The TV video clips of the fighting were not balanced. They were impersonal, catastrophic, horrible imagery of a losing army—intentionally cast that way, it seemed to me. My memories of our Army in Vietnam were of dedicated men doing dangerous work.

I stopped reading the papers, and at home we did not watch the evening news.

After two weeks of home leave, I flew to Lincoln and picked up my car for the drive to Fort Ord. Pete's parents met me at the airport and listened carefully to my version of the stories about Pete and the action on the day he was wounded. Mrs. Peterson held my hand in the car as we talked and said how fortunate that we came out of that chaos alive.

We went down to the filling station where my Mercedes was garaged. As we drove up I saw it parked off to the side, cleaned up and serviced for my arrival. How handsome it looked. I thought about the day I saw it sitting on the edge of the farmer's lot. It still looked as good a year later. They also serve who sit and wait—that car had soul. I had the feeling that it was glad to see me, too, as it jumped away from the service station—like a young kid, I thought, happy to be on the road again.

Though winter was setting in, I put the top down, turned the radio up loud, and streaked across the wheat lands. I felt great. "Nothing could be finer than to be in Carolina, in the morn . . . ing."

I passed through Cheyenne, Wyoming, where we had stopped for a rest during our train move to Oakland en route to Vietnam. I'm lapping the world, I thought. Small place.

—— FOURTEEN ——

The Best Job in the World

Pete was asleep in his BOQ room when I arrived in Fort Ord. We embraced, but Pete said that was generally frowned on between two men alone in a BOQ room. I had brought along a six-pack of beer, and we sat talking, laughing.

Though late, we decided to visit Bob and his bride Linda, who lived in a Monterey apartment. We bought a bottle of champagne on the way and jumped over the back fence of the apartment house. The sliding glass door was unlocked, and we barged in, catching Bob in his shorts. I said that only six weeks out of the combat zone and already Dunn had dropped his guard. He promised to sandbag the patio over the weekend and post Linda guard. She said, "I can do that. Got my broom and my hair spray, they'll never take us alive."

We liked Linda right away. Perky, bright, personable, and attractive, she filled out the group. We sat around their living room and out by the pool of the apartment house that evening. Finally everybody had to show their battle scars. Pete's shoulder looked terrible, with lacerated, pink skin stretched over what looked like the end of a coat hanger. Bob had been wounded in so many places, we tried to count all the scars, marking them with a ballpoint pen. For me, Pete and Dunn held me down and pulled my pants to my knees. There isn't much honor in getting your butt shot in war, although Linda said, "Well, Jimmy, at least you weren't facing the other direction."

I officially signed in at Fort Ord the next morning. Within the month I was officer in charge (OIC) of the 6th Army Area Drill Sergeant School, the boot camp for drill sergeants in the Northwest. Sergeant Vick was the noncommissioned officer in charge (NCOIC). There were seventeen senior NCOs on my faculty, all impressive soldiers. Each carried a riding crop, the symbol of authority of a drill sergeant school instructor.

The school was a showcase for the post commander when VIPs toured, and the staff and I were called on almost weekly to conduct 6th Army Area award and retirement ceremonies. As the OIC, I sat on NCO promotion panels, prosecuted summary courts-martial, and was a mainstay on OCS review boards.

I taught two classes, conducted Saturday morning inspections of the drill sergeant candidates, and had the final word on who graduated.

It was the best job in the Army, at one of the most sought after posts, and my closest friends were nearby. Pete and I roomed in the same BOQ. He was assigned to a line unit that went to a field garrison every Monday through Friday. On the weekends we spent time with Bob and Linda, playing bridge and doing the Monterey Peninsula. Carmel and Big Sur were incredibly beautiful and we were particularly enthralled with the area in between—the Carmel Highlands—where we could drive to scrub-lined vistas high in the hills and look out over the rocky coast littered with rafts of seal otters and herds of sea lions far out into the Pacific where migrating gray whales passed. Late one afternoon, Pete and I, with dates, were on an overlook when a storm came in from the north. Under the threatening sky the waves broke angrily on the rocks and lightning flashed in the distance. The old evergreen trees in the Highland swayed in the wind. There was salt in the air, the smell of nature.

"This is what we were fighting for, this is America," I said.

"Boy," Pete said, "how times change. We used to say America was those people back in that honky-tonk bar in Junction City, Kansas. Remember?"

"Aug," I mused, "fuck 'em, I hadn't seen this yet."

My sister Judy, married with a couple of kids, lived in the San Francisco area. Pete and I occasionally drove up to the Bay Area on the weekends and hung out, at Judy's and in the Fisherman's Wharf area.

Pete Javit, another OCS graduate and Vietnam vet, told us the ins and outs of off-post housing. We applied, got preapproved for a substantial allowance, and started looking for a place—with what we would be given, the three of us could live almost anywhere on the peninsula. I was for something along Cannery Row in Monterey because I was a John Steinbeck fan. Javit wanted something near Pebble Beach.

Pete, however, found the best place—a furnished three-bedroom house in the Carmel Highlands owned by a local professor on a year's sabbatical somewhere. To reach it we had to turn off the ocean highway and climb a winding road halfway to the top of a hill and then down a small one-lane road behind an Episcopal bishop's house. Our house faced the ocean and jutted out over a ledge so that standing in one of the front bedrooms there was nothing but ocean to the front. Below, the distance of five or six football fields, was the rocky coast where seals and otters and sea lions played. The sound of waves crashing on the rocks was a pleasant background to the noise of birds in the trees behind the house. It was as near a perfect setting as three boys in their mid-twenties could hope for. On the weekends it became "party central" to all levels of the local community, although there was a tendency toward Vietnam veterans and zingy, hippie girls. One-on-one, the braless wonders of northern California got along with the short-haired GIs of Fort Ord, especially when they found out some of us had war wounds. Linda Dunn did not approve of most of the girls who hung around the house, however.

"Jimmy Parker, and over there, you, Larry Peterson, you both are bad. Bad. And Bob Dunn, you listen to me, you are never, ever allowed up here without me."

Kim Novak lived two houses down from us. Everyone I knew had seen her in *Picnic* with William Holden. She lived by the ocean in a compound with a gate. Almost every day we stood on our terrace, looked down toward her house, and quoted William Holden's lines to her. Sometimes at night before going to bed, we went outside and said, "Good night, Kim."

Our mailbox was near the cutoff by the bishop's house. The mailbox for the house across the street hung on the same board. The woman who lived there often worked in her garden, and she would wave at me. Occasionally we met at the mailbox or in the local supermarket. One day I was coming in from the drill sergeant school in my dress uniform. She hailed me from her yard as I checked the mail.

She was in her late forties or early fifties and looked bookish, like a New Englander, I thought. Obviously she had been working in her garden for some time that day; she was dirty and rumpled. After she asked me about the plumage on my uniform and I explained it briefly, she told me that she was having a garden party that weekend and wondered if I would be able to come. Possibly the other men in my house would also attend. I said I couldn't speak for them, but I'd be there. She asked if I would wear my uniform because, she said, I looked so handsome in it.

Pete and Javit had no interest in garden parties. Bob and Linda said they would go with me, but then something came up and I went by myself, still dressed immaculately from Saturday morning inspection at the drill sergeant school. About thirty people were gathered in the side garden. A bar stood under a small tent in the rear.

The Episcopal bishop was standing near the lattice entrance portal, and we spoke. He did not seem as warm and engaging as the ministers I remembered in North Carolina, but rather of the arty sort. Beyond him I saw several people moving in our direction, drawn, I was sure, by my uniform.

"These medals," one woman said to me, "what do they mean? What did you do to receive them?"

I began explaining the campaign medals, and the bishop asked to be excused. As he was breaking through the crowd around me, he looked back in my direction and nodded, smiling sweetly.

"Tell me about this ribbon," said a woman. "What did you do, personally?" She wasn't friendly. Her tone was hard, her gaze steady and accusing. I looked around, surprised to see that the other people were glaring at me.

"Did you kill any women and children for that?" someone asked.

"Be quiet, Helen," said the first woman, turning quickly to the new questioner. "I have him first. He answers to me first. What did you do that got you that medal?"

I scanned the crowd again for one friendly face. Finally, I looked at a man standing behind some women on my right. He had a round, happy face and looked a little drunk. I continued to look at him until he spoke.

"Did you carry a bayonet?" he asked with a slight lisp.

Where was Duckett when I needed him? They wouldn't attack a black man like this.

I talked about some of the personalities I knew—Pete, Dunn, Woolley, Bratcher, Spencer. It wasn't what they wanted to hear. One woman told me that she had heard we gassed whole villages, the Air Force bombed populated areas with napalm, and we had body count quotas on operations.

Smiling at her, I said the public perception of the war in Vietnam was distorted because it had been sensationalized by the media. They had an attitude when it came to coverage—get as much blood in the frame as possible—and they always ended with the message that it's a bad war. It seemed to me that they never ever had a feel for the GI. One reason, I guessed, was the men doing the reporting could not relate to the poor and the black from our society who were doing the fighting and the dying over there. I also guessed that no one present knew anyone fighting on the ground in Vietnam. No one they knew, knew my war.

"War," a scrawny little man said, "corrupts the human experience. Failures in statesmanship lead to war. It is an enormous waste."

"It is disconcerting," a woman close to me said, "your contention that there is a separation between us and the soldiers over there. That's what happened with the Nazis. No one knew what the soldiers were doing in Treblinka. It's a government gone mad. Leads to things like the Holocaust where mass murder was sanctioned. Body-count murder in Vietnam is very similar, it seems to me."

I looked around. My way out of the gate was blocked. Perhaps they sensed that I might try to make a break for it. I stood there, like a bear in a bear baiting, nodding to the people who were talking, but it was hard to focus on one person. So many were talking in a breathless frenzy.

Finally noticing a path open toward the bar, I excused myself and made my way to the rear of the garden.

"Very mean scene, man," said the smiling young bartender. "They were on you like a mob. Like they were waiting for you. Why did you wear your uniform, for Christ sake?"

"She asked me," I said, looking at the guy with eyes wide, "the hostess asked me to wear my fucking uniform. Jesus, I didn't know that she was an antiwar piranha."

I took a deep breath and asked the boy for a beer. Someone walked up beside me. A woman. I could smell her. She placed her arms on the counter. I looked at her wrist to see if there was anything I recognized about her jewelry to tie her to the women behind me. Nothing was familiar, but I decided not to make eye contact so as to avoid any further confrontation. The woman asked for wine. She had a soft, cultured voice, not harsh and raspy like the voices in the crowd by the gate. I fingered the rings of water on the bar and debated whether to look at her. Acting on a sudden impulse, I turned my head at the same time that the woman turned hers. We were no more than ten inches apart.

Kim Novak.

Honest to God, Kim Novak. I looked at her eyelids, at the pores of her cheek, at her full lips. She smiled, warm and friendly, and said softly, "Hello."

Kim Novak.

My mind froze. I couldn't think of anything to say. I didn't even think about thinking about something to say.

Kim Novak.

We were so close that I couldn't even tell if she was beautiful. I looked at the forehead and the eyes and the nose and the lips, but I didn't know what the whole face looked like.

Except for my eyes, my body was rock still. Saliva collected in my mouth, and a little drained out and ran down my chin. Kim lowered her gaze but continued to smile. She looked up at the bartender when he handed her the glass of wine, thanked him, turned to look back at me quickly, and then walked away.

I stood there in shock, my head still turned to where she had been. First the screaming liberals and then Kim Novak. Get me outa here, I said to myself. I turned, walked through the house, passed the hostess without comment, and went out the front door and down the road to my house.

That night, I told Javit and Pete about the party and meeting Kim Novak, but I did not tell them that I had been frozen speechless. I said that we had a little chat, and she was nice, very soft, very different from the other hard cases there. I told them I thought I had made an impression. She knew where we lived, and

I wouldn't doubt that she might someday just pop in for a drink. Or invite us down. Whatever.

Several nights later, Javit and I were at the Matador Bar in Carmel. We were sitting at a table for two against the wall, near the front. Javit looked up and said that Kim Novak had just walked in.

I said, "Yeah, sure. I bet she'll come over and hug my neck when she sees I'm here." Shortly afterward I was walking near the row of bar stools on the way to the men's room. A woman swung around as if to leave. I was close, and she looked at me.

Kim Novak.

Veering off to the left away from her, I walked right into a table and spilled all of the drinks on it. Fortunately, apologizing and righting people's drinks gave me something to do, so that I didn't have to turn back to Kim. No one at the table understood how I could have "accidentally" walked into their table—it wasn't like they were in the middle of the aisle.

Kim Novak notwithstanding, it was a very good year. In March 1967 a representative from the Army's Personnel Section at the Pentagon visited Fort Ord and told an assembly of company-grade officers that most of us would be going to Vietnam after our Fort Ord tour. We were infantry officers, and the Army needed infantry officers in Vietnam. Pete put in for helicopter school. Dunn said he was getting out.

Lenore wanted to visit the Monterey Peninsula. I told her that if I got out of the service, she could fly out and we'd drive back across the States together. A grand idea, she said.

But I told her I hadn't decided to get out yet. I'd let her know.

I wavered for days.

I did not want to go back to Vietnam as a replacement. If I had been offered a proposition to take my drill sergeant school staff to Vietnam, I would have gone. If I could have gone back and taken over my old platoon with Bratcher and Spencer and Rome and Manuel and Ayers and Castro and Lyons, I would have gone. Neither was a possibility.

I also considered the soldiers who had been in that Quonset when I left. And the news. It was not a very good war. The United

States was not winning on anyone's scorecard and, more important to me, did not appear intent on winning. There was no groundswell of public support for the fighting GI.

Plus, Dunn said there were bullets with our names on them over there. As long as we stayed here, we were out of range. Dunn knew I felt an unusually strong sense of duty—I told him in Vietnam about the personal way I took the OCS graduation address, how I accepted responsibility to protect the dignity of the United States for all of time. Bob's comments at the time had been, "It was just gas. You were excited, all pumped up, Momma and Daddy and your little sister in the audience. Had some champagne I bet. Just gas. It does that . . . distorts your thinking. Besides, Parker, like Pete and I have told you often, you are one of the most unashamedly self-serving individuals we have ever known. You are not one to go into the priesthood, or to be believed about dedicating your life to some principle, other than 'Jimmy first.' So I don't know where all this comes from. Forget it. Do what's expected. That's enough."

When I told him in Monterey that I was thinking about getting out, but felt guilty about forsaking my duty, abandoning my obligation to country at a time of war, he said, "Listen, my friend, you have served one tour in Vietnam. That's enough. You wanta die, go back. You wanta live, get out. Remember when Haldane ordered us to battalion operations from our platoons? Remember? Did you say, no, my duty is to my men? Of course not. You said, 'Yes, sir.' Went with the flow, right? Plus you ain't got your college degree, because you're stupid. You stay in the military, you'll get to about captain and they'll say, okay, go stand over there, you ain't going to get promoted again because you're stupid and don't have a college degree. That's the way it works. There is no question in my mind about this. Get out and go home."

I agreed with him for the most part. But there was in me a compelling notion about the flag, about duty to country. So I wavered, feeling guilty. Then Lenore said she really wanted to come out, and I said, okay, I'm getting out.

It came down to that. Bigger decisions have been made for lesser reasons. Plus the lease was up on our house, so if I stayed we'd have to find a new place. So I went with the flow. I put in my discharge papers.

I went through the giveaway, throwaway, and send-away selection of personal stuff and was down to a suitcase when Lenore arrived.

On my last day in the Army, 2 May 1967, I cleaned out my desk at the drill sergeant school. Vick had the seventeen staff NCOs standing at attention when I was ready to leave.

A very fine honor guard for my leave-taking, I said. As I stood in front of them, I remembered when I had joined the Army, three and one-half years before—just a faceless "INductee," shaven-headed, in an ill-fitting new uniform, scared out of my wits.

It had worked out altogether better than I could ever have imagined. I was fortunate to have served in Vietnam when I did and to have led 1st Division soldiers in combat. And I ended up in charge of the seventeen NCOs standing in front of me— among the best in the Army. I would have liked to work with them for the rest of my life. I told them that I had learned most about life from my father, who grew up on a North Carolina farm. But I had also learned from Cottonpicker and Willie O. McGee and Bratcher—all three of them Army sergeants—and I had learned from that staff. I saluted them, wished them the best, and left.

Unfortunately I forgot my hat. Couldn't very well go back and get it, however. Last impressions are important in benchmark events like this. I left it and drove off base as a civilian.

I said good-bye to Pete and Bob and Linda that night. Nothing would ever be the same with us again; we were on different tracks. There would be new situations, new friends, new places. We told each other that we were thankful that our lives had crossed and that we had spent some time together when we were young and full of energy, hope, and humor. Bob, Pete, and I had fought a war together.

We were all over the place with our comments that night trying to say it all. It was as if we were back on the top deck of the USNS *Mann* trying to figure out where we were going based on where we'd been.

Bob finally said, "Be happy, nothing else matters much. That's what I've learned. One little word is the key to a successful life. And it's, 'Be happy.' "

Pete, drunk, said, "Pardon me. Pardon me, please. But, ah, ain't 'be happy' two words?"

Three weeks later I reported to work for Dad at a North Carolina timber mill he had just bought that had turn-of-the-century equipment. Despite our best efforts and the long hours of our thirty-man workforce, we had trouble competing with new, high-tech mills that were also suppliers to the North Carolina furniture industry.

I started work for a hundred dollars a week, enough to pay for room and board in the small town of Sanford, where the mill was located, but not much else. I worked ten to twelve hours a day, first manhandling logs in the yard, then behind the lathes, and finally in the splicing and grading room.

At Christmas we were down to a few weeks' worth of orders. Money was slow coming in. We stopped buying logs so Daddy could give each man in the mill a Christmas bonus. In our efforts to keep up with the lower prices offered by the modernized mills, we were not meeting cost.

I drove up to New York City to spend the holidays with Lenore. Bravely she introduced me to her friends at a neighborhood restaurant and at a party in her apartment house, but she was obviously uncomfortable when I told people I managed a veneer mill in Sanford, North Carolina. The New Yorkers invariably asked, "VAneer?" and I said "VEneer" and nodded. It seemed to me everyone was very opinionated and loud. Different cultures, Lenore said, different ways of interacting.

Our time alone was pleasant. Briefly I forgot about Sanford and the problems with the mill, but after a couple of days I was ready to leave. I was out of place.

Lenore was not surprised when I said I was going back home before Christmas. She said she understood. Our parting was tender and final.

—— FIFTEEN ——

Nothing Could Be Finer

Driving south, I listened to country-and-western music and occasionally sang, "Nothing could be finer than to be in Carolina, in the morn . . . ing," but the tune was melancholy that night. I didn't have much to look forward to. The orders at the mill were good only through January, I was out of touch with most of my friends, the girls I dated in the Carolinas were of no interest, and a return to college was a difficult proposition.

I would have liked just to turn the car west and find my place in life by chance, if it weren't for Dad and Mom. Dad was overwhelmed by the mill, but he wouldn't just walk away from his investment. He needed help.

With the dark winter highway stretching out ahead, I felt very much alone in the little two-seater. I was twenty-five years old, maybe time to take stock. Two years of college, Army, no conspicuous talents or well-placed friends. I was getting beyond that point where I could rationalize that I was still growing up, kicking around. Shouldn't I be seeking a stable course, looking for a place to settle down? What to do?

Looking back on Vietnam, I liked the dangers and I missed the patrols, the comradeship, and leading men into combat. For a fleeting moment I wanted to be back in the jungle with my platoon. I remembered the rush of adrenaline when a round zinged overhead and how I crouched, all senses alert, when a sudden exchange of gunfire erupted nearby. That was my element, I thought. Great risks, great rewards.

Not necessarily what I had at hand. There wasn't much of a future with the mill. When the mill had run its course, I would move on. I had liked Havana, Monte Carlo, and Bangkok. Maybe I'd head to Thailand and look for work. Something would turn up.

By midday on Christmas Eve I was back in Sanford. I stopped at the mill to ensure that steam was up in the boiler before heading to Southern Pines, thirty miles away. After leaving the mill I stopped at Lee Drug Store on Main Street, the only store open. I hadn't bought any presents for my parents or sisters. The day was dreary, cold, and wet, and I was tired.

A lanky, very attractive girl with a warm smile waited on me. She was soft-spoken and had a wholesome manner. She started working in the drugstore when she was in high school, she said. Now that she was living in Raleigh, North Carolina, she returned to work in the store every Christmas. It was part of her holidays. I tried to make eye contact as I described my parents and sisters, and asked her to suggest presents for them. She acted flustered; I wasn't sure why, but she did not lose her smile. As she gathered things from around the store, she explained why she thought that each one would be a great gift. I told her I had to write a check for my purchases because I didn't carry much cash. I was trying to maintain eye contact. It had been a long night on that lonely highway. She was such a welcome, uplifting change. She was so fresh and beautiful.

After scanning my check, she asked me to have it approved by the owner in the back. He initialed the check and I returned to the counter. The girl smiled and asked to be excused for a moment. She was very sweet.

She went back to the owner. "Mr. Joe," she said, "see that guy up by the cash register? Did you just approve this check of his?"

Mr. Lazarus, a portly, balding, gentle man, looked at it briefly and said, "Yep."

"I'm not so sure it's a good check. I've never seen this guy before. Said he just drove down from New York City but works here in Sanford at a mill. Acts like he's God's gift to women."

"He looks okay. It's all right," he said and went back to work.

The girl came back, smiled sweetly, and asked if she could gift-wrap the presents. I said of course, and we chatted as she wrapped them. She told me her name was Brenda Joyce Denton and reluctantly gave me her telephone number.

As she helped me take the gifts to the car, she noticed that I had a Carmel, California, city tag on the front bumper. "California," she said. "You do get around, don't you?"

I held her hand and told her how much I appreciated her help. I kissed her lightly on the cheek, for Christmas, and left for Southern Pines. For all that was going on—coming home so many miles through the night, the mill, the holidays, Lenore, New York, my future—that lanky, sincere girl in the drugstore was suddenly a major consideration, and I smiled.

Back in the store, Brenda quickly walked to the pharmacy in the rear and stood beside Mr. Lazarus. When she saw my car turn the corner, she said, "Mr. Joe, I have been working here for several years and I have had my share of bad checks and I know that guy is a con man. He didn't fool me. He's got charm he can turn on just like that. New York and, and, listen to this, his car is a white convertible sports car, with California tags. California. In Sanford, North Carolina? Works at a mill? No. That check is going to bounce. Yes, sir, he's a crook. I can tell. It was the way he smiled, like a carnival barker. He's as shady a character as I have ever met."

Brenda Joyce Denton accepted my proposal of marriage on Valentine's Day, fifty days after we met.

The mill continued to do poorly. With our old equipment we had no reason to hope for a reversal of fortunes in an industry that was becoming fully automated. Our principal customers began to cut back on orders, and it was becoming a problem to make the payroll.

Brenda noticed that Daddy was struggling under the load. If there was no hope of things getting better, she reasoned, we should cut our losses, close up the mill, and go on to something else. She suggested that I go back to school, that we could make ends meet after we got married. I qualified for the GI Bill, and she could get a job in Chapel Hill or we could live near Raleigh. The bright side was always clear to Brenda. She had an uncommonly clear sense of direction and vision.

I talked about going to Central America and she would say, "Okay," and I'd say, "You want to go?" and she'd say, "Sure, I just said okay." Then I would say, "We'd have an exciting time and a better opportunity to make a future for ourselves than here, you know?"

"Yes, I bet so. We'll have so much fun."

Then somehow—she wasn't leading me, I don't think—I don't know how, but we would get back to the subject of UNC and I'd be talking about going back to school. She'd say, "We'll rent an apartment, and you can read to me, and I'll help with your studies, I will. I'm so excited."

After a late-night discussion with Mother, Dad also came to the conclusion that there was no hope of keeping the mill going. On April 1, 1968, we shut down. We let the fire in the boiler die out for the first time in decades, laid off the workers, and locked the gate.

Admission officials at the University of North Carolina said I could return to Chapel Hill in the fall if I made up my grades during the summer sessions. I signed up for summer school and paid my tuition.

One Friday night on the way to see Brenda in Raleigh, the Mercedes overheated. I was late and anxious to get back on the road. When I filled the radiator with cold water, I heard the engine block crack and the sound of steaming water running onto the ground. My car died like a tiger, hissing and blowing as though it were angry because I was more concerned about someone else.

It was probably best. A Mercedes convertible was not the car for a struggling college couple. Plus, it held too many memories of a different time. I sold it to a collector for five hundred dollars and watched sadly as a wrecker pulled it away. That car had soul and personality. Men are seldom so well served by their machines.

Cool Springs Baptist Church was filled to capacity for the wedding. Dad was my best man. Brenda's oldest sister Betty Jo was maid of honor.

We honeymooned at Hilton Head, South Carolina. With part of the money we received from Mom and Dad as a wedding present, we bought a trailer and had it moved to a trailer park south of the Chapel Hill campus. It was my idea, and Brenda said having our own place was a good way to start. We enjoyed choosing colors and accessories, the way young people in love take pleasure in doing these things.

Brenda obtained a job in the Education Department at UNC and began work as I started the first session of summer school. We drove to the campus together every morning. Down the road in the other direction from campus was a large chicken farm, and trucks loaded with crates of chickens came past our trailer park every night to catch the interstate near Chapel Hill. Occasionally some chickens got out of broken crates and fell to the road. We saw bloody chicken carcasses along the road every day as we drove to school.

One morning Brenda remarked about how gory the scene was, like driving through Gettysburg the day after the battle. I said the real problem was with the chickens that got away, and then in my most sincere voice proceeded to tell her the story of "Redleg."

"Those on the side of the road are dead and gone," I said, "but some chickens survive the jump. There's a herd of the wild chickens now, west of the road, deep in Chatham County. Grow to be three-and-a-half, four feet tall. Leader of the pack is called Redleg, must weigh thirty-five, forty-five pounds. Three times as big as the biggest turkey there ever was. He and some of the chickens in his pack killed a goat down near Pittsboro a couple of weeks ago. Pecked the goat to death. Wild chickens of Chatham County."

Brenda was looking out the window at the carcasses as we passed. She had a frightful look on her face.

It wasn't nice to exploit the trust of a loved one, but I smiled to myself. Like Pete and the insurance years before—sometimes I am not a nice person.

I pulled in $125 a month under the GI Bill, and Brenda made little more than $100 a week. At the end of the first month I figured how much we needed to pay for tuition and books, and how much to put aside for gas, food, mortgage for the trailer, and a Christmas fund. We had something like $13.50 to last the rest of the month. Brenda said that would be enough, and it was. We met others on the GI Bill and had BYOS—bring-your-own-steak—parties, although it sometimes turned out to be chicken.

"Road kill!" we all yelled.

Classes, mostly political science, were exhilarating, challenging, interesting. I enjoyed going to the library and doing extra reading. I made all A's during the summer. It would have been difficult to go to Brenda, who was working to send me through school, and explain anything less than good grades. She wanted her money's worth.

We were getting gas in the car one day on our way home when

Brenda saw a box filled with small puppies at the side of the service station. The lady behind the cash register said we could have one, they were free. Some were furry, some had short hair; some were larger than others. The lady said it was the damnedest litter she had ever seen, looked like there were three or four different daddies. Brenda picked out one of the small furry males and we headed home to the trailer. Getting a little puppy was just right for our situation.

I had been talking about former President Harry Truman's famous 1951 confrontation with Gen. Douglas MacArthur over the Korean War when we pulled into the service station. We decided to name the pup "Harry."

He peed on the floor for a few days before getting the message that even a small puppy was expected to do his business in the woods, where the Wild Chickens of Chatham County lived.

While I studied at night, Brenda and Harry played on the floor and on the bed and in the backyard. The dog slept on the foot of the bed at night. At first light he woke Brenda, and she would take him to the sliding glass door in back and let him out. She left the door ajar for him, then returned to bed for another thirty minutes or so of sleep.

One morning Harry returned with a farm dog friend that had been rolling in cow manure. The smell prompted Brenda to wake up. Within three inches of her face as she opened her eyes, a huge, black, smelly dog was looking at her. She screamed and, using her elbows, the back of her heels, and her butt muscles, shot toward the ceiling and landed on the other side of me.

What was happening? My wife was screaming, and at least two animals were spinning in place, their feet trying to get traction on the linoleum floor. A helluva racket.

For a second I was sure that ol' Redleg and his Chatham County Wild Chickens had gotten in and were coming after us.

On my way to class one morning I was walking past the administrative buildings where the resident war protesters usually congregated. A pimple-faced youngster was dragging the American flag behind him at the rear of a demonstration.

I had stood, bemused, on the edge of campus demonstrations before as protesting students marched around in tight circles and chanted such things as "Hell, no, we won't go," and "Ho, Ho, Ho Chi Minh." It was street theater, I thought. I considered the U.S. government policies in Vietnam well-intended—they obviously weren't popular—but our government had served us well over the years, and we went to South Vietnam to stop that country from being overrun by its neighbor to the north. A noble endeavor, and I felt no regret for my part in it.

Why, I wondered, do these youngsters take such issue with the war? Probably because it was all the rage across the country. It was very hip to be antiwar. As a popular song of the times proclaimed, this was the dawning of the Age of Aquarius, and moral outrage with our traditional culture and our government was acceptable. Plus the youngsters did not have a vested interest in our society, and that encouraged alternative lifestyles. I had taken a vow once to uphold the dignity of our country, so, only five or six years older than these Carolina protesters, I felt like I had come from another age. Like an old codger, I would stand, watch, and smile.

But, to my mind, that young man who was dragging the American flag went beyond hip Age of Aquarius free expression. To me, the red of that flag represents the blood shed by my friends in Vietnam. That kid dragging it on the street denigrated their noble sacrifices. Ahead of him other students were cheering "Ho Chi Minh." Without thinking I yelled out, "Hey Shithead!" and the boy turned in my direction. He had a smirk on his face.

I dropped my books and charged after him. He bolted away, collecting the flag as he went. I followed him, but he was too far ahead. I lost him in the crowd. Standing in the middle of the demonstration, with my fists balled up, wearing my old fatigue jacket, angry—indistinguishable from those around me—I shouted profanities, which added to the hue and cry of the crowd. People near me were supportive until they saw the look in my eyes, and then they moved away. When I stopped yelling and walked back to my books, the crowd was quieter than before.

Later, in a speech class, I try to articulate my thoughts. I pointed out that the war is being fought on our side by people too stupid to stay out of the Army and, once in the Army, too stupid to get out of the infantry. They smell bad and have rotten teeth, tattoos, bad grammar, and no future to speak of. They are on the point out there, doing their duty, and if we appreciate the traditions of our country, then those American soldiers deserve our respect. They are the most honorable people on our side of the war—those young men in harm's way, in that foreign jungle. They answered their country's call, and in the years ahead they will take great pride in that. It will give them sustenance. I had been there, I know those men love their country, respect its laws and traditions in a way all Americans should. No one should drag around the American flag.

A glib senior from New York dissented, respectfully, presenting a sophistical argument against the war based on the premise that all people are well-intending. He proposed that we give world peace a chance. It was a far more noble thing to do, he intoned, for our government to seek peace rather than war.

My final comment was that peace is a good idea—in concept— but the Communists won't buy it until they get what they want.

By a voice vote the class decided that the peace position was stronger, and I lost the argument.

The Carolina basketball season began with the Blue/White game on Thanksgiving. Bill Bunting, Rusty Clark, and Charlie Scott, among other notables, played for the Tar Heels. On the night of every home game I met Brenda at her office and we walked downtown to Zoom-Zooms, a pizza/steak house. We ordered "The Special," a strip steak served on a sizzling platter with a mountain of fries and all the iced tea you could drink for under three dollars each. Most of the customers were also going to the game, and there was always electricity in the air. Carolina basketball generates excitement.

Brenda and I walked across campus and took our seats in the student section long before the junior varsity game began. We liked all the young Carolina freshman players, every single one, and we knew all their names. They were good at the game and usually beat the opposition, sometimes doubling the score, often reaching a hundred points. Carmichael Auditorium was small; no matter where we sat we had good seats, close to the floor, in the middle of the noise and the action. We were enthusiastic about the freshman games, lopsided as they often were, because of the players' high spirits and promise. The varsity games, however, were more serious entertainment. ACC (Atlantic Coast Conference) basketball is high drama. At that time Lefty Driesell was coaching for Maryland, Bones McKinney for Wake Forest, and Vic Bubbas for Duke. We believed them to be evil people with their lanky, towheaded, awkward players. And the Carolina team, Bunting and Scott and the others, seemed so clean-looking—they had a certain sweetness about them. And they were very good, especially when they played in Carmichael.

In one game, Bunting slapped the ball away from a Duke player, grabbed it in the same motion, and threw it over his head downcourt in front of Scott, who had broken toward the other end. Chased by Duke players amid the deafening roar in the auditorium, Scott came to the top of the key and stopped. Running hard on the fast break, he stopped dead. And jumped in the air to shoot the ball. Out in the open. He didn't want to go in for a layup, maybe, because he would be lost behind the backboard. He wanted it out there, in the middle of the noise, at the top of the key—sure of himself. The ball arched perfectly and swished cleanly through the net, without hitting the rim. With his fingers sticking forward like chicken feet in his follow-through, his white Carolina uniform so perfect on his dark skin, his feet landing lightly back on the floor, the Duke players running by him, he was framed in our minds for all time as the perfect Carolina athlete. We adored him. Charlie Scott. Gave up a sure layup and shot it from the top of the key. How audaciously grand. Jumping into the air and pumping our fists, we felt pure joy. "Nothing could be finer than to be at Carolina. . . ."

I continued with my political science major throughout the year, went to summer school the following summer, and was taking extra courses the following fall so I could graduate in January 1970, a year and a half after returning to school. Although I toyed with the idea of going to law school, I had turned twenty-seven that fall and was anxious to get into the workforce. I was interviewed by several firms that offered me jobs, but I turned them down. Making paper boxes or selling baby products didn't seem right for me.

To kill time before picking up Brenda one afternoon, I went by the student placement office to see what companies were interviewing. I had a chance encounter with a recruiter from the Central Intelligence Agency (CIA), who was on campus despite the student demonstrations. The recruiter said that the protesters notwithstanding, many people expressed interest in working for the CIA, but very few were hired. It was actually a small organization, he said, and employment standards were high; however, he indicated that my combat experience was a positive factor if I was interested in paramilitary work. The agency had openings in its Special Operations Group.

He gave me an application. I filled it out and sent it in within the week. I tried not to be excited about the possibility of working for the CIA, but it seemed so perfectly suited to my interests. Also, I had just happened on that recruiter. "Destiny is involved here," I told Brenda.

Within a short time I received notice that the CIA had my application and that the next step would be a battery of tests at the Carolina testing center. A couple of months after I took the tests, the CIA invited me to Washington, D.C., for more testing and an interview.

I came away from my trip to Washington with a good feeling that I would be hired. The interviewer said my application looked solid. Back in Chapel Hill, I stopped looking for jobs. I'm going to work for the CIA, I told people. Sure you are, they said. The CIA was not a common employer in North Carolina.

Then Brenda said she didn't think I was supposed to tell people that I was going to work for the CIA if, in fact, I had planned to do so. So I told people that I was going to work in the government, maybe the State Department. Sure you are, they said. I was not known for having a diplomatic style.

I graduated from the University of North Carolina in January 1970 with a bachelor of arts in political science. Another Vietnam vet, Dennis Myers, graduated at the same time. He liked the idea of the CIA, but getting a law degree, he reasoned, was like putting money in the bank, so he decided to go to law school at UNC in the fall. We sought gainful employment together. Our first idea was "Myers and Associates, Private Investigators and Bodyguards."

That didn't work. No one responded to our ads. Mighty safe state, we assumed.

We heard that volunteers were needed for experiments at Duke Hospital. We did not particularly want to work for Duke, the evil empire, Carolina's archenemy, but the pay was good, something like four dollars an hour. Dennis and I signed up. My first session was a Pavlovian-based drill that tested concentration. A technician taped little wires to the ends of my fingers and told me to indicate the different colors projected on the wall.

"Okay," I said. "What are these little wires taped to my fingers?"

"Oh," said the technician, "if you make a mistake you get a little shock. Just a tiny, little shock."

This was not good. They knew I had gone to Carolina. We were in the basement of Duke Hospital, and a Duke Blue Devil was strapping me to a chair—big, no-nonsense straps—and the chair had wires running to it, and the Duke devil was saying I was liable to get a "tiny, little shock." I imagined cadavers upstairs, other Carolina graduates who had received the same shocks.

It was the longest hour in my memory. I was shocked every minute for a total of four dollars.

That was enough for me. I quit but Dennis continued. He obviously had a higher pain threshold. This was found most often, I told him, among primates. Sensitive people avoid situations where they regularly receive electric shocks.

I got a job at a garment mill in Sanford through the help of the assistant manager, Don Harding, an old friend. Sam was king in the washing/drying room where I was assigned. He had been working in the mill since before there were blueberries, he said, and before there was sin. Teg was another member of the washing/drying room gang. They said that no one with a high school education, as far as either of them knew, had ever worked in the room, much less a white man who had just graduated from college. The job was simple. Trolleys delivered yarn dripping wet to the back room from the dying vats. We grabbed handfuls of yarn and loaded first the large washers and then the dryers with the clean yarn. The dried yarn went into clean trolleys that we pushed into the processing room.

Teg and Sam sang, laughed, and danced all day. Most of the others in the room, about eight people altogether, were quiet. Teg and Sam were often moved by the spirits, especially when they knew the words to the songs coming from the radio that sat on a high windowsill. It was a hot, wet, happy, and honest workplace.

The workers brought me documents occasionally that I read and, if they asked, made recommendations on. They were mostly tax forms, alimony payment requests, voter registration forms, and the like. Once, Sam received a personal letter from a union representative in New Jersey who asked him to meet another representative who would visit the area to contact people willing to form a union of the mill workers. I told him that was risky business, and it wouldn't make their lives much happier either. It would cause a lot of confrontation, and something like that ought to be left to people who liked confrontation.

A garble of our conversation reached the front office. Later Don called me outside. He said word was circulating that I was talking with Sam about unionizing the mill. The mill manager was so angry he couldn't talk; he was just standing in his office and mumbling. Don said he was on the block for hiring some college fellow and putting him in the back to stir up union sentiments. I finally convinced him that he had bad information, but the front office was never completely convinced. Everyone in the front office stopped talking and just looked at me when I walked in. Management personnel in garment mills in the South had a paralyzing fear of unions. I finally just kept to the back room. Front-office people had different priorities from us in the back. They weren't nearly as much fun either.

In March 1970, I went back to Washington for more tests, including a polygraph examination and another personal interview.

On the drive back to Chapel Hill my thoughts raced over a thousand scenarios of how my application would work out, and what I would be doing if hired. I had become more aware of agency news items and noted that it was well-represented in all provinces in South Vietnam, and worked with the South Vietnamese intelligence service, the police, and the military in a variety of jobs. The agency was also running a "secret war" in Laos, but there was little reporting on how they were doing that. The rules of engagement in Laos did not allow for U.S. ground troops, so maybe the agency put civilians like myself in the mountains to work with the hill tribes. The agency liked men with "hang," a CIA interviewer had said. I assumed that meant men who could "hang in" when things were tough out in the wilderness.

I also worried about the polygraph examination I had taken. What a terrible, intrusive test. Was it exact? Could it misread reactions? There were so many shades of meanings to things I had done in my life. The examiner had asked if I had ever been involved in a felony. Growing up I had been rowdy and done a number of things. Had any of those "things" been against the law? Well, maybe, yes, a little bit. Were they felonies? I didn't know. The obvious answer that they wanted was, "No, I haven't committed any felonies." So that's what I said, and then I worried about my answer during the rest of the test. Did the fact that I worried indicate on the polygraph machine that I was lying? Please no, I prayed. It was out of my hands now. Please, Lord, let these things pass. Let them find out quickly that I am a good, God-fearing patriot, that I would make a good employee.

In mid-June I received a telephone call. The CIA offered me a job starting 2 August 1970. I hung up and yelled, pumped my fist in the air, and then started jumping around. I jumped up and down, up and down and up and down—through the kitchen, down the hall, into the bedroom. Jumping and yelling. In the bedroom I calmed down, stood still for a minute to regain my composure, and walked casually back into the kitchen to call Brenda.

We quit our jobs, sold the trailer, and packed our few remaining items in the back of the smallest rental trailer available. With Harry riding at Brenda's feet and the back seat of the car loaded with houseplants from Brenda's mother, we left North Carolina in late July. Shortly after our arrival in Washington we found a small, unfurnished two-bedroom suburban townhouse, rented some furniture, and moved in. Two days later I reported to work for the Central Intelligence Agency in Langley, Virginia.

— SIXTEEN —

Holding the Line in Laos

I had been hired on contract to work in the CIA's Special Operations Group (SOG), the section that had given the American people the Bay of Pigs and the U-2 program. Most of my compatriots were former military people with Vietnam combat experience. There was an innate feeling among them that they belonged in the CIA. They exuded self-confidence.

In September 1971, after a year of intelligence and paramilitary training, I received my first assignment, as a case officer in the Lao program, the CIA's largest covert operation.

During the late 1950s, Laos, a small, indolent, landlocked country, was on the verge of a civil war that could have brought about a confrontation between the world's superpowers. The ragtag forces of the pro-West government of Souvanna Phouma were opposed in the countryside by the Pathet Lao, a Communist group supported by North Vietnam and the Soviet Union. In 1962, to defuse the situation, a senior U.S. State Department official, William Sullivan, helped structure the Geneva Accords, which prohibited foreign forces from fighting in Laos. The intent of the accords was to get the North Vietnamese out of the country so the Lao could determine their own fate. The North Vietnamese signed the accords but did not leave. A "tacit agreement" ensued. The North Vietnamese would remain in Laos to help the Pathet Lao; the United States would support Souvanna Phouma but would not commit ground troops. The United States subscribed to this agreement because the CIA had contact with Vang Pao, leader of the Lao hill people (Hmong), and U.S. policy makers were confident that he could carry the fight to the Communists. With CIA support, Vang Pao's forces fought and died bravely during the mid-1960s as the war in Vietnam took shape, and they quietly contained the North Vietnamese in the mountains, away from the Laotian capital of Vientiane. By the late 1960s, however, Vang Pao's forces were exhausted and there was some question about their ability to continue the fight. Paid volunteers from Thailand were brought in to shore up the Hmong. In 1971, as I prepared for my Lao assignment, the North Vietnamese were deploying two divisions to destroy the CIA's combined Hmong/Thai paramilitary force encamped on a high mountain plateau—the Plain of Jars—in an effort to move on the capital and bring Laos into the North Vietnamese sphere of influence. The future of the country was in doubt.

The rear headquarters of the CIA's Lao program was at a U.S./Thai Air Force base in Udorn, Thailand. Brenda and I arrived there in mid-November 1971. CIA intelligence indicated that the North Vietnamese would probably launch their offensive before Christmas. I was anxious to get to the field and learn the lay of the land before the North Vietnamese attacked, but I was assigned to a desk in Udorn instead. While I was busy with paperwork and briefings, my friends were bracing the Hmong and the Thai mercenaries up-country for the battle ahead. Unhappily, I was on the sidelines as the game was being decided.

Early one morning in mid-December 1971, the first day of the smoky season, when haze from slash-and-burn farming in South China enveloped the mountains, the North Vietnamese attacked the CIA forces on the Plain of Jars with human waves of infantry supported by deadly, railroad-car-size 130mm artillery. The Hmong and Thais fell back several ridgelines before consolidating on a ridge called Skyline. The North Vietnamese pursued them and, on New Year's Eve, 1971, started an advance up Skyline as dozens of 130mm rounds landed on the ridgeline and in the Long Tieng valley beyond, where the CIA had its up-country base camp.

The CIA forces held Skyline on New Year's Eve and inflicted heavy casualties on the North Vietnamese. The next day the North Vietnamese attacked again, and the day after, and the day after that, but the Thais and Hmong did not break. The North Vietnamese pulled back, regrouped, and started to attack again—they had been ordered to take the ridgeline at all costs. On 14 January

1972, every newspaper in Hanoi announced that Skyline had been overrun and the CIA forces in Laos destroyed.

But the Thai mercenaries and the Hmong had not been overrun. They still held out. The North Vietnamese continued to attack Skyline, occasionally capturing Thai positions before being repulsed. The CIA forces were stretched to the limit.

The last all-out attacks before the smoky season ended were pending when I finally received a transfer up-country. I joined CIA men known by their call signs: Hog, Digger, Clean, Ringo, Zack, Hardnose, Dutch, Kayak, Tiny, Electric, Bag, Shep, Bamboo, and Greek. Hog, who had been in up-country Laos for ten years, gave me my call sign—Mule.

Like Hog, the CIA people tended to stay around in the mountains of Laos for years. They had good rapport with the Hmong and Thai mercenaries; they knew the territory; and, although they looked like weathered, backwater cowboys, they were effective. It was a closed society. Hog, the senior case officer, was the unquestioned leader. He had a keen, woodsy intelligence—he set the tone, he was our soul. Over a beer some night he might say, "Need to have all you girl singers on the dreaded ramp 'fore sunup. Bring a little hang."

"Girl singers" was a Hogism for prissy men, and he used "dreaded" somewhere in every other sentence. "Hang" was courage. Hog had hang and he expected each of us to demonstrate the same virtue.

I also met two stalwart groups of pilots, the mighty Air America men and the fighting Ravens. Air America was the CIA airline. Its fleet of helicopters moved case officers, troops, and supplies from mountain to mountain. There were also fixed-wing, STOL aircraft, mostly Porters that could land on extremely short, dirt runways. Air America also had large fixed-wing planes for airdrops and for moving troops forward from rear bases. No roads led into the area where we operated, and everything had to be flown in. The Air America flying machines were the lifelines to the fighting units.

Probably no other profession was as dangerous nor could any other organization attract such stout hearts as did Air America. Compared to the ten dollars a day GIs were making in Vietnam, the pilots and the kickers were reasonably well-paid, but they were not there for the money. It was the adventure. They were not sentimentalists. In fact, Air America people showed little emotion; every pilot had lost dozens of friends in that war. Their employer's reason for being there did not matter to them. They simply wanted the action of combat flying for the CIA, and they wanted to be on the winning team. All of them had been in Vietnam, with its complicated rules of engagement, distracting media kibitzers, and lack of purpose. In Long Tieng, Laos, there was no politics. Air America did its job, and we were successful in Laos. We held the line. We did not lose. Air America helped make the difference. The U.S. government has rarely employed such irreverent, hard-living, competent patriots as the Air America pilots.

Although my CIA training and all the stories I had heard prepared me for the case officer corps and Air America, I had to go back to my military days, to the U.S. Air Force forward observers, to find people comparable to the Ravens.

U.S. ground troops were prohibited from fighting in Laos, but U.S. warplanes were not. Flying unarmored, light 0-1 observation planes called Birddogs, the Ravens challenged death every day to lead U.S. warplanes in on targets. If an Air America pilot knew an enemy position was on a ridgeline, he avoided it; the Raven went looking for it, in the hope of drawing fire. As military officers, the Ravens put great value on comradeship and each accepted his own death as the possible consequence of a mission. They were, it seemed, more willing to die than the Air America pilots and CIA case officers. God, were they impressive. Coming in from a reconnaissance, their little planes shot up, they coolly got out and walked proudly across the ramp. That day the rounds might have missed them by feet. Tomorrow it might be by inches, but they would still get out of their planes at the end of the day and calmly walk away, heads up, apparently unfazed. They looked like lawyers or preachers, but they were cool, committed killers, a breed apart, extraordinary risk takers.

As were the Thai volunteers. Most came from humble, rural backgrounds in Thailand. They had tattoos, criminal records, and disrespect for authority, but put them on top of a mountain in Laos, surrounded by North Vietnamese, and they would fight and they would die. Every day we sent body bags to Thailand.

Every day we received replacements. When they arrived, CIA case officers moved among those tough men to prepare them for deployment. They also smiled at the danger. Between attacks we sent them up to Skyline and, sometimes within hours, put what was left of them in body bags and sent them south on planes that had just brought in more replacements.

Six battalions of Hmong worked out of Long Tieng. After ten years of fighting they were happy to see the Thais taking the brunt of the attacks, so that they could act as guerrillas, the maneuver elements in our little war. Many of the Hmong soldiers were young, but they all had hang. Recalcitrant, unorthodox, dirty, tenacious, they were defending their homeland, and they were good soldiers.

What army in the world could beat people like Hog and Air America and the Ravens and the Thais and the Hmong?

Not the North Vietnamese in Laos. They never took Skyline.

As I was getting into my first job up-country, locating, organizing, and training the Hmong village militia north and east of the fighting on Skyline, the North Vietnamese pulled back. They had suffered heavy casualties in unsuccessful efforts to rout the CIA men. As the North Vietnamese retreated, the Ravens pursued them every step of the way. The North Vietnamese were a shattered, defeated force when they reached the Plain of Jars.

On Christmas Day, during a break in the fighting up-country, Brenda and I visited the Catholic orphanage in Udorn and in a second's time, she fell in love with a runty, sickly, ugly little two-year-old Thai boy who was recovering from an operation and had been left out of the Christmas party. I saw it all happen.

We had brought some fruit as a token gift and were being escorted to the back play area of the orphanage by one of the Catholic sisters when we passed the nursery. This kid—the only child in the room—was standing up in his bassinet and rocking from side to side, looking mean and sad. Brenda and he made eye contact and something happened. She walked on a couple of steps, leaned back into the doorway, and saw the boy leaning to the side to see her. They were at crazy angles—he and she—like yin and yang, and Brenda straightened up and asked the nun if she could bring that lonely little boy out back. The nun extended her arms out as if he were hers for the taking, so Brenda went into the nursery and picked him up and joined me outside. As we sat on the edge of a picnic table, she bounced him on her knees. She got him to laugh and she looked at me, that woman I loved so much, and her eyes were twinkling and her smile was radiant and she looked back at the boy—the nun said his name was Joseph— and he smiled again and she hugged him so hard he cried out.

There were so many other kids there that after a while Brenda began to feel guilty about focusing so much attention on one, so she tried to set Joseph to the side and he cried out in a lonely, desperate wail. Forever bonding their relationship, he then reached out his hands to her. Brenda picked him up and he stopped crying, snuggling into her arms.

We adopted Joseph two months later.

Two days after that a man appeared on the doorsteps of our house on the outskirts of Udorn and asked if we'd consider adopting an American-Asian girl. We followed the man back to his home—he was leaving for the States soon and was not able to bring Mim, his foster daughter, with him. He was looking for a good home for her. Mim was escorted into the room and I was smitten—she was so beautiful a child that she was startling. She had been the center of attention all her brief life and did not take my adulation as anything out of the ordinary.

A week later Mim was adopted and our family was complete. We were so proud of our children. They held such promise. There was so much more to life with them around.

Because of the fighting up-country, I was not able to spend much time at home in Udorn. My family had grown considerably since February so we decided to move to Vientiane. Brenda rented a house; hired a cook, a maid, and a gardener; and settled in. She was comfortable in her surroundings and was not afraid of things that went bump in the night.

Up in the mountains, I expanded my contacts with village militia north of Long Tieng and had positioned Hmong irregulars on a mountaintop in preparation for a move into a village previously held by the North Vietnamese. After training that group, my Hmong ops (operations) assistant/interpreter, Va Xiong, and

I were resupplying them when the plane he was on hit a mine as it took off. Va barely escaped with his life. My parents were visiting us in Vientiane and Va went back with them to the States.

In late summer 1972, I received a Hmong battalion, GM 22. With Digger's GM 21, we came down out of the mountains for training and refitting prior to what would be our dry season offensive against the North Vietnamese dug in on the Plain of Jars.

We returned to Long Tieng in September to launch our attacks. A fellow case officer was killed in the first week of the offensive. We eventually established positions in a crescent south, southwest, and west of the plain. Digger's GM to the west, my GM in the middle, and Kayak's GM to the south. The other Hmong battalions and the Thais were in reserve. Digger's forces were hit first and pulled back. Kayak's forces were hit and held.

My forces were hit and fell back one ridgeline as we pounded the North Vietnamese with artillery. Air Force fast movers came in to help us, and the Hmong's prop-driven T-28s flew through the smoke and haze of the battle to deliver treetop support. The converted trainers were equipped to carry bombs and .50-caliber machine guns. Flown by the heroes of the Hmong nations, committed only on Vang Pao's order and often directed to targets by the Ravens, they were a very effective fighting element. My GM eventually pulled back to a staging area some distance from the plain, but we returned later.

I went down to see my family every ten days or so, often leaving directly from the field and arriving home in my dirty and bloody field clothes. Brenda would know when I was coming and started a homecoming ritual with the children. Each kid had his own group of light switches to turn on so that, when I came in, every light in the house was on. The house would be aglow, and tunes from Walt Disney musicals would be playing on the reel-to-reel tape recorder. It was wonderful, coming in the front gate, the kids excited, Brenda smiling, the dog barking, the lights, and the music. Home from the hills. Home from the fighting. All I could do was stand there and smile.

Mim and I developed a particularly close bond. It was her job to take my boots off, and that seemed to give her first rights to my attention. She snuggled up to me on the couch, sang along with the Disney songs, and told me about things that had happened while I was away. Brenda sat nearby with Joseph on her knees, both of them listening, laughing.

What other citizen/soldier in our lifetime could have it so good? Fighting a winning war, coming home nights. On every family visit I said to myself, I am the luckiest man in the world.

The war in Vietnam, that odd, politicized, hackneyed, never-ending embarrassment to America, was coming to an end. Secretary of State Henry Kissinger was making deals. After years of U.S. support—the last ten years with up to half a million GIs in-country—the South Vietnam government still did not rule the countryside. The Saigon leaders, most of them French- or American-educated Catholics, had little in common with the unsophisticated Buddhist farmers in the provinces. The North Vietnamese Army remained strong. Every year, two hundred thousand young men in the North came of military age. Although they might be killed by the tens of thousands, the North Vietnamese leaders were prepared to deploy every one until the South fell. They knew that the Saigon government would never control the hearts and minds of South Vietnamese peasants, and they knew the United States would not stay forever.

The United States and Kissinger simply wanted to get out, but leaving South Vietnam to its own destiny was difficult, and it would require, at minimum, a decent interval between the withdrawal of American forces and the certain collapse of the country so as not to implicate the United States as a fair-weather friend.

Disengaging from Laos, however, was easy. A "secret war" did not require a decent interval. A cease-fire was called in early 1973, negotiations ensued, and, in short order, the Communist Pathet Lao, hosts to the North Vietnamese, overflew Long Tieng to quarters in Vientiane. Although the government that was created was ostensibly a joint pro-West/Communist coalition, Pathet Lao soldiers stood on every street corner of Vientiane, making it clear that the Communists were in control.

Up-country at the CIA base in Long Tieng, we said among ourselves: "Hey, wait a minute, what the hell have we been doing here for ten years?" "Why did we fight so hard?" "Who gave it all away?" "How could they do that?" "What was the value of all those young men dying?"

A new CIA boss came up-country and told us to get on with disbanding the Hmong and sending the volunteers back to Thailand. Pack up your base, he said, and go on to something else. It's over. Air America understood and left without a word.

So did we, finally. In November 1973, Hog drove me down to the ramp where I was to catch a plane south. I was going to pack the family out of Vientiane, go back to the States for some home leave, and return to Indochina. I had requested and received orders to Vietnam.

Hog parked his Jeep in the shade of the air ops building and squinted into the sun. In his slow Montana drawl, he reminded me what our chief had said, that the fighting was all over. He thought a tour in Vietnam was after the fact.

"Nope," I said, "it's my war now. It seems to me the Americans on the scene there now don't understand what we've gone through fighting this war—the human price we've paid. To them, it's just some other man's war. Someone who was around early on ought to be there now to speak for the Americans who died. Don't you think?"

Hog, tough and unsentimental, shrugged.

We sat side by side in silence. I had requested an assignment to Vietnam because I was frustrated with the way things had turned out in Laos and, as naive as it might sound, felt I could make a difference in Vietnam. There was no question that I enjoyed paramilitary work, but I was also motivated by a sense of unfulfilled duty. Perhaps my feelings had been fostered by General Heintges when, at my OCS graduation, he had said that I was among a group chosen to uphold the dignity of our country. Perhaps it was because I had gotten out of the military when our country was still at war. Maybe because I had come to realize that I had a lot invested in the war: Memories of my friends and compatriots who had died—Patrick, McCoy, Goss, Ayers, Castro, Slippery Clunker Six, the Hmong, the Thai mercenaries, the Ravens, the Air America pilots—stayed fresh in those baskets at the back of my soul, where I had put them so I could get on with my life. Sometimes when I was alone I would take down one of the baskets and look at the contents, and then put it back. I felt a soulful obligation to ensure that the sacrifices of my friends in this war were not overlooked.

"Just something I got to do, I reckon," I told Hog. "Just got to do it."

Hog looked away, but smiled. "The dreaded Mule," he said.

On the way back to the States, Brenda, Mim, Joe, and I stopped in Hawaii and stayed in a beach bungalow at the Kahala Hilton. Bob and Linda Dunn were living on Oahu at the time, and they showed us the island as if they owned it. We went on to Los Angeles, California, where we made the obligatory two-day Disneyland visit. Then we drove a car across the southern United States for a company that transported cars from coast to coast. It was an almost new Mercury that was being repossessed from a sailor in San Diego. We returned it to a car dealer in Charleston, South Carolina, and then went on to North Carolina in time for Christmas. The kids assumed that everyone traveled around the world the way we had.

After the holidays, I went to CIA headquarters in Langley. I spent a month on the Vietnam desk and read up on the deteriorating situation there.

On 3 March 1974, we departed for Taipei, Taiwan, where Brenda and the kids would stay while I served in Vietnam. The wife of a man whom I had known in Laos and a CIA support officer met us at the airport and delivered us to our quarters in a comfortable housing enclave in downtown Taipei. A neighbor said the name of the development was "Mortuary Manor," after a funeral home at the head of our street.

The kids were not sure that this was the best place in the world. When I left for South Vietnam, Brenda was in the process of moving to another development of forty or fifty houses on Yangmingshan Mountain, which overlooked Taipei.

At Tan Son Nhut Airport in Saigon, a CIA station driver met me. He drove to the U.S. Embassy through streets clogged with traffic—motorbikes darting in and out among the larger vehicles, bikes, and pedicabs with passengers sitting in front all competing for road space.

Standing in front of the main gate of the embassy, I remembered that Duckett and I had stood in the same place seven years before. We had been intimidated by the embassy then and reluctantly gone inside, only to jump out of the way when embassy staffers came by. It seemed less forbidding in 1974.

I met with the CIA's deputy chief of station, who told me that I was assigned as a case officer to the Mekong Delta, which included all of the area below Saigon. He said, in the way of an overview, that what was happening in the Delta countryside was of extreme interest to policy makers in the States. I was to work hard at developing new sources of information on enemy political and military activities, get as many reports as I could from the existing agents whom I would be handling, and work closely with the Special Branch of the South Vietnamese police, but I was not to let them lead me around or recruit me to report the war the way they saw it. My job was to work on building up unilateral—not liaison—operations. He said that I was needed and there was much work to be done. "Plus," he said, "your presence out there reassures the South Vietnamese that the United States is still at their side."

Later I took a pedicab to the Duc Hotel, a residence hostel used exclusively by the agency. Sitting in the front of the three-wheeler with the wind in my face, I smelled the city, the exhausts, the cooking odors, and the ripe human smells brought out by the tropical sun. Horns blew. Bikes whizzed by. The street noises induced a sense of excitement and vitality. Most of the people did not look at me or show any expression—hundreds of thousands of Americans had come that way before.

—— SEVENTEEN ——

CIA Work in Vietnam

In mid-March 1974, almost four months after I had said good-bye to Hog in Laos, I jumped off a helicopter in Chau Doc, South Vietnam, a Delta province capital bordering Cambodia. My new boss, Don K., was waiting on the tarmac. A tall, lean, goateed intellectual in his early thirties, Don K. was a career intelligence officer who had been busy in another part of the world when he was drafted into the CIA's clandestine corps to serve in Vietnam. He had little in the way of a military background, but he knew people and he was adaptive.

Don drove me to our downtown office/living quarters compound on the Bassac River. By the standards of the Lao program, we had palatial accommodations as well as a large service staff, mostly Chinese, of cooks, maids, mechanics, and drivers. Our guard force was all Nhung, descendants of Chinese mountain tribes, who had served with the CIA for years. Several interpreters and translators worked in the office. The office staff was multilingual, and English, Vietnamese, Cambodian, and Chinese were spoken.

Among my assigned contacts was a squat and unusually quiet Cambodian, "Ros" [alias]. He had been a CIA agent for years and had done everything asked of him. If he understood what his agency case officer wanted him to do, he did it. He traveled on intelligence missions into Cambodia under a number of guises, often as a hawker selling sundries he had purchased in the local market. Ros lived by his wits. He carried a knife, among other weapons, and had killed when cornered and questioned about his activities.

His reports of missions into Cambodia were detailed and informative. Initially it took me hours to debrief him because I had no background on the interplay among the various groups in Cambodia, which included the Khmer Rouge, Khmer Krom, North Vietnamese, Viet Cong, and Cambodian government forces. But Ros was patient and I soon became conversant with the border situation and the stark, brutal realities of life in Cambodia.

On the South Vietnam side of the border, the Chau Doc office collected both military and political information from a variety of agents. The military information was straightforward. North Vietnamese forces dominated the countryside. They moved with impunity from sanctuaries in Cambodia through Chau Doc Province and throughout the rich farming region of the delta. The Government of South Vietnam (GVN) forces held all of the cities south of Saigon, as well as the lines of communications, roads, major waterways, and other components of the infrastructure, but the GVN's influence in the countryside was limited. In some areas it was restricted to the ground under the feet of its Army.

For the most part, the farmers around Chau Doc didn't care about the war or, for that matter, the government in either Saigon or Hanoi. If they took sides they were at risk of being killed. The farmers wanted to farm, and they had no interest in politics. Their traditions were nondemocratic. They didn't understand the reasons for U.S. involvement, and they didn't make eye contact with soldiers moving through their areas. The country people did what they were told by whatever force was around at the time.

I liaised with the military and, because I knew most of the Air America pilots, became the outrider for the office. Often I went to Ha Tien on the coast. Once, while waiting to talk with the district chief there, I walked out to a cemetery on a windswept knoll overlooking the ocean. On some of the tombstones were names of Frenchmen, most with military rank. French Foreign Legion perhaps. "Mort pour La France" was inscribed on the tombstones. A beautiful place that country, that hill overlooking the ocean. Vietnam was a country worth fighting for. But what was that Kipling poem the cavalry sergeant quoted about Westerners making war in Indochina?

At the end of the fight is a tombstone white
With the name of the late deceased.

And the epitaph drear:
"A fool lies here
Who tried to hustle the East."

I thought the epitaphs were correct, and the poet wrong. Those Western men who died in Vietnam were not fools, they were patriots, men who died in the service of their country. The fools were Western politicians and bureaucrats who did not know the beauty and vitality of that land, who thought it was a little, insignificant "pissant" country where it would be easy to impose the Western will.

When I went back to Taipei for my first family visit, I found that Brenda had moved the family to the development on Yangmingshan Mountain. Our house, tucked in behind the Chinese Cultural College, was only a five-minute walk to a spectacular view over the city. At night the lights from Taipei went on as far as we could see.

The kids had started kindergarten and Brenda was working part-time. Her life was more hectic than it had been in Vientiane; more to do and more wives around as friends and neighbors. The development swarmed with children and our kids had no lack of playmates. Brenda played bridge and handball and had evenings out with the other wives. My family was very much at home in Taipei.

After I returned to Chau Doc, I spent my days developing information on Cambodian and Vietnamese political and military activities. Part of the conventional wisdom in 1974 was that the North Vietnamese military was stronger than the South Vietnamese, but the long-term consequences of that were not widely discussed. That was because the CIA station in Saigon, an insulated, bureaucratic, personality-driven institution, held the notion that the future of South Vietnam was assured because of secret, off-the-battlefield developments that they were following but of which the field officers were unaware.

As a direct consequence of that perspective, CIA officials in Saigon did not encourage military reporting, particularly reporting from GVN military sources, "liaison sources" as they were called in the trade. Station personnel in Saigon considered

GVN information biased and unreliable. I found it strange that people in my organization in Vietnam did not have the same trust in our South Vietnamese allies as we had had in our Lao compatriots. Maybe because in Laos we ran the war and had a vested interest in winning. In Vietnam, 1974, we only monitored the situation. And those who managed the intelligence collection effort for the most part had political backgrounds and did not care about the opinions of military commanders. That message was conveyed to us in the field by the use of the CIA intel grading system.

Each intelligence report submitted from the field to Saigon and to Washington was eventually given a grade, from "ND" to 20. If a field report was not disseminated to customers in the intelligence community, it received an ND (nondisseminated). A report that was disseminated but judged by the analysts to be of marginal interest received a grade of 1, a disseminated report considered to be of some value received a 5, and a report of significant value received a 10. If a report attracted significant notice and had some hard, critical information that would have an impact on policy, it received a 20. Most liaison reports were graded ND, 1, or at most a 5. On the other hand, political reporting from unilateral agents received 5s and 10s.

The troubling aspect of the political reporting from the South Vietnam countryside was that unilateral Vietnamese agents run exclusively by the CIA were found, time and again, to be fabricators.

There were a number of reasons for that. Most of the CIA case officers who served only one tour in Vietnam did not speak the language, were poorly trained in the esoterica of Vietnamese operations, did not fully understand the complicated interactions within the Vietnamese political arena, were manipulated by their translators and interrogators, and, despite all that, were pressured to produce intelligence reports. The CIA officers who put out the most reports were the ones promoted. Numbers—reports and grades—spoke more clearly than the reports themselves.

Over time, a subculture of professional Vietnamese fabricators, "intel producers," had developed. Operating in the alleyways of Saigon and on the fringes of the American community in the provinces, they satisfied the CIA's need for political information— any information. As they moved from province to province they created agent nets, cultivated relationships with translators, found out what was needed, developed their contacts with CIA officers, and convinced the latter that they had privileged access to Viet Cong or North Vietnamese political plans. When they were placed on a salary, they began selling fabricated reports. They based the information on local newspaper articles or marketplace rumors, or, more often than not, on just pure invention.

It was hard to believe that CIA analysts in Saigon, inundated beneath all that manufactured mush, could have had any idea of what was really happening. Or perhaps the invented political "intelligence" from the phony field sources was so broad that the analysts could choose their own conclusions.

In June, after I had been in-country four months, the CIA base chief called me to his office in Can Tho and asked if I would like to take over a province by myself.

"Yes, sir," I said. "What province?"

"Chuong Thien."

"Chuong Thien?" I asked incredulously.

Zee, an old friend, had just been assigned to Chuong Thien. Some people had given him the nickname "Deadman" because, on most people's maps, Chuong Thien Province was VC-controlled. Only the capital of Vi Thanh, the location of the ARVN's 21st Division headquarters, was under South Vietnamese control.

"Zee is being transferred out of Chuong Thien," the base chief said without elaboration. "It is yours if you want it. Go down and show the flag. The 21st ARVN Division has the security responsibility for most of the delta. Even if Saigon Station doesn't want to know what the ARVN are doing and what they think about the enemy, I do."

So I took the job and flew down in an Air America Porter airplane that afternoon for a short overlap with Zee. As we approached the town of Vi Thanh, I told the pilot that we were awfully high if that little airport way down there was indeed where we were going. He showed me his map. It was all red around the town, which indicated enemy control. There was no approach area. The only way to get in was to get directly over the town and spiral down. That we did, and he delivered me dizzy to Zee below.

Terry Barker, the local State Department/USAID (United States Agency for International Development) representative, was also on the ramp when I jumped off the Porter. He and Zee were the only Americans in the province, a point they emphasized on our way into town—that the whole American community had shown up to welcome me. They said there was a siege mentality about the place. ARVN forces did not leave town unless they were in battle formation. The badlands began right outside the city gates.

As close as we were to enemy forces and as dangerous as the place was supposed to be, the compound was surprisingly open. A barbed-wire fence ran around the football field-size area where I was to live and work. A single Nhung guard stood by the main gate. I was to inherit a staff of ten local workers, two of whom were translators and ops assistants.

After dropping off Terry at the compound, Zee took me to meet General Le Van Hung, commanding officer of the ARVN 21st Division, who welcomed us warmly. Speaking English slowly but clearly, he said that his division was responsible for the whole lower delta. They were outnumbered but he did what he could, picking and choosing his confrontations. He could not go charging every enemy bunker, because he would lose his men quickly. Because he was in the war for the duration, he had to husband his forces and his resources. He said, matter-of-factly, that he could not turn the tide there. If he began to get the upper hand, he reasoned, the North Vietnamese would bring in more forces.

"Why fight a losing battle?" I asked.

"What are my choices?" he asked, smiling. Slowly, he added, "This is my country."

On the way back to the compound, Zee began talking about the realities of the war in the same way we had talked about it in Laos. He said Vi Thanh was the worst place in South Vietnam. There was no reason for hope in Vi Thanh. The enemy was all around. He said he had argued with the base chief in Can Tho that we should pull out. Why risk the capture of Americans during the eleventh hour? It is all over, he said. The country is lost.

As he continued to talk, I thought, Well, I know the reason this guy's leaving. His doomsday reporting contrasted too sharply

with the enormous number of other—primarily political—field
and Saigon-based reports that said everything will work out. Zee
was calling the cards as he saw them at a time when Saigon Station said the real game was being played under the table, out of
sight.

After Zee left, I moved into his room in the two-bedroom main
house on the compound. Terry had the other bedroom. That night
after supper, Terry suggested that we sit on the front porch.
Slumped in a rattan chair, I balanced a glass of tea on my stomach. I couldn't see Terry sitting half hidden in a chair to my right.

"We're surrounded by VC and North Vietnamese regulars.
Just you and me, you know," he said. "There are no other Americans around to bail us out if the bad guys come after us."

"Yep, I'm getting that message. Just you and me down here in
godforsaken Vi Thanh."

"Yep, and I'm a draft dodger," Terry said quietly.

Because my companion was out of sight, I just stared straight
up at the ceiling. Draft dodger? What's he doing in Vi Thanh with
me, surrounded by VC?

"How'd you get here?" I said aloud.

"Damndest thing. I was in college in Texas in 1969, and I
didn't have a clue what I wanted to do with my life though I was
aware of what Uncle Sam was doing with uncommitted youngsters over the age of eighteen. I was thinking, I want no part of
going to war in Vietnam. Hell, I'm from Texas, Alamo country,
but try as I might I couldn't justify our military involvement here
and I was certainly not going to participate as a U.S. soldier. So
out of college, to avoid the draft, I joined the Peace Corps. It's
that simple. For the same reason some people went to Canada, I
went into the Peace Corps.

"Got sent to a small island on a Micronesian atoll—one hundred by five thousand meters. That's all. Just me and 350 natives.
A resupply ship came by once every two to three months with
mail; sometimes it forgot to stop. But on the positive side, I wasn't
in the Army, wasn't in Vietnam. Then one time when the resupply
ship stopped—I had been on the island for a year and a half then,
I think—it stopped and there was a letter from my draft board
back in Texas, saying, come on home son, your number's coming
up and you got to go do your duty. Whatever you might think,

here in Texas we don't consider Peace Corps work a deferment."
He paused a moment. "Want some more tea or something?"

"No, I'm okay," I said. The sun was almost completely down
and it was pleasant on the porch. Cool. Terry's slight Texas drawl
wore well, and he told an interesting story. Although he was de-
scribing himself as someone very unlike myself, he was a kin-
dred, rational spirit.

"So I went home," he continued, "took a physical for the Army
on a Friday—passed it, unfortunately—and was prepared to go
in the Army on a Monday. But Saturday, now I know this is hard
to believe but it's the truth, on Saturday, I got a call from a U.S.
Agency for International Development fellow who offered me a
job. I called the U.S. Army on Monday and told them to stick it.
This was late 1971. Took training for about ten months and
USAID sent me to Vietnam. Trying as hard as I could to stay
away, it's where I ended up. I've been here in Chuong Thien
Province ever since." He paused.

"And you know what, I've become very proud to be part of the
U.S. effort to keep this country free. I believe our intentions are
noble, and I have humble respect for the soldiers fighting for
freedom here."

"What changed your mind?"

"Being here, knowing the people—they're good people, you
know, hardworking, family oriented, proud. You met General
Hung. Colonel Canh is the province chief. I'll introduce you.
These two are dedicated South Vietnamese patriots. And the
others here in Chuong Thien, the farmers out there, they have it
so tough, but you know, every encounter I have with them, they
smile. Every time I fly out to the districts, they seem glad to see
me; they smile and ask me to eat with them. They are so humble,
so easy to like. And they just want to farm and family. That's
pretty much what they do—farm and family—and I'm a big fan.
I think they should be able to do that without the Communists
telling them what to do, who to share what with. I can understand
why I was unconvinced about our warring effort when I was in
college, but I know for sure now that we were right in coming
here to help these people stay free. What we're doing here is
worth dying for."

Texas Terry Barker, I thought, did not betray his Alamo roots.

He was a tough guy, and I was lucky to have him with me in Vi Thanh. He had been there for three years. Wonder if he thought I was Alamo/Vi Thanh material?

I asked if the local security situation was as bad as everyone said.

"Yep," he said, "maybe worse. The enemy owns the countryside. But I don't think they are going to come across the field in the back and attack this compound because," he paused, "they never have. They don't want to. The Communists want Americans out of South Vietnam, and capturing or killing civilians like ourselves might change Washington's resolve to get out. Attacking us here would make the papers back home, and the North Vietnamese don't want negative press. They're not stupid. They read the papers, too. Even the VC out there in the Chuong Thien boonies know what's going on in *The Washington Post*. And you know what, we're low priority to them. What damage do we do? I don't harm them myself, my USAID programs probably indirectly help the local Communists. And nothing that you do is apparently disruptive.

"So we get along, out here as far from Washington as you can get, we and the bad guys get along. There's something like a truce between us. Zee didn't believe it. He thought the end was near, that he was at risk of being attacked on the whim of some local VC commander."

Sitting in the half light on the front porch that night, I thought a case could be made for both sides. I agreed with Zee that there was a short future to South Vietnam, but my sense was that we would not be attacked there, that I was safe as long as I didn't threaten the local VC. However, it wouldn't hurt to double the size of the night guard and keep a loaded gun at my bedside.

That night we decided that if the bad guys did sneak into the compound and come into the house, they would probably be gunning for me, Parker, the CIA guy. I figured that I had to convince them that they didn't want me, Parker, but Barker in the next room. Barker, not Parker. Maybe it was a typo, maybe they had just misunderstood their orders, which I would try to say was easy to do, confusing the names of Americans.

Right, said Terry.

Over the months that followed, I worked to develop information on the situation in the lower delta. I spent hours at 21st Division headquarters and finally obtained a permanent pass to visit the G-2 and G-3 sections. General Hung spent most of his days in the field. His command helicopter left early most mornings to make the rounds of the isolated positions so he could talk with his field commanders. I met him most often at night, sometimes over supper, sometimes for drinks. Occasionally we met during the day in his office. Over time our contacts became relaxed and comfortable. We enjoyed one another's company.

Terry introduced me to the province chief, Colonel Canh. He was the ARVN "soldier of the year" prior to coming to Chuong Thien, an honor he received in part because of his heroics in a battle with North Vietnamese mainline forces near An Loc. Terribly wounded, he had lost part of his face. When I met him, his disfigurement had been corrected to some extent by plastic surgery, although the first thing my eye went to was the long scar running along his jaw. Canh had a positive attitude about the war, as dismal as it was in Vi Thanh. He was a soldier's soldier, brave and incorruptible. He traveled alone by sampan at night to remote outposts to deliver salaries and supplies and to lift the morale of his soldiers. He said that he had good men and they would fight the Communists until they died or until his country was free.

At night, Terry and I had to work hard to entertain ourselves. Our favorite pastimes were playing rummy and watching 16mm movies. During our rummy games Terry got up to owing me eighteen zillion dollars. Then we played one hand double-or-nothing and he came back even. We received only five or six movies every other week. The first time we showed each movie we invited our Vietnamese counterparts. Although Terry and I watched the same movies again and again, we never tired of the musicals.

My parents wrote that everyone in the States was talking about Watergate and the prospects of Nixon's impeachment. Everything was a downer. Fortunately, some distance on the other side of the world from those sordid goings-on, we blissfully played cards and watched musicals and did not feel deprived.

We also played tennis at the old MACV compound across the

street and read several books a week. And we played chess—conventionally at first, and then battle chess. We placed a thin piece of board across the middle of the chessboard so we couldn't see the placement of the other person's pieces. After arranging our pieces any way we wanted, we lifted the board and flipped a coin to see who went first. Those were bloody skirmishes. Each lasted fifteen minutes or less.

General Hung's outlook did not change while I was in Chuong Thien. He was convinced that the real struggle for the delta was under way in other places, possibly in Saigon parlors. A Buddhist, Hung believed in fate; whatever happened with whatever consequences was the natural order of things.

Hung thought his role as 21st Division commander was to keep his division together, to maintain communications and keep everyone alert, to fight for survival, and to take the net advantage from any engagement. He did not believe in trying to win the war or in squandering supplies. Survive and things will take care of themselves, he said.

I usually called for an Air America plane and flew into Can Tho once every two weeks. During alternate weeks I tried to find time to visit a neighboring province, either Rach Gia or Bac Lieu. A person could get cabin fever by staying in Vi Thanh too long at a time, plus it was safer to meet away from Vi Thanh the few unilateral agents whom I handled. I maintained a schedule of twenty-eight days in-country and six days with the family in Taipei.

There were no direct flights from Saigon to Taipei, so I always transited Hong Kong. Sometimes I lay over in Hong Kong for a few hours on a shopping errand for Brenda. On those excursions, as I had done on my R&R from infantry days in Vietnam, I took the Star Ferry back and forth to Kowloon. The cruise was soothing, and I always compared those times with my life in Vi Thanh. There was so much industry and energy there, so much to see, so much going on. I felt so safe on the edge of the crowded Star Ferry. In Vi Thanh, life was very quiet. Its days were measured, and gloom and doom permeated the place. And danger always lurked nearby. Hong Kong was a reaffirmation of life. One round trip on the Star Ferry convinced me that a world, prosperous and alive, lay beyond Vi Thanh.

Homecomings were also uplifting. I could see how much the kids had grown between my visits. Their lives were full and challenging. Undeniably American kids by that time, they had their slang and their favorite junk foods and their Hollywood heroes.

Mim and I still had our special times together. She appeared honestly disappointed that I wasn't wearing boots for her to take off when I came home, but she took off my shoes anyway. Once when I came in she took off my shoes and socks, and because she was in a playful mood she ran into her room, came back with fingernail polish, and painted my toenails red. I never removed the polish but just let it wear off in time. It was Mim's special mark on me.

Brenda's sister Betty Jo came to Taipei for a visit during the fall of 1974. After dinner one evening she and Brenda went to the Grand Palace Hotel to buy postcards. When they had finished shopping, Brenda pulled away from the curb near the entrance as she chatted away with her sister, made the first turn leading out to the street, and found herself going down the stairs from the hotel to the street below—in our 1971 Oldsmobile.

The doorman came running up to the driver's door and with his hands over his eyes shouted, "No, no, no, no!"

The car wouldn't back up. The rear tires were lodged against the top step. So the doorman called everyone in the area, workers, guests, everyone—the car was surrounded by Chinese. Brenda put the car in reverse and gave it the gas as they pushed it up the stairs. When she drove off they all applauded.

Back in Vi Thanh, I continued to send out dispatches on the situation in Chuong Thien and the lower delta to what I perceived to be an uninterested readership in Saigon and Washington. My grades were mostly 1s and 5s. I tried for balanced reporting, without sensational language, but the message was clear that the Communists dominated the countryside and the long-term prospects for GVN forces were bleak.

One day field officers were called to Can Tho for a briefing by the CIA's chief analyst in Saigon. I had heard that he was from North Carolina, so I was looking for an educated redneck in the hope that we could have a substantive give-and-take on the situation in the delta. I was excited about the visit. It would be my first opportunity to give my views of the situation directly to someone in a position to make a difference.

As it turned out, I was very disappointed. "Terry Balls" [alias] was a condescending, pedantic elitist who ventured south to give us a "big picture" lecture, resplendent with insignificant order of battle information and minutiae on North Vietnamese personalities, trivia gleaned during his years in the air-conditioned confines of Saigon.

Balls's talk did not reflect the realities of the countryside. It had no sense of sweat and no military or historical perspective on what was going on where we worked, where the war was being fought. Plus, he didn't ask us any questions. Despite the recent setbacks to the South Vietnamese troops in the central and northern parts of the country, the southern area, especially the delta, was secure, he said. Generations of case officers would follow in our footsteps in the delta. Eventually there would be tacit understandings to the negotiated cease-fire, signed in 1973, with which both the North Vietnamese and the South Vietnamese could live. There were factors at work, not apparent to us in the field, that ensured this to be the case. There is no question, he said, that South Vietnam will survive.

It occurred to me much later that no reasonable person could have believed that the North Vietnamese, who had suffered a million casualties in that war, were going to stop short of complete victory. Maybe, I thought later, Balls was part of a U.S. government conspiracy to keep us at our posts in the field while we waited out that decent interval until North Vietnam took over the South.

Then, I thought, no. Our government isn't that smart when it comes to Vietnam. The prediction of a North Vietnamese–South Vietnamese coexistence is just foolish enough for our policy makers to believe.

At the bar later that night, I told Balls that despite what he might think, the North Vietnamese were not going to stop this side of a complete victory in the South. The South Vietnamese military could not stop them. Hung's 21st Division was among the best the ARVN had, but it was outgunned and only waiting for the end. There was no democratic future for South Vietnam.

Balls, accustomed to briefing world leaders, looked at me strangely and turned his back to me without comment.

On my return to Chuong Thien, I was in a gloomy mood so I decided to visit the local orphanage, one of my all-time favorite places. The small Catholic chapel and orphanage complex was on the edge of Vi Thanh, across a small river. I drove a motor scooter to the river and yelled to a boy who poled a boat across to pick me up.

Most children orphaned in Vietnam were taken in by members of their immediate families because it was part of the culture and it was common for extended family groups to raise orphaned relatives as adopted siblings. The children taken to an orphanage were often deformed, sickly, or disturbed, and beyond the ability of their families to care for them. Many of the children in the Vi Thanh orphanage were horribly disfigured. The nuns gave them loving care, which was reflected in the faces of the kids. The children were always either happily at play outside or sitting dutifully on little pots—all in a row—doing their daily business.

When I visited the orphanage and sat under the trees to watch those scrawny, deformed kids laugh and play, I always felt better. It was often the high point of my day, to go over to the orphanage after work, and I frequently carried the kids around the play area on my shoulders.

For Christmas, Terry and I enlisted the help of our parents in the States and Brenda in Taipei to get enough gifts for all the kids. We bought cases of ice cream and candy in Can Tho and invited everyone in the orphanage to the compound. Remembering how excited the children were in Udorn, Terry and I sought to make the Vi Thanh Christmas party just as joyous.

The party was grand—a wonderful holiday.

—— EIGHTEEN ——

My Bodyguard

The North Vietnamese launched a coordinated offensive in the northern areas of South Vietnam in December 1974. There was no subtlety. They got their conventional forces on line and charged straight at the South Vietnamese positions. After each attack it appeared to us that they waited for a response from the United States. When there was no response, they attacked again. On 6 January 1975 the North Vietnamese captured Phuoc Long Province, north of Saigon.

Finally, the U.S. government did something. It reduced the size of the official American community in Vietnam, which clearly indicated that our government had no confidence in the ability of the South Vietnamese to survive.

In late January, as a consequence of the reduction, Terry was transferred out of Vi Thanh. I would be the only American left in the province.

Jim D., the new CIA base chief in Can Tho, asked if it was tenable, and I told him it was and that the only thing I feared was fear itself. If the local Communists had not attacked when only the two of us were there, I figured they would not attack now just because I was alone.

After I put Terry on the plane, I called aside the chief guard, Loi, and told him that his job was being changed from ensuring that his men changed shifts on time, stayed awake at night, and received correct pay. From then on, his main job was to be my bodyguard—that is, *body*guard. He was to think about the safety of my body at all times. He was to move his bed to the room of the guardhouse nearest the corner of the main house where I slept, and he was to be within several steps of me all day. If I was in the office, he was to be in the office. If I ate at noon in the house, he ate at noon in the house.

Loi stood almost at attention. Wide-eyed, he took in everything I said.

If I went to division headquarters, I wanted Loi to go to division headquarters. If I rode the motor scooter at night, he rode his motor scooter with me. If there was any danger, anything out of the ordinary, he was to get between me and it. I wanted him to take spears in the chest. I wanted him to die before I died. I wanted him to be a living, walking, talking shield. That was his job. If he didn't want it, I would get someone else, either there or in Can Tho.

Loi, after waiting a second to be sure I was finished, said he understood. He said he would take spears in the chest if he had to.

"What are spears, anyway?" he asked.

The first night after our talk I was riding my motor scooter, with Loi right behind me on his. The route, which I had taken before, ran past the market and out to the northern edge of town, then on a built-up road to a bridge and back by the orphanage and home.

At the edge of town, Loi came up beside me and sputtered, "Where are you going?"

"Down to the bridge."

"No, no, no."

"Why not?"

"Bossman, the bridge belongs to the local VC," he said.

When I told him I had been going there for weeks, he slapped his forehead with the palm of his hand and said, "Are you crazy?"

So I didn't go there anymore, but I checked Loi's information and found that it wasn't entirely true. The VC tax people were there only some of the time.

Also, when Terry left I asked one of the interpreters to help me have a talk with the cook. The kitchen had been Terry's responsibility. He paid the cook and bought the things she needed in Can Tho. Her name was Ba Muoi. In English that's number ten. She was the tenth child born in her family. Naming children by number is an ancient Vietnamese custom that promotes family unity by giving each child a place. Ba Muoi knew how to prepare about nine dishes, which she served on a rotating schedule. We almost knew what day it was by the meals she prepared. I asked her to vary the menu. It would make my stay much more pleasant. I liked Vietnamese food. Don't always cook Western, I told her, give me some down-home Vietnamese food. For example, I said, I pass the market often and see these giant frogs. I used to hunt frogs as a kid, and I want some frog legs. Try fixing me Vietnamese frog-leg food.

There was some distance between what I intended and what I had for my next meal. I think maybe the phrase "down-home" got garbled in translation.

Ba Muoi went down to the market and bought some frogs. She put them on her cutting board, chopped them up from the heads to the ends of the legs, and served them in a soup.

I had frog soup. Not fried frog legs, but frog soup, with frog lips, frog eyes, and other green stuff swimming around in it. I had lived with the mountain people of Laos for a couple of years and eaten some odd things, but I had never seen anything as unusual as that woman's frog soup.

I told her to go back to her nine meals.

She was walleyed. When I told Brenda, she said that was what she expected me to say—my maid was a walleyed older woman—but I said it was true and that she was a grandmother, too. Because Ba Muoi's eyes looked out opposite sides of her head, she had a blind spot in front and had to walk with her head cocked to one side.

Ba Muoi had been working at the U.S. compound in Vi Thanh since it was built years before. Someone, sometime, had told her to make up the beds at eight o'clock in the morning, so she would come into my bedroom to make up that bed at eight o'clock, whether I was in it or not. And I swear she went into Terry's room to make up his bed for months after he left. She'd go into his room and say "Oh," and then go into the kitchen.

One weekend morning at eight o'clock, I heard her come into the house while I was still in bed. I got up and walked over to the closet to get dressed. Intent on making up my bed, she walked into the bedroom. Because the curtain was still pulled, it was dark in the bedroom and she apparently did not see me. She headed for the light on the bedside table where I kept a 9mm pistol, loaded and cocked, when I slept. I had been reading late the previous night and had dropped my glasses on the floor beside the bed. They were in Ba Muoi's blind spot and she stepped on them, mashing them flat. She stepped back and cocked her head to one side to see what she had crushed. When she saw that it was my glasses, she backed out of the bedroom, leaving them flat on the floor.

I went outside a few minutes later with my flat glasses and I said, "Hey, what happened to my glasses?"

She said she didn't know.

One night some VC came into the cluster of houses across the field from the compound. They carefully put together wooden troughs, aimed them across the field, placed rockets in them, and fired the rockets in our direction.

What we pieced together later was that some merchants had slipped through the VC checkpoints without paying taxes on the goods they brought into town. The VC tax collector was letting the merchants know that he wasn't happy with this.

The first rocket whizzed over the compound, exploding in the market beyond. Loi came tearing out of his room and ran to my bedroom window.

He started yelling, "Hey Boss, Boss, Boss, Boss!"

Another rocket came zinging overhead and Loi dropped to the ground, but then he was back on his feet by the window, yelling, "Hey Boss, hey Boss, Boss!"

Another rocket whipped by overhead and Loi kept yelling, but I didn't hear anything. The air conditioner was going and I was in a deep sleep.

One of the guards at the rear of the compound had a night-vision scope. He yelled to Loi that he could see the VC across the field. It looked like they were getting ready to fire again. Loi ran around to the front of the house and hit the screen door to the porch with his shoulder. It flew open, but the front door was secured by a small bolt lock. Loi slammed against it as another rocket flew overhead.

I began to come awake as Loi burst through the front door, and I was wide awake when the rocket exploded in the market behind him. When Loi charged across the living room into my bedroom, I was certain that he was an attacking VC or North Vietnamese. I reached for my 9mm and Loi saw me going for the gun. He screamed and jumped to stop me from shooting him.

Adrenaline was surging through my body. I had the strength of a thousand men, and Loi and I wrestled mightily—until I recognized him and calmed down.

Another rocket went off in the market. Trying to protect my body, as I had ordered him, Loi was lying on top of me.

"Get off me, you fool," I said.

My routine during the day remained unchanged. I would wake up around 0730, breakfast at 0800 while I listened to the news on the radio, and then take a Jeep ride to the operations section of 21st Division headquarters to get a report on military activities in the lower Mekong Delta over the previous night. If there was a serious incident, my subsequent visit to the intelligence section would usually focus on the implication of the incident to the overall security of the region. I often visited the Special Police offices on the way back to the compound. If they had a VC suspect in the interrogation center or if they had special intelligence on VC/North Vietnamese intentions, I would go over their reports. We also ran several joint operations and I would meet with the individual South Vietnamese case officers to discuss developments. Some of the bilateral operations were substantive, but most were obviously fabricated to get money from me or to give the Special Police an excuse to travel out of Vi Thanh. As I reported to Can Tho once, "Some of their stuff is chicken salad, but most is chicken shit." They produced little intelligence.

In the afternoons I usually went back to the division, but most of the time I wrote reports and managed the few unilateral CIA operations run in the province. The Air America courier flew in from Can Tho twice a week. I would go days without seeing an American.

At night I refused to be idle. If I grew tired of reading, I invited the guards and translators to play chess. As a group, collectively, they knew how the pieces moved. I faced Loi across the board and the guards and translators stood behind him. Talking fast in Vietnamese among themselves, they discussed every move, sometimes arguing, sometimes poking at different pieces on the board. When they finally came to a consensus on a move, Loi slowly and cautiously advanced a piece. As I reached toward the board to make my next move, often without much of a wait, they looked at me and back to the board, paused, then started talking again. They never won a game.

On the other hand, I never beat Loi at tennis. Once or twice, deep into the game, I managed to even the score. Then it was as if Loi said, "Oh, what, even?" and he'd slam a serve back at me so fast that I couldn't react, as if to say he was still in control.

I asked the compound manager to build a Ping-Pong table so we could play at night on the porch. All my people were very good at Ping-Pong; unfortunately, I was not. One night I said to Loi, who was toying with me as we played, "Loi, I can't see. The light is reflecting off my glasses. We're going to have to move the table so the light is over my side." Loi said okay, so we moved the table down the porch. Not only did Loi's side have much less light, but we had moved the table so far that he had little room to maneuver. The end of the table was less than four feet from the end of the porch.

"Hey Boss, this not fair," Loi said. "I can't see. I can't move."

"I can't hear you. Whose serve?" I asked.

I began to win a fair share of the time, but I constantly had to put up with, "Hey Boss, this not fair."

My evenings with General Hung were more serious. He would ask about my family, about the United States, and about current events. He had an interest in American literature and I would often talk about American authors and their works. Although I read two or three books a week in Vi Thanh, I had not read many of the books Hung asked about. For his part, Hung would talk about Vietnamese history and stories of Indochina wars. He always spoke deliberately, slowly. He smiled often, even when discussing serious issues. He was uniquely self-confident and had a calming aura about him. He was very easy to like, and we developed a deep friendship.

In February, at the insistence of his superiors in Can Tho and Saigon, Hung's forces attacked a large North Vietnamese unit on the eastern fringe of Chuong Thien, in the infamous U Minh Forest, long a Communist stronghold. The attack was Hung's largest operation since I had been in the province, and he agonized over the operations plan. He used what South Vietnamese

Air Force he could get. Although he had an abundance of artillery pieces left by the U.S. Army, he had difficulty moving the equipment into place because of the paucity of flyable helicopters, and he lacked the right supplies to adequately outfit his attacking force. For example, he had plenty of claymores but no activators, and plenty of artillery ammunition but rusty fuses.

As it turned out, he suffered extensive casualties.

His men fought bravely. Reports coming from the field reminded me of skirmishes in Laos. I could understand his anguish, and I knew how proud he was of his men, who were taking casualties but continuing to press the attack.

When the battle was over and the North Vietnamese had been pushed back into the U Minh Forest, General Hung was not sure if he had, in fact, secured the net advantage. He had used much of his limited resources. For what?

A few days later the most god-awful odor drifted through my compound. I had smelled it before—rotting flesh, dead people. An interpreter said the division morgue was located between our compound and the orphanage.

The bodies of many of the soldiers killed during the operation were waiting to be shipped out. In addition to limited transportation, there was no refrigeration and some of the dead were from areas completely controlled by the North Vietnamese. Mercifully, Hung managed to move the bodies within the week. We were almost to the point of abandoning the compound.

In late February a team from the International Commission of Control and Supervision (ICCS) arrived at Vi Thanh. The team consisted of four nationalities—Hungarians, Poles, Indonesians, and Iranians—westerners, most of them, with round eyes. I was excited and went to see them the same day they came in. They were civil but obviously uncomfortable with me because I was CIA. I was not to be put off, however, and went back the next day. They were correct but unfriendly.

So Loi and I went out and hit tennis balls. I felt like Robinson Crusoe with his man Friday.

The following month, Ban Me Thuot fell, and ARVN Supreme Headquarters in Saigon had to realign the standing forces under its command to protect what remained of South Vietnam. Elements of General Hung's command were transferred to protect the northern edge of Can Tho and the general was asked to accompany the detachment. He was assigned as the deputy ARVN commander for the area south of Saigon.

On 20 March, Hue fell.

On 30 March, Da Nang fell.

In Can Tho, General Hung was courteous to Jim D. and the officers working in military liaison out of the American consulate, but his remarks made obvious that he was more likely to be candid with me than with officers he was meeting for the first time.

With the collapse of the ARVN forces in the north, military reporting suddenly became job one in the delta. Jim called me to Can Tho on two occasions to meet with Hung for a briefing. The second time he told me to move up permanently so that I could meet Hung on a regular basis. Another reason was that consulate staffers often found Air America pilots uncooperative, and many of the pilots were my friends. Jim thought that I could improve the overall relationship.

I planned to visit Vi Thanh weekly or biweekly thereafter to check on the compound and get a briefing from Colonel Truong, commander of the 21st Division element left behind. My departure was an ominous sign to my interpreters and the staff, especially Loi. As long as an American was on the scene, they weren't going to be forgotten. They had a fatalistic view about the future and wanted to be at a launch point when the light went out. They were aware that the North Vietnamese were pushing down the coast above Saigon and that most South Vietnamese forces were falling back.

Promising them that I would not forsake them, I said I would be back as often as I could. They were to continue doing the job and let me know what was going on. I left that day with most of my personal items. I had been in Vi Thanh for nine months, most of the time as the only American. As the Air America Porter was making its tight spiral to gain altitude over the city, I saw the staff standing silently in the compound as they watched the plane leave.

My work routine in Can Tho differed greatly from that in Vi Thanh. The nights, however, were about the same. Wasn't much to do in Vi Thanh at night, and in Can Tho everyone went to ground early because of the 2000 curfew. Each morning I walked to the consulate from my apartment down the block, and it was crowded with people trying to get in to get a visa for the States. I had to fight my way through the crowd, past the local guards and U.S. Marines, into the secure base area. The first person I always saw there was Jim D.'s secretary, Phyllis F.

The general drawdown of official Americans continued. Every morning as I passed Phyllis's desk I saw piles of automobile, office, and apartment keys from people who had left the previous afternoon or evening.

After the fall of Ban Me Thuot, the North Vietnamese were moving south without much resistance. Sometimes no one was sure exactly who controlled what area. Some South Vietnamese military forces in the delta deserted their positions. Some South Vietnamese military and provincial officials just walked out of their offices and headed to Saigon to catch planes out of the country. Air America pilots did not want to take just anyone's word on the security of an area where they were asked to fly or land. Relying on the trust that we had established in Laos, most of the pilots worked with me, as well as "Mac" [alias] and "Sarge" [alias], two other CIA officers at the Can Tho base. Mac, another North Carolinian, had previously worked with Air America in southern Laos and knew most of the pilots. Sarge spoke fluent Vietnamese and was a longtime adviser to the Can Tho interrogation center. He had been in South Vietnam for years and knew the lay of the land in the delta better than any other American in-country.

The principal officer at the consulate, Consul General (Congen) Francis T. (Terry) MacNamara, had the unenviable job of trying to identify all U.S. citizens in the delta to ensure that they had some way to leave if they wanted to. He was assisted occasionally by Lacy Wright in Saigon, previously a State Department officer at the consulate in the delta. It was difficult to determine sometimes who was entitled to U.S. citizen status. Some Vietnamese women had returned from short marriages with GIs in the States. Even if their status was clear, the eligibility of their extended family was always fuzzy.

In one case, MacNamara was required to fly to a province

close to the Cambodian border for a personal interview. He tried to arrange this directly with several Air America crews, but they either told him to get someone else or said that their helicopters were down for repairs. MacNamara, in fact, had a history of altercations with Air America pilots. Once, he had asked a pilot to shut down in a field in an area that the pilot thought was not secured. After a loud shouting match, the pilot said he was leaving. MacNamara could come with him or walk back. MacNamara, of course, left with him but was fuming.

MacNamara asked Jim D. to intervene on his behalf with Air America so he could get out to the province close to Cambodia. The next morning I went with MacNamara to the airfield at Can Tho and waited for the Air America helicopters to come down from Saigon. Cliff Hendryx, an old poker-playing friend, was captain of the first chopper to land.

I asked MacNamara, who had a scrubbed, neat, office-look about him, to wait in air ops until I had talked with the pilot, and I walked up to the helicopter as it was shutting down. Cliff opened the door. His helmet was lying on the console beside him.

His eyes were bloodshot and he hadn't shaved in several days. He had a thin, gaunt face, and his stubble made him look like a mountaineer. He also reeked of garlic. The kicker in the back was handing him a slice of watermelon.

"Muley, how you doing, fuckhead?" Cliff said. Most Air America pilots did not know my real name.

As he ate the watermelon, with juice dripping down his chin and onto his shirt, I explained what MacNamara wanted and what I knew about the area where he wanted to go, which appeared safe. Cliff picked up a *Playboy* magazine and put it in his lap to catch the juice. I said I would go along because I knew some of the ARVN in the area. Cliff didn't voice any objection to the mission. He finished his watermelon and lit a cigarette. He was smoking and spitting out watermelon seeds when MacNamara walked up. The Congen looked at Cliff—the smelly mountaineer—for a long moment. He finally said he had changed his mind, turned on his heels, and left.

"Well, fuck him," Cliff said.

— NINETEEN —

The Light at the End
of the Tunnel

An area of increasing concern was Route 4, which ran west and southwest out of Saigon, north of the Bassac River, and down into the delta. Elements of the ARVN 7th Division protected the road, and General Hung arranged for me to be briefed by General Tran Van Hai, the 7th Division commander. Hung said that he had served in the 7th Division himself when he was younger. The American adviser at that time was the legendary Lt. Col. John Paul Vann, a man who became an authority on the ARVN and eventually died in South Vietnam.

I flew out by helicopter to 7th Division headquarters and met with Hai in his office. An Oriental copy of a U.S. Army officer, he was a neatly dressed chain-smoker with his sleeves folded up above his elbows. He spoke excellent English.

The eyes in his pudgy face were hard and he was not friendly. I asked him about the situation.

"You want information, U.S. government man. I want helicopter parts. I want ammunition."

"You're talking with the wrong man, that is not my job."

"You are U.S. government. The U.S. government promised to keep us supplied so we can fight. We can do it, we can continue to fight, if we have bullets and planes. Tell your government that and I will tell you what is happening here."

"I will. I will report that you are short of supplies."

Hai looked at me for a long moment. Finally he said, "You Americans don't always keep your word to us Vietnamese 'slope heads.' " And he continued to look at me through his cigarette smoke as he waited for my reaction.

When I did not respond, he shrugged and started his briefing. He said his men had interlocking positions down Route 4 and out to the Cambodian border to protect the underbelly of Saigon. The area was mostly open rice fields. Morale was good, and he could hold out against a division-size North Vietnamese force for a short period of time. Morale would collapse, however, if his division was set upon by a larger force and if its ammunition began to run low, and he expected that a large North Vietnamese unit would attack soon and that he would have no source of resupply. He faced the NVA 9th Division commanded by Maj. Gen. Di Thien Tich, who had been fighting in that area since before 1965.

"Tich is maybe the best field general the NVA has," he said. "You know what the slogan of his division is? 'Obliterate the enemy.' That's me. You know what the slogan of the Army helping me is? 'Fuck your friends.' "

There was venom in his voice. The ARVN was collapsing in the North, and he was sullen, bitter about his fate. Unlike Hung, Hai was not philosophical about the future. He was angry.

I suggested that there might be a negotiated cease-fire that would protect the sovereignty of the Government of South Vietnam. The general looked at me without speaking. I had no idea what he was thinking.

Later, back in Can Tho, I reported on my meeting with the 7th Division commander to Jim D. and told him, in conclusion, that the general wanted more bullets and spare parts. Jim D. knitted his brow and looked at me. "Put it in your report to Washington, then, don't tell me."

I went downstairs to the base map room, where I had set up my work space, and wrote a cable for dissemination to Saigon and Washington. I thought about Balls's overview that things were okay and his prediction that South Vietnam would survive. Who was right, Balls or Hai?

Every morning the crowd in front of the consulate got larger. Every morning there were new keys on Phyllis's desk. Every morning there was bad news about the North Vietnamese push down from the north.

Sarge, Mac, and I continued to travel throughout the delta as we gathered information and looked after the local staffs in compounds that had been abandoned by departing CIA and USAID officers.

Wherever we went we promoted the line from our Saigon Station that the delta of South Vietnam had nothing to worry about—there would be a negotiated peace. I repeated this message time and again without blinking my eyes. It was a better out than saying what I believed—that the clock was ticking and the end was near.

After consultation with CIA management in Saigon, the base chief decided to close some of the compounds in which there were no Americans. Rather than return the equipment in the compounds to Can Tho, Jim decided to turn everything over to the South Vietnamese government officials in the provinces. He told those of us going to the field to terminate all local support staffs, and he instructed the base finance officer to draw a large amount of U.S. and Vietnamese currency from the Saigon Finance Section to cover their termination and separation pay.

The agency, however, had long-term responsibilities to some of the special agents who worked out of the compounds to be closed. Jim told the deputy base chief, Tom F., to draw up a list of those key indigenous personnel (KIP) who had tenured employment with the CIA and work on ways to protect them.

Tom was uniquely suited to the task. He was one of the most experienced agency paramilitary hands in Indochina. In his first CIA assignment in Thailand during the 1950s, he handled a one-man office in a small town on the Thai-Cambodian border and met other Americans only on quarterly trips into Bangkok. His total immersion into Asian culture served him well. He knew the soul of the Indochinese farmer.

Although Tom had tough standards, he was compassionate and fair when it came to dealing with the Vietnamese and deciding who deserved our special consideration and protection. Because the number of KIP had to be realistic—we couldn't take everyone who wanted to leave the country—Tom included on the KIP list only those staffers and agents who had done sensitive work. Maintenance staff, guards, and cooks were not included. In Vi Thanh the only people who qualified were my two interpreters. Loi, the senior guard, did not.

Before leaving Can Tho to close my old compound in Vi Thanh, I drew a cardboard box full of Vietnamese piasters and a box half full of American currency as an advance from the finance officer. Loi met me at the airfield and peppered me with questions about the situation in the North. As we drove into the compound, I told him that we were closing down and I wanted him to prepare a list of all the equipment—every typewriter, every rifle, every knife and fork, every towel, every pencil. The interpreters were sitting on the porch of the main house when we pulled in. I told them to work on the employment histories of all the employees. I wanted to know when each man started to work and his terms of employment. I told the two interpreters that they were being transferred to Can Tho. Loi was carrying my bag into my old bedroom and overheard me. He stopped and looked at me in the hope that I would say, "Loi, too, you're going to Can Tho," but I did not. I turned and walked toward the office. Tom had said, "No guards."

I was going to have to pay off Loi and let him fend for himself. If there was a negotiated halt to the North Vietnamese advances, he would face the prospect of finding a new job. If the GVN was near collapse, as I believed, Loi would almost certainly have a bleak future. Either way he was on his own. He was despondent and dejected, and he thought that I, personally, did not want him. Loi had worked for the Americans for most of the previous ten years, but he wasn't on the first team, with the interpreters. I avoided Loi, although there were times that afternoon and evening when he tried to talk with me alone.

The next day we resumed our inventory, and I started individual meetings with the staff members so that I could pay them off. I sat behind a desk in the open bay area of the office, with the boxes of money on the floor beside me. As each worker came up, usually with one of the interpreters standing by to ensure that there were no missed communications, we discussed their employment history to arrive at the exact length of service with the U.S. government. Most had termination bonuses of one month's salary for each year of employment, plus there were other considerations, such as leave earned and not taken, outstanding loans, breaks in service. Another factor that confused the exact termination figure was a period during which contracts had been written in U.S. money amounts, which implied that U.S. rather than Vietnamese money was owed. When we arrived at a final amount, usually in two currencies, I counted out the money from my boxes. Then the worker counted it out and signed for it.

Finally, everyone was paid except Loi. I called him into the office, and the interpreters left. With his hat in hand, he stood in front of my desk and cried. He said that he didn't want his money, he didn't want to be laid off, he wanted to continue working for the U.S. government.

I told him that it wasn't in the cards. My chest hurt and my eyes watered, but there was nothing more to say. Loi wiped his eyes and looked at the floor.

My voice breaking, I told him to sit down and we would figure out what he was owed. I gave him every consideration and added six months' salary as a bonus for being my bodyguard over the last few months. I laid an impressive amount of money on the desk. He signed for the money and stuffed it into his pack.

That night I went by the orphanage for the last time. I said good-bye to the sisters, and they told the kids that I was leaving. One boy with crossed eyes, who was possibly retarded, shook his head no. A sister was holding him. I tickled him under his arms, and he laughed.

The province chief arrived the next morning, and I asked that his staff check the serial numbers on all of the items before he signed for them. By midday everything had been accounted for, and the province chief signed for the compound.

As a final piece of business, I asked Loi to drive the two interpreters and their families to Can Tho. I was thinking that maybe I could find something for him to do later, but did not tell him that. He looked closely at me to see if there was hidden meaning in my request, sensed there was, and enthusiastically said he'd get the men there safely. I could trust him.

They arrived in two days, having fallen in with a military convoy. I sent the two interpreters to General Hung's headquarters, where I had located office space for them, but I had found nothing for Loi. Mac and Sarge, also closing compounds, were having similar problems in dealing with longtime staffers who had done nonsensitive work. Large numbers of Vietnamese, who had been good loyal employees of the U.S. government, were looking for seats out if the Americans were evacuated. I told Loi to go home in the truck that he had brought from Vi

Thanh and see his wife, do something with his money, and come back in one week to my apartment. Good plan, he said, relieved to have continuing contact with me.

By the first of April, all CIA compounds in the delta had been closed except for My Tho, Chau Doc, Rach Gia, and the base offices at Can Tho. Including immediate families, we had a list of fewer than 150 KIP.

Bill A., another base officer working out of Can Tho, located an American with a Vietnamese girlfriend who claimed to know of an island out from Rach Gia that was loosely controlled by the GVN and did not have a Communist presence. The island might be useful as a temporary safe haven for our KIP if we needed a staging area away from Can Tho. Conceivably, if South Vietnam fell, we could move the people to this island for later pickup by the U.S. Air Force or Navy.

In early April, My Tho was hit with rumors that the VC were ready to launch human-wave attacks on the city. The men in the agency compound finished shredding classified documents and left for Saigon in the fastest vehicles available. The compound was ransacked that night before the Nhung guards could get control and roust the intruders. I went up the next day to close it permanently.

The staff was assembled in the courtyard when I arrived, apparently ready for what they anticipated would be an inquisition into how the compound walls had been breached and some of the compound property stolen. I listened patiently to their stories and sent the senior Vietnamese staffer at the compound to get the province chief's aide-de-camp. When he left, I told the remaining staffers to line up outside the office and come in to see me one by one. With four exceptions I was going to pay off all of them and dismiss them from U.S. government employment.

I had finished paying off the staff, who were quickly leaving to put away their money, when the aide-de-camp arrived. I told him that I was turning the compound over to the province chief in forty-five minutes, and I wanted someone there to take responsibility, plus a guard force. The aide-de-camp left, and I dispatched the four men who had been designated KIP to get their families and start making their way to Can Tho. I had closed the compound in a little over two hours, compared with the two days to close Vi Thanh.

As I waited for the province chief, I walked around the compound. My Tho, the first province south of Saigon, had been used as a support base for some Saigon operations. The compound was an old French villa, comfortably outfitted with nice furniture. A dozen vehicles were parked in the motor pool/garage, the offices had typewriters, copying machines, and photo equipment, the game room was filled with movies and recreational equipment, and the kitchen had a vast inventory of stainless steel cookery. The province chief arrived, out of breath; I told him that I was turning the compound over to him. He signed a receipt handwritten on a piece of notebook paper and I left with the remaining money and the staff receipts in a box.

As I was being driven out the gate I observed the province chief, anxious to see exactly what he had been given, hiking up his pants and walking into his new facility.

A few days later I left the consulate in Can Tho with Sarge at the end of a long workday and we went to the Delta Club for dinner. Glenn R., one of the senior officers at the base, was the club manager. For weeks he had almost given away perishable items. A T-bone steak dinner with a bottle of wine cost less than a dollar. Mac joined us and the three of us had a feast. In pain from overeating, I returned to my apartment before curfew and went to bed early.

The first explosion jarred the apartment building, and I was awake immediately. Several more explosions followed. I decided that the explosions were on the other side of the consulate, and my apartment wasn't in danger. Jim D. came on the handheld radio and called Don K., who was on duty in the base area of the consulate. Don said the explosions were artillery rounds landing in the shanty area down the road. He couldn't imagine why the VC were firing there.

Jim asked for a head count. As we were calling in, Don broke in to say that a fire had started near the impact area. It was growing fast and coming toward the consulate.

With almost everyone accounted for, Jim received a preliminary report from a base asset at General Hung's headquarters.

The South Vietnamese military's best guess was that the VC were firing rockets randomly into town as harassment.

Don came back on the radio and said the fire was building in intensity. He could feel the heat when he opened one of the rear windows by Phyllis's desk. We heard several more explosions.

I got up, dressed, and went to the roof of the apartment building. The flames raging beyond the consulate were higher than any building in the area. The street below was becoming clogged with people trying to get away. Sirens went off on the other side of my building as fire trucks tried to make their way through the mob.

The wind was swirling and tossing around ashes and bits of charred wood. The fire was so intense that it was pulling air into it, but a natural breeze was blowing our way and the wall of flames was leaning in our direction. There was no doubt that the fire was heading toward the consulate.

Several helicopters with searchlights passed over. The noise from the street below competed with the loud popping from the fire.

Glenn lived in an apartment immediately across from the consulate. He confirmed to Jim over the radio that the fire appeared to be heading in their direction.

Don, knowing Glenn lived close by, said, "Ah, good to know I'm not alone in this part of town."

I said that I was also nearby.

Glenn volunteered to go across the street to help Don. Jim told the radio communicator and me to join them so that, if the consulate had to be abandoned, we could shred the files in the vault and remove or destroy the communications equipment.

The fire was getting closer, Don said, and the building was getting hotter.

I went down to the street level, and the guard in front of the building helped me open the door against the screaming people outside. Suddenly I was out in the middle of the masses. I was initially carried away up the street before I got my feet under me and began pushing my way against the crowd. It was like swimming up a raging river. If I stopped pushing forward, I was swept back. People were carrying personal items on bikes and carts, on top of their heads, in baskets. Children were screaming. Several pedicabs, filled with household items, were mixed in with the crowd. An armored personnel carrier, leading fire trucks, came down the street. Sirens were wailing. People were screaming.

The guard at the front gate of the consulate helped me get inside and pushed away people who were trying to get in through my legs. Glenn had already arrived, after a struggle just to get across the street. In time the communicator also arrived.

It was hot in the base offices and even hotter near the rear windows. The fire covered the whole skyline to the west. Ash swirled around the building. We heard loud popping and burning noises. Sirens were still going off pell-mell in the street over the roar and screams of the crowd.

The communicator went into the commo room and Don, Glenn, and I went into the vault and began shredding the personnel files on the most sensitive of the active operations in the delta. We had a sense of urgency and moved quickly and quietly. Periodically we ventured out of the vault to look at the fire. It was still intense, but, as we finished shredding, it did not appear to be gaining on the consulate.

Don went down to the commo room to help the communicator prepare items to be destroyed or removed.

After he left, Jim called and told us to destroy the money in the safe. The finance officer gave us the combination over the radio. Soaked in sweat, we went into the finance office where, against the near wall, sat an old black Wells Fargo–type safe, with a dial on one of the double doors and a heavy brass handle on the other. We tried the combination and pushed the handle down after spinning the dial for the final turn. Slowly we opened the doors and there—from the bottom to the top of the safe—were stacks of money.

Glenn whistled and we both stared inside the safe. I had never before seen that much money in one place—U.S. tens, twenties, and hundreds, plus Vietnamese piasters. A person could work hard all his life and never make the amount of money that was on even one shelf in that safe. It was a sight right out of Hollywood, a CIA safe filled with money.

We could hear the popping from the fire. I wiped sweat from my forehead. Glenn picked up the radio and asked Jim D. if he was sure he wanted us to destroy all this money.

"Yep," he said.

Picking up a box of piasters, we went to work at the shredder, but it was quickly obvious that it would take us hours. We had to take apart each bundle and separate the money into piles small enough to get through the shredder. So we rolled a couple of fifty-five-gallon drums equipped with thermal chemicals for emergency destruction of paper into the finance office and filled them with the remaining Vietnamese money.

We put the American money into cardboard boxes. There seemed to be something patently wrong about destroying hundreds of thousands of dollars of U.S. currency. We told Jim that if we had to abandon the consulate, we would destroy the Vietnamese money in the drums and take the U.S. money, with the communications stuff, to Glenn's apartment across the street.

Don came back upstairs and said we were crazy if we thought we could get across that street, still clogged with people, while carrying boxes of money.

"It's only paper, burn it, shred it," he said, looking at Glenn and then me.

Standing in front of the safe, I said, "We can't do that."

"Why not?" asked Don.

"Just can't. It's not right. I come from the South and we just don't do things like that down there. Just look at all that money. We'll put it in the trunk of one of the cars down by the motor pool and we'll drive across the street. It's taxpayers' money."

"It's paper," Don yelled.

"It's money," I said.

So we carried the U.S. taxpayers' money down into the commo room and stacked the boxes alongside the equipment Don and the communicator had prepared for removal. We went back upstairs. The fire had not come closer and appeared to be diminishing, although a wall of flame still covered the area behind the consulate. We had done all we could.

I got a cup of coffee and slumped in a desk chair. Glenn went to the roof where the Congen had set up a crisis center to watch the fire. MacNamara was wearing a flak jacket and a helmet with a large white star painted on the front. He told a consular officer later that he considered himself equivalent to a brigadier—one-star—general in the U.S. Army.

With the fire in the near distance, the star on that man's helmet looked to Glenn like a reflective bull's-eye. Apparently Mac-Namara was seeking some visual inference of rank at that significant point in his life, but "foolish" was the only word that came to Glenn's mind. Glenn told MacNamara that he was leaving the consulate to see that his Filipino engineer contractors were safe. Seeming to take that as a request, MacNamara was debating the safety factors of someone's leaving the consulate as Glenn turned and left.

The fire eventually subsided and the crowd in the street in front thinned out. As we found out later, the fire came to the edge of a small river and burned itself out. Shortly before dawn I returned to my apartment for a few hours' sleep.

When I returned to the consulate at mid-morning, the finance officer told me that he thought my concern about destroying taxpayers' money was silly. He said it was newly printed currency that could just be written off the books. Since the U.S. government still controlled it, the money was just paper.

"Easy for you to say," I replied. "You have never been told to shred a million dollars before, or however much was there. To you it might be just paper. Not to me. You don't burn money."

"You serious?" asked the finance officer.

"Yep," I said. " 'Cause you know what, one of these days I'm going to be low on funds, maybe broke, and I don't want to feel any worse, knowing I once just burned money. Besides, look at me! Listen! You don't burn money."

Later that morning an officer in from Chau Doc who had been unaccounted for the previous night—he had slept through everything—came into the consulate. Still unaware of what had gone on, he told me I looked like hell; life in Can Tho was obviously too hectic for me, and I ought to go back to Vi Thanh.

I continued regular visits to General Hai, commander of the ARVN 7th Division. He rarely smiled. Usually he was sitting in a wooden lawn chair beside his desk, half hidden in cigarette smoke, when I visited his field headquarters near the Cambodian border. Our times together often involved his recollection of what he described as the "USA's haphazard" military involvement in his country.

His words usually ran something like: "There is enormous difference between our cultures, yet you Americans expect us to think and to act like you. In fact, we do not like you or your policies . . . you hear me? We don't like you telling us what to do. But we need your help in order to survive and we know that it is to your advantage to see us survive. That shouldn't give you a right to meddle in our affairs, our culture. You are here like a visiting three-ring circus. Who asked for the newspeople? And USAID? We were doing okay before. Where did all these 'civic action' things come from? What were they? Nation building? The Vietnamese culture goes back to the beginning of time, and you are telling us how to live and work and govern? Does this make sense?

"And why wasn't your military in Cambodia? The North Vietnamese were, why weren't you? If you came all this way to stop the spread of Communism, why didn't you go on into Cambodia, where there are Communist camps, and knock them out? Why aren't you in Laos? Why don't you use some of your big equipment to plug up the Ho Chi Minh trail through Laos? It's a simple military situation here. Simple. Why are you acting like such fools?

"We Vietnamese think you are fools. What do you say to that, CIA man? You are a fool, working for a fool organization."

I sat quietly, although I thought, Where did this word "fools" come from? The poet Tennyson, and now from this South Vietnamese general. Tens of thousands of U.S. servicemen had died trying to keep his corrupt government afloat. They were not fools.

In time, after the general had called me names, after he had ranted about the way the war had been fought, often repeating himself, had blown himself out, we talked about the here and now—the situation in his area of operation.

In those meetings at his headquarters the general and I had become comfortable with one another. Not friendly, but comfortable; we knew our place. Possibly that was the result of my two years in Laos, where I had made many Oriental friends, or maybe it was that the general noticed my sympathy and respect for his sense of duty, honor, and country at a time when others were thinking only about themselves. Perhaps we were comfortable with each other because I was his most frequent visitor.

Throughout early April the North Vietnamese Army met only occasional resistance and continued to close on Saigon from the west, north, and east. Although some ARVN forces, especially the Hoi Chanh special units and elite regulars, went down fighting, the South Vietnamese could not stop the NVA's progress.

Sen. Frank Church, speaking for the U.S. Senate on 10 April, said that enough was enough, the South Vietnamese military was on its own. Congress rejected President Gerald R. Ford's request for $720 million in military support and $250 million in economic support to South Vietnam. It allocated money only to evacuate Americans from South Vietnam.

The next day I flew by Air America helicopter to meet with Hai. He did not rise from his lawn chair to greet me when I walked into his office. Almost out of sight in a smoke cloud, he said slowly that my government stank like leper shit. Senator Church was worse than Hitler. Americans had no honor. Our military violated the universal soldier's code of conduct by turning its back on a comrade in arms, abandoning him on the battlefield.

He stood up and came up close to me. His eyes were red. His hand rested on the grip of his pistol and he stared at me, loathing and anger visible in his expression. He tensed, reached a point of action, and his fingers tightened around the gun handle. Then the moment passed and he sighed. "I should kill you," he said, "in the name of all the good men who died in this war. I should kill you because your government did not try to win this war."

I stood my ground, but I was shaken. Quietly I said, "The war is almost over. The fighting has been done. You have to accept the ways things turned out. You have to accept fate."

"I heard your Kissinger said the other day that Vietnam was finished. Does he know we're still here?" Hai asked.

I did not respond. The general finally shrugged and, speaking in a voice that displayed no energy, he gave me an update on enemy deployments he had obtained from an aircraft observation of the Cambodian/South Vietnam border.

When there was nothing more to say, I took my leave.

— TWENTY —

Promises and Confrontations

Every morning more and more South Vietnamese gathered at the front gate of the consulate in hopes of arranging travel to the United States. As news spread about the NVA's advances, the crowd became more desperate. Reaching out to show me letters and pictures, many people pleaded with me. Anxious to avoid involvement, I never paused or made eye contact. I worked my way to the front gate and a local guard opened it slightly to let me through.

Glenn R. approached me in the consulate one day and asked if I would consider adopting two kids. He knew that my wife and I had adopted two Thai children. Sarcastically I thanked him for thinking of me, but I had too much work to do to get involved in something that personal and told him no. He insisted and said that the mother of the children was in a small interview room off the lobby of the consulate. It wouldn't take long to hear her story.

Glenn led me to the room, where I met a beautiful Vietnamese woman in her late twenties wearing a demure *ao dai*, the traditional local dress. Speaking softly in broken English, she said she had two American-Asian children, a daughter age four and a son, two. She loved them very much and was concerned that the North Vietnamese would treat them badly when they took over the country.

"The Communists slaughtered all half-French children when they won in North Vietnam," she said. "They will do the same in the South with children who are half-American. I do not want my children to die." She started to speak again, opened her mouth, closed it, and then, still looking at me, started to cry, wide-eyed and sorrowful.

278

After five years in that war, I knew the only way to keep my sanity was to avoid agonizing over the suffering of others. So I remained detached and told the woman that we did not know for sure that the North Vietnamese were going to occupy the delta. People in Saigon who knew more than either of us had said we were okay down here.

"You do not know," she said. "I know that in a matter of weeks a North Vietnamese man will be sitting in this room, talking with me, deciding the fate of my children—like you are now. Please take them. Please. Let them live. Send them to your wife."

I finally said that I would come by to meet them but could not promise anything. My main interest was in getting out of that room and back to my work.

I'm not sure why, but I did stop by her rowhouse that night. She had drawn a map. The house was on the way to the airport and easy to find. The two children were outside. The little girl, with her intelligent, sincere eyes, reminded me of my daughter, Mim. The boy, a toddler, was active, loud, inquisitive, and unafraid. They were grand-looking, healthy, everyday children. The girl escorted me inside, but the mother was sullen and did not move to greet me. Without smiling, she flicked her hand toward the couch, motioning for me to sit. She took a chair across the room and introduced the children. The boy finally broke the awkward silence by climbing up the back of his mother's chair and falling, with a thud, into her lap.

The woman ruffled the boy's hair and renewed her efforts to get me to take her children. I told her that I could not do that now—the North Vietnamese were not at our doorsteps; they were to the north. She would not want to send the children away unless she knew the Americans were leaving. Because I was still here, I reasoned, no decision had to be made now. We could wait.

"Okay," she said, "but, if before you come back, the delta is attacked by the North Vietnamese, I will take my children to you at the U.S. consulate."

At the consulate that night I got a telephone call through to Brenda in Taipei. Excited to hear about the kids, she started asking questions and making plans at the same time. Then she paused and said that the woman must understand that, if we adopt her children, she cannot come back later and say, "I got out and I want them back."

"I will not be used," Brenda said. "Look after yourself, and tell that woman I understand her terrible anguish and we will give those children a good home."

I relayed this to the woman the following night when I went back to visit. She whispered, "Thank you."

The next day, 15 April, I flew back to the 7th Division at first light. As usual, the general harangued me for the conduct of the United States. "Where are South Vietnam's friends now when she needs them? Who can I call on? The enemy is at our door, my country is on the verge of being occupied by a hostile neighbor. Who will come to our aid?"

On the other side of the Cambodian border, his observation plane had noticed a concentration of North Vietnamese that was beginning to swell in number. He said new heavy equipment was arriving twenty-four hours a day.

"Where are your bombers? We have them in the open. Now is the time to get them. They are marshaling in front of my men. I need help. Help me, CIA man."

As usual, I left him sitting in one of the wooden lawn chairs in his office, looking at me through his cigarette smoke.

Returning to the base, I was late for a general meeting with the chief of station, Tom Polgar. We were to learn later that Polgar had come to Can Tho specifically to investigate the reason why General Timmies, his principal liaison officer with the ARVN, had changed his assessment of the defensibility of the delta after a recent visit to the base. I had spoken with Timmies and had gone with him when he met with General Nam, ARVN commander for the delta, for a briefing on the military situation. Timmies, a venerable old soldier who had been around the South Vietnamese Army for decades and had known most of its commanders since they were junior officers, had developed a Saigon attitude—elitist, urban, theoretical—about life in the countryside. He did not want me in the room when he met with Nam, but I knew that Nam was giving Timmies a picture of the situation that tracked with what his commanders at Supreme Command in Saigon wanted the U.S. government to hear.

Later, on my own, I arranged for Timmies to meet with Hung, whose briefing differed from the normal ARVN party line. Hung said that the South Vietnamese could not defend the delta, and the North Vietnamese knew that. If all the South Vietnamese Marines and Rangers and other regulars and irregulars, who had lost their positions in the north and were streaming into Saigon, were brought to the delta, organized, and put in fighting position, they could not hold. They did not have the right supplies and felt they had been abandoned.

Polgar wanted to neutralize this opinion at the source. His position was that the North Vietnamese would not occupy Saigon and could not take the delta.

As I walked into the meeting I had to take a seat close to the front. Like Balls before him, Polgar said there would be generations of other case officers after us assigned to the delta, that thing about future generations of case officers apparently being a catchphrase in Saigon. He said, unequivocally, "South Vietnam will survive."

From the back of the room, Tom F. opined that the resolve of the ARVN to hold out was in question. I agreed, adding that I thought the North Vietnamese were certainly intent on taking Saigon and the delta by force. North Vietnam was run by military people who had been fighting the war for decades. They were unlikely to sue for peace when they could win.

Polgar was unmoved and ended the meeting with a positive statement about the rocky but generally bright future of South Vietnam.

Later, after Polgar left, Tom F. sulked at the Coconut Palms Bar. "Either that guy is crazy or we are."

I said, "He's the chief of station, Tom."

"Well," he conceded, "then we're crazy. But crazy or not, I know this, the North Vietnamese are going to win this war, flat out, whether that desk warrior likes it or not."

We eventually heard an interesting story. Polgar spoke fluent Hungarian and was meeting privately with Hungarian members of the ICCS, the peacekeeping force in Vietnam. They told him the North Vietnamese had no plans to occupy Saigon or the delta. This same information was being passed by Anatoly Dobrynin, the Soviet ambassador in Washington, D.C., directly to U.S. Secretary of State Henry Kissinger. This apparently orchestrated disinformation from two separate sources made a convincing case to American policy makers on the viability of the South Vietnamese government.

The information was not totally incorrect. The North Vietnamese did not hope to take Saigon within the year and had no occupation plans for the delta. But they never wavered from their intent to occupy all of South Vietnam in time. And the Government of South Vietnam was not viable. Corrupt and totally out of touch with its farmer citizenry, there was no hope that it would survive.

Polgar, however, and possibly Kissinger believed the Hungarians and the Soviets against all reason.

On 17 April 1975, Phnom Penh fell to the Khmer Rouge—Cambodia was in the hands of the Communists.

I began visiting General Hai every day. He reported that North Vietnamese forces continued to assemble just over the Cambodian border. They were bringing in armor, portable bridges, and artillery. He also said fresh troops had arrived, probably, he thought, to lead the attack forces against Saigon. It was the only realistic target for them, the general said. They were assembling more of a force than they needed just to attack the 7th Division or to secure Route 4. Once they launched there was nothing but open marshy country—the Plain of Reeds—between the border and the southern city gates of Saigon.

Jim D. put his hands over his ears when I briefed him on Hai's prediction about a pending attack on Saigon. He didn't want to hear it. Saigon Station continued to put out intelligence reports supporting a negotiated cease-fire, and there were enough other pessimistic reports out of the ARVN. Possibly, he suggested, the North Vietnamese planned to use that force as a cocked gun at the head of the South Vietnamese government to force negotiations. I said, nope, those NVA troops out there in front of General Hai were going to occupy Saigon. I suggested to him that U.S. politicians in Washington and the U.S. government people in Saigon, who were calling the shots, thought only in terms of indoor work such as negotiations and compromises. "I know this war out here in the countryside," I told him, "and it's about over."

A U.S. Navy armada was assembling off the coast of South Vietnam. It could have been considered a deterrent to major North Vietnam attacks in the Saigon environs, but we understood that its primary function was to ensure the safe evacuation of Americans from the country. Mac, flying along the coast one day in an Air America chopper, said he could see Navy ships to the edge of the horizon.

Under pressure from Washington, U.S. Ambassador Graham Martin ordered all but essential personnel to leave the country. We were reduced to twelve officers at the CIA base in the consulate—the only U.S. government facility still open outside Saigon.

I visited General Hung occasionally in Can Tho. He was aware of the military situation throughout the country, but he remained calm and resigned as he waited for the outcome. Not one of the delta's sixteen provincial capitals was under North Vietnamese control. Possibly half of the population of South Vietnam was there and out of harm's way. He would sit and wait.

During our 19 April meeting, General Hai told me there did not appear to be as many new additions to the North Vietnamese forces collecting across the Cambodian border. They were repositioning in their assembly area. He thought that when they began to line up with the new troops close to the border behind the bridge units and heavy attack tanks, their push to Saigon would be imminent. It would take them seven days to get from their sanctuaries in Cambodia across the Plain of Reeds to the underside of Saigon. The general's 7th Division forces could only slow their progress.

"We cannot stop them," Hai said. "There are too many, we are too few."

On the morning of 21 April, Xiam Luc, one of the last ARVN strongholds north of Saigon, fell after a heroic stand against a vastly superior North Vietnamese force. The president of South Vietnam, Nguyen Van Thieu, resigned later that day.

I flew out to 7th Division headquarters 22 April. It was dark inside Hai's office. He was sitting in his regular chair near a small table and couch, and smoking.

"The NVA's heavy tanks are lining up. The new, young troops are falling in formation behind them. They are getting ready to launch. Saigon will fall to the North Vietnamese in seven days," he predicted. "29 April 1975."

Raising his cup of lukewarm coffee, he proposed a toast to all the soldiers who had died and to our future, but he did not smile.

The remaining base officers were in the consulate when I returned that afternoon. They gathered in Jim's office and listened quietly when I reported on my visit with General Hai.

"A week," Jim D. said when I finished. "He's saying attacks on Saigon will start next Tuesday, 29 April." Over the past month, he had developed an appreciation for the 7th Division commander's reporting. Although Hai was morose, the information obtained by his observation planes and his analysis of that information had proved to be accurate, corroborated by overhead and other special intelligence.

"That's a shame," the base chief continued to muse as he looked off into space. Finally, he said, "Saigon doesn't want to hear this. They've sent out more developments on the negotiated peace theme today. Do we try to get anyone's attention back in Washington?" He paused. "As if they care. They've already given up on South Vietnam."

"First," Mac asked, "do we believe it?"

"I do," I said without hesitation. "Saigon will fall in seven days." No mysterious force, no promise by the Hungarians, nothing the CIA leadership in Saigon could imagine would prevent it. The North Vietnamese had more than one hundred thousand soldiers in an ever-tightening circle around Saigon. North Vietnamese would occupy the city in seven days. Standing in the base chief's office, I was sure of it.

Jim polled the others in the office. No one doubted Hai's information.

We had seven days.

In the map room I sat down at my desk and began to draft the report of my meeting with Hai. Jim asked that I keep it lean, leading with the general's statement that he believed Saigon would fall in seven days, followed by the general's reasoning that the North Vietnamese were preparing to launch from their sanctuaries in Cambodia west/southwest of the city and that they would be moving through an area where they could not hide. Their intentions were clear to Hai. They'd get to Saigon in seven days because ARVN 7th Division forces would not be able to stop them.

At dusk, after some small changes to my draft, we sent the report to Saigon and Washington.

We gathered in Jim D.'s office the next morning to receive our work assignments for what we considered to be our last week in Vietnam. Jim told me to continue visiting General Hai until he evacuated his headquarters, which was on the edge of the North Vietnamese advance, and to work out arrangements with Air America to have enough helicopters on hand for evacuation in the event of an attack against Can Tho. The South Vietnamese military's ability to provide for our safety could suddenly deteriorate. Mac and the Sarge would continue to collect most of the KIP in safe houses around town and in outlying areas.

Tom was to work on ways to get the KIP out of the country. He told Bill A. to pursue the possibility of a back-door escape route through the island off Rach Gia suggested by the ex-GI and his Vietnamese girlfriend. In developing that option, Bill was to truck the base's speedboat from Can Tho to Rach Gia and position barrels of fuel on the island for possible use by Air America and boat crews.

Jim would work with MacNamara to come up with a practical evacuation plan for the remaining Americans at the consulate. We were to stay in contact with Phyllis. It was no time for performing missions of mercy or focusing on anything but the job at hand. Jim wanted us to coordinate with him on everything we did. We were to carry our diplomatic passports wherever we went. We were to leave no loose ends. If we had to go "right now," we would just get up and go.

"There is to be no 'Oh, wait, there's something I've got to do across town,' " he said. I thought about the two children.

Our primary rally point for the evacuation was the CIA housing compound and club, the Coconut Palms. Tom sent a work crew there later in the day to cut down all the trees around the tennis court in order to facilitate helicopter landings.

After the meeting I helped arrange with O. B., the CIA air operations officer in Saigon, for three Air America helicopters to remain in the delta twenty-four hours a day, with at least two parked on the Coconut Palms tennis court at night. Pilots would rotate back to Saigon every other day.

I visited General Hung in Can Tho later that day. He reported that North Vietnamese forces had launched across the border near General Hai's forces early in the morning and were heading toward Saigon. Hung had begun to direct the limited South Vietnamese Air Force and artillery resources available to him in the delta against the advancing enemy, but, as yet, the North Vietnamese advance had not been impeded. He remained calm but kept his family close by.

Jim D. and MacNamara were not able to agree on a joint evacuation plan for the consulate. Sitting around Phyllis's desk, we sometimes heard them yelling in MacNamara's office below us. One confrontation went something like this:

JIM: "The safest, surest means of evacuation is by helicopter."

MACNAMARA (louder): "There are not enough helicopters to go around, there are too many Vietnamese that we must get out."

JIM (louder): "What Vietnamese do you have to get out?"

MACNAMARA (still louder): "I do not answer to *you*. Listen to what I'm saying. If we have to evacuate, this consulate goes out by boat down the Bassac River. Period. End of discussion."

JIM (softer): "That is ridiculous. We might have to fight our way out, and we are not combatants. We get up in the air, and we go out by helicopters."

MACNAMARA (softer): "We cannot control the helicopters. I have had my experiences with your Air America helicopter pilots. They have the last say. They could leave us all here. They are wild, uncontrollable animals, the Air America people. We control our own destiny if we go out by boat. I have many, many Vietnamese—and Cambodians—I am obligated to get out, and going by boat is the only way we're going to do it. I am the senior man on the scene here, do not forget."

JIM (even voice, determined): "I have my people to protect, and I have helicopters. My people go out by helicopter."

MACNAMARA (screaming): "You will do what I say or, God as my witness, I'll have you out of here. You—hear—me? [We heard a crash, like an ashtray hitting the floor.] Get out of my office."

In normal times the shouting and bitter wrangling would not have happened. But it was a situation of unusual proportions, and in view of the personalities of the participants, it was not unexpected. Jim D. was a large, forceful, competitive Irishman, a Georgetown law school graduate and a world-class tennis player. Two of his sons were All-American tennis players at Stanford University. Terry MacNamara, a career diplomat, had firm ideas of his responsibilities and powers as the senior American official on the scene. He was intelligent and tenacious, and he did not back down. Both men sincerely believed in their separate positions.

MacNamara's plan, however, was dangerous. It was sixty miles from Can Tho down the Bassac River to the South China Sea, and a boat filled with Americans certainly would draw attention. It could be overtaken by South Vietnamese forces or, worse, attacked by VC or North Vietnamese who occupied positions along the river. Not long before, a base officer had been shot in the head while riding on a boat near Can Tho.

Second, MacNamara was not an experienced boatman. He had no idea how to negotiate the navigable channels or of their locations, especially where the river lets out into the ocean. And he didn't have access to the radio frequencies of Air America, the U.S. Navy, and ARVN units. He would have been completely out of communication during his sixty-mile run down the river. Obviously his plan had not been developed by anyone with a military background.

Third, MacNamara's plan did not provide for the safety of the CIA officers. We had no official cover. If we were captured by the North Vietnamese, as was entirely possible, MacNamara suggested we tell them that we were USAID engineers, which would not have held up during any type of serious interrogation.

Although Jim explained all those points, MacNamara was not to be dissuaded. He approached some of the base officers in an effort to obtain their support for his plan. Each one told MacNamara that his plan was crazy. He did not approach me, but possibly saw me as an extension of Air America and a certain adversary.

Our original support officer had recently left to take his family out of the country and was replaced by an officer from one of the abandoned CIA bases to the north. When the old support officer departed, he left all the keys to the supply warehouses with Phyllis. She tried to get the new man to take them, but he told her to get rid of them herself.

"Get rid of them?" she asked, not knowing exactly what that meant.

"We're only twelve here now. We aren't running any operations. We don't need supplies. I'm busy. Help me here." And he walked into Jim's office.

She was standing by her desk, looking down at the pile when Sarge and I told her we'd take care of them for her. We raked the well-marked rings of keys, plus a book listing safe combinations, off her desk and into a shoe box.

"Whoever owns these keys," I said, "owns what's inside those warehouses."

Phyllis said, "I don't bloody care. I just want to clear my desk. Thank you."

There were a lot of keys, maybe a hundred. Glenn, as head of the Delta Club, was aware of an impressive amount of supplies on hand in the warehouses. He was the custodian of a few storage bins which held equipment passed down from club to club. During the height of the war, when hundreds of thousands of American troops, officials, and contract workers had been in Vietnam, there were clubs in every province—USAID clubs, officers clubs, enlisted clubs, Special Forces clubs, MACV clubs, private engineering company clubs, hospital clubs, and so on. As the Americans began to pull out, various clubs were consolidated, and the best items, including jukeboxes, slot machines, bar accessories, restaurant equipment, lights, signs, and stereo components, were turned over to the consulate clubs that remained. As the last club proprietor in the delta, Glenn was now owner of the primo of primo equipment left behind. Other merely very good bar equipment was stored in the warehouses.

So, if there was so much interesting stuff just from the clubs, who knew what else was out there in the warehouses. We could only imagine all the sexy CIA stuff we would find.

When we arrived at the compound, the guard at the gate wanted to see some identification. We showed him our embassy badges, but he said it was a restricted area and that we needed special permission to get inside. We fished around in the box of keys until we found the badge of the departed logistic chief, which satisfied the guard. He waved us through.

We drove up and down past the warehouses as we tried to reconcile the building numbers with the tags on the keys. Finally we stopped and opened one warehouse with a key that was clearly marked. It was filled with weapons—crates of carbines, M-16s, Swedish Ks, AK-47s. In a fenced-off area were special sniper rifles. There were pistols with silencers, pistols with scopes, and pistols that converted into rifles and concealed weapons. In another warehouse we found knives, machetes, night-vision equipment, more scopes, binoculars, and web gear.

There were refrigerated warehouses and air-conditioned warehouses. We discovered electronics equipment—what looked like hundreds of different types of radios—projectors, furniture, typewriters, pool tables, linoleum tile, baby cribs, kitchen stoves, furniture, generators, crystal, silverware, maps, uniforms, claymore mines, books, Bibles, and hundreds of unmarked boxes. The motor pool had new Jeeps and cars, some with armor, some with oversized engines, and some with oversized tires.

"It's all ours, Sarge, all ours," I said. "I think that when I was a Boy Scout, if I had known there would be a chance to go through something like this and pick out anything I wanted, I couldn't have waited. You know what I mean? I would have been anxious all my life to get here. Is this a boy's dream or what?"

Eventually we left the complex and tipped our hats to the guard. We had not taken a single thing; there was nothing there we needed.

Amazing, I thought as we drove back to the consulate. All that money we were told to destroy, all the goods in those warehouses—amazing. The sheer volume was staggering. And all of it would be left behind in seven days.

── TWENTY-ONE ──

KIP Collection

I visited the mother and her kids almost every night. At first the children were suspicious of me because their mother was so distraught when I was around, but the boy's natural curiosity brought him closer and closer to me until he came naturally into my lap when I arrived. Before long he was taking off my glasses and investigating what I had in my pockets. The girl often sat beside me and held my hand. She examined my fingers and occasionally looked up at me. She spoke some English and usually looked at my lips as I talked.

The mother always sat in her chair across the room. She had taken the kids out of school and kept small plastic suitcases packed with their clothes by the front door. On advice of the Consular Section, I had her sign a note giving up her rights to the children. The note and the children's birth certificates were in one of the bags.

It was clear after a few visits that the mother hated me. My countrymen had gotten her pregnant, twice, and left, twice. Both men had said that they would marry her, but they had dropped out of touch. And now my country had abandoned her country, had dropped out of touch, and broken its promises.

Her comments were in this vein, "Is this the American way to be a friend? You don't care about us. You used us. You. Yes, you. You and your countrymen. I cry inside all the time. I will die soon because of you. You have destroyed my life. My country. We trusted you. You used us and now you leave. 'Good-bye, Vietnam. Sorry.' "

I told her I could not explain how the war had turned out the way it had, but I promised her that, if I had to be evacuated, I would come by for the children. She would probably know if an evacuation was under way. I told her to stay in the house. She was not to try to bring them to the consulate because I could miss them on the way. If we left, I told her, I would have little time. The kids had to be at home.

Sometimes the girl went over to her mother as we talked and wiped her eyes or held her hand or leaned against her. She looked back at me, confused, unable to understand what made her mother cry, why exactly she and her brother might be leaving with me someday.

The boy could not remain serious for long, and he squirmed. When he slowed down, his body tiring from a full afternoon of rowdiness, I knew it was time to go home.

After a while the woman stopped seeing me off when I left. Usually the girl was the last one I saw as I got in my Jeep and left. She stood with her arms wedged in the door frame, her brightly colored suitcase near her feet. She waved as I turned the corner and looked back.

We had four days to go. All of our delta KIP were identified and in separate areas. Bill A., assisted by Larry D., an officer from a closed base to the north, had visited the island off Rach Gia several times and made a convincing case to Jim D. that it was ready to receive our KIP if evacuation through Saigon or by boat out to sea was not possible.

Jim sent Glenn to Saigon that day with what turned out to be three missions. One was to arrange for the evacuation of fifty delta KIP who had homes or families in or near Saigon. He was to try to put them and their families on aircraft leaving Tan Son Nhut Airport in Saigon. His second mission was to arrange for a U.S. Navy ship, with a landing platform, to position itself off the coast somewhere near the mouth of the Mekong as a receiving station for Air America helicopters shuttling people out of the delta. The third mission was to talk with CIA management in Saigon and, if possible, Ambassador Martin, in an effort to get permission for us to evacuate our KIP to the Navy platform, to the island, or through Tan Son Nhut.

The same day, I went out to the 7th Division area on an Air America helicopter. General Hai's headquarters had been evacuated. The tents and building of the command complex had been torn down. All I could see on the ground were scars from the old structures. Deserted bunkers ringed the area. Off in the distance, near the North Vietnamese line of advance, I saw large dust columns like those made by armored vehicles crossing open fields.

Returning to General Hung's headquarters at Can Tho, I found the general serene, as usual. He said that the 7th Division was mobile and that the North Vietnamese forces were large and not temporizing. They were moving aggressively toward Saigon.

Glenn telephoned Jim from Saigon. He said there was bedlam at the embassy. Everybody was talking; no one was listening. No one, other than a few close associates, was able to see Ambassador Martin. Word was that he was not acting rationally; he was walking around in a daze and unresponsive. His secretary had been asking people for amphetamines. No one wanted to make decisions, so the ambassador's existing orders not to facilitate evacuation of Vietnamese civilians by any element of the embassy had not changed. People were getting out, however, through Tan Son Nhut, Glenn said, and he had been successful in getting the fifty delta KIP placed on a nonscheduled flight that would leave the country within the next couple of days.

Jim told Glenn to continue working on getting a Navy platform and permission to evacuate our KIP. He added, "Oh, and Glenn, don't let them forget about us down here."

Early the following morning, Sunday, 27 April, the few of us who were left gathered in Jim's office.

He began by saying, "Things are deteriorating as fast as we predicted. Cable traffic this morning indicates to me that no one knows what's happening. Everyone in Saigon is breathless, confused. As far as I can tell, here, we're ready to go. We'll have two Air America helicopters working for us today, and Parker says we have good pilots. If we get the word to evacuate right now— Parker, Mac, Sarge will work on sending the KIP out of the country by helicopter. Everyone else goes to Coconut Palms." He paused and looked around the room. "We assemble there and we go out with MacNamara by boat. That's the plan for now. We send the KIP out by helicopter and we go out with the Congen by boat. He has a couple of landing craft tied up at the State Department compound that are ready to make the trip down the Bassac.

He's got the Marines and boat pilots, and God knows he needs our help. That's what happens if that telephone rings right now with orders to get out of Dodge." He looked down at a pad on his desk and made a check mark.

"Number two. But we can't wait for that telephone to ring to do something. We got to decide what to do with our KIP, and we gotta do it. Our options are: One, we can move them to the island off Rach Gia. Two, we can send them out to the U.S. Navy. Or three, we can send them to Saigon in hopes of getting them out through Tan Son Nhut. We can just start doing one of these three things or we can try again to get Saigon's permission. What do you think?" he asked the group.

Tom suggested that sending the KIP to the Navy ships immediately was best, going to the island was number two, and sending them through Saigon was a distant, improbable third. He agreed that doing nothing—waiting for the evacuation order—was waiting for events to overtake us. Mac suggested that we get Glenn in Saigon to try one more time to get permission to move the Vietnamese out to the Navy and, if he couldn't, that we move them to the island.

Jim said Mac's plan works. Glenn would be contacted that morning with instructions to get permission from someone in the embassy, or at Tan Son Nhut airfield, for us to move the KIP to U.S. Navy ships offshore.

As a backup, Bill A. would take a helicopter to Rach Gia and continue work to prepare the island as a safe haven. In either event, we were moving our KIP the next day, 28 April. We had them at launch sites, we had two helicopters at our disposal, and the clock was ticking.

In the morning I would load up one helicopter with the group from Chau Doc and either head east to the armada of U.S. Navy ships at sea or go south with the group to meet up with Bill A. on the island. So as not to cause panic, all the KIP would be told that they were being moved to an evacuation point near Tan Son Nhut airport in Saigon.

Jim said, "There it is. Go out and make it work."

Several days before, I had moved from the apartment near the consulate to the Coconut Palms, the agency compound in Can Tho, which was on the way to the airport and convenient to the kids' house. I had left instructions with the guards at my former apartment house to send Loi to the compound when he returned from visiting his family.

Loi was waiting beside his truck in front of my apartment when I pulled into the compound later that morning. He had a pensive look and tried to make eye contact as I got out of my Jeep and walked over to him. I told him that the situation was deteriorating. He was to get his family and return to my apartment there the following evening. He hugged me and left. We were together only a few minutes.

For the rest of the day I collected KIP from separate safe houses and moved them into groups. I told them they would be moved to Saigon the following day for eventual movement out of Vietnam by airplane from Tan Son Nhut.

Jim telephoned Glenn at the embassy in Saigon and passed on our plans. When he finished, Glenn hung up the telephone, took a deep breath, and went outside to the parking lot. He found a Jeep with keys in it and drove out to the MACV compound at Tan Son Nhut, where he met with Rear Adm. Hugh Benton and asked him how long it would take to have a U.S. Navy ship within reach of evacuation choppers from the delta.

Benton, claiming surprise that someone was taking action on a sealift, said, "You are the first embassy person to come to me with a request for U.S. Navy support. The first. I've had ships steaming around in circles for five days waiting for instructions. Let's get on with it."

Glenn asked for a time and place where the Air America helicopters could find the U.S. Navy platform. Benton said he'd have something ready in a few hours and promised to advise us of the coordinates when he got them. With that information, Glenn tried to telephone Jim in Can Tho but was told by the operator that the lines to the delta were down.

When Glenn returned to the embassy in the commandeered Jeep, a red-faced, angry George Jacobson, the ambassador's special assistant, confronted him. "What the hell is going on? What is this request in to Admiral Benton to evacuate people out of the delta? On whose authorization? And why didn't this request go through this office or through MacNamara? You people know anything about proper channels? You taken leave of your senses?"

"They're Vietnamese," Glenn said. "Longtime CIA agents. That's who we're evacuating. We don't have access to the Tan Son Nhut gateway for these folks like you do. Or are there other plans to move our key local people from the delta that we don't know about? And MacNamara knows about this. He has been moving his people out of country for days through the airport here. Well, ours are old CIA agents. They don't have a clue, we don't have a clue how to move them through Saigon and get 'em booked on flights out. Our people have no passports, no destinations, no nothing. No one's helping us. We're just doing what we can. That's all."

"I beg your pardon, MacNamara didn't know about this," Jacobson countered. "He blew his top when I called him a few minutes ago and asked what was going on. Blew up. He said you have been trying all along to make your own evacuation plans, to take over, and he was going to put a stop to it."

"Look," Glenn told Jacobson, "Saigon's gonna fall in two days. Two days. Forty-eight hours. Pooof. Gone. No chance to get our people out then. It's now or never. MacNamara can rant all he wants but this thing is bigger than he is, there's more at stake. We're just trying to do in the delta what you're doing up here . . . getting people out while we can."

Jacobson seemed understanding although he was oddly unaffected by Glenn's report that the NVA would be in Saigon soon.

In parting to answer an anxious call from a colleague down the hall, he said, "Well, good luck. I'll try to help with MacNamara."

Glenn took the ambassador's special assistant's manner to indicate that he supported our effort to move the KIP to the U.S. Navy.

While this conversation was taking place in Saigon, MacNamara was calling Jim into his office. He yelled that he had just heard from Saigon that Jim was acting as if he were the law unto himself in the delta. Jim called MacNamara hypocritical—everyone in the consulate knew that MacNamara had facilitated the evacuation of his Cambodian in-laws, plus cooks and drivers and others of questionable eligibility through Tan Son Nhut while refusing to allow the base to evacuate its more vulnerable KIP.

MacNamara yelled that he was in charge and that Jim was "fired."

Jim returned to the base offices and cabled the Saigon CIA Station.

Unaware of the problems that Glenn and Jim had encountered that day, I returned to the consulate in the early evening before curfew and called Brenda. I told her that I thought I would be home soon, that I would be flying out of the delta the next day but that things were under control. She wasn't to worry. On the way back to the compound I drove by the kids' house but the lights were out. I hesitated before going in, then decided that I would see them the next evening and give the mother a radio.

Returning to the Coconut Palms, I learned about the latest developments in Jim's continuing problems with MacNamara. As we were discussing the ramifications, Jim walked in and said MacNamara had just been told in State Department communication channels to continue working with him—he wasn't "fired"—and to stand down on objections to evacuate CIA KIP. Tan Son Nhut was mentioned in the text. Although there was no reference to taking the KIP directly out to the U.S. Navy, Jim said that's what we're going to do, first thing in the morning.

At first light the next day Monday, 28 April, I went by the State Department club complex. One of the Air America helicopters was going to land that night on top of the compound, and several trees had to be cut down. The tree-cutting crews were at work as I left.

Air America pilots George Taylor and Charlie Weitz were flying for me that day. They were just coming in from Saigon when I arrived at the airport and I briefed them on our plans. Sarge, who would be getting KIP ready to go at the different launch sites, had already left on a chopper to meet the group driving in from Chau Doc.

The airport was quiet. There was nothing to do but wait for Sarge to call in that the Chau Doc group was ready. Standing on the tarmac, near the radio room, I had the sense of impending conflict, not unlike the feeling I had here in Vietnam ten years before as we staged for heliborne assaults. There were so many unknowns about the day ahead. We had to pluck people from rooftops and empty fields, and then head out to sea. Was the

Navy going to receive us? Had they gotten the word? And it was hard to tell what was happening around Can Tho. Would we be overrun by fleeing South Vietnamese soldiers or attacked by North Vietnamese? Where exactly was that large force of North Vietnamese moving on Saigon? At last report they were only a few miles to our northwest. Had an element been sent to occupy Can Tho?

I had worked with copilot Taylor, an implacably cool individual, going on four years. He said, "Mule, I've never seen you so tense." Trying to reassure me, he said that we could stay in contact with everyone from the helicopter so we decided to take off and see how the tree-cutting was going. Taylor said it would stop my pacing. As we were gaining altitude, Sarge called in to say that he had the Chau Doc group in a field west of Can Tho and was waiting for us.

We headed due west and soon landed where Sarge was waiting for us. The Vietnamese agents and their families—wives, children, and some unexpected parents—scrambled on board with their luggage. We lifted off with twelve people, including Ros, my former Cambodian agent. Flying high, we headed due east down the Bassac River to the South China Sea. As we neared the coast we could see U.S. Navy ships.

I had on the customer headset. Taylor contacted a Navy air controller and told him that we had Vietnamese on board and that U.S. embassy officials had directed that they be taken to the U.S. Navy evacuation force.

—— TWENTY-TWO ——

Broken Promises

As we left the coast and flew toward the Navy ships, the Vietnamese were becoming agitated. I told Ros to let them know that we had to change our plans. We were not going to Tan Son Nhut. It was for their good. They had to trust me. I did not want any problems from them.

One KIP moved beside me and yelled in my ear that he had to get to Tan Son Nhut, that all his money was being brought from Chau Doc by a relative. He would go back with me on the helicopter. He insisted that he could not leave Vietnam without his money.

I looked at him for a long moment and told him to shut up. I saw no need to be diplomatic.

The Navy air controller asked Taylor again who had authorized the evacuation. Taylor said, the U.S. embassy, and he added that an embassy officer was on board and could explain. The air controller told us to circle between the Navy fleet and shore.

As we circled we saw one ship, with two distinctive helipads marked on the rear deck, move out from the armada. A radio operator from that ship, the USS *Vancouver*, came on the guard frequency. He told us to come in and for the U.S. embassy officer to meet with the captain before anyone else got off.

Armed U.S. Marines surrounded the helicopter as it touched down. A couple of Marines quickly approached one side, and I got off to meet them. They escorted me off the helipad and up a flight of stairs. A Navy officer with an unfriendly expression then took me to a stateroom and asked for identification.

Producing my diplomatic passport and U.S. embassy pass, I explained that the people on this helicopter and other groups of people on their way were delta KIP.

"Delta KIP?" he asked in a flat voice.

I told him I was with the CIA and that these people were agents who had worked for our organization for years. Their evacuation had been coordinated with MACV and the embassy in Saigon. I said he could get confirmation by contacting the embassy, but could rest assured that this was authorized and necessary. If these people did not get out, they would be killed when the North Vietnamese took control of the country.

The officer looked at me without expression. Obviously the Navy at sea had not gotten the word because our KIP were unexpected.

This guy decided their fate and it was up to me to win him over.

I said I had to return to coordinate the evacuation of the rest. We had about 150 total. Time was critical. I encouraged him to check with his superiors. I did not blink.

He reluctantly agreed to take the Vietnamese, although he never smiled.

I thanked him and went back to the helicopter. Ros was the first one off, then he helped a woman who had been sitting wide-eyed near the door of the helicopter to the deck. The remaining Vietnamese seemed reluctant and hesitant, but they followed. As the helicopter revved up and lifted off, the Marines were lining up the people beside their luggage.

In the air, Taylor said he had no doubt that Muley could talk the Navy into taking on some passengers without tickets.

We flew back to the airstrip in Can Tho. Mac came running out to the tarmac and gave Taylor instructions on where the next KIP group was to be picked up. The other helicopter was already en route to the Navy ship.

Throughout the day we moved KIP offshore. I was at the airstrip as the people in the last group were being assembled for what they, too, thought was a flight to Tan Son Nhut. The pilot, Bob Hitchman, was to return to Can Tho after that last flight to the Navy ship and land on top of the club, where the trees had been cut down that morning. It was going to be dark when he returned, and he was unsure if he could find the exact building. I told him I'd go along, that I could find it in the dark. Mac was on the tarmac, and I asked him to tell Jim that I'd be in later.

Like the group from Chau Doc, the people in the last group

were also upset to see us flying toward the South China Sea instead of Saigon. I had fallen asleep on the flight and was awakened by one of the Vietnamese at my side who wanted to know what was happening. I told him curtly to calm down, everything was going to be okay, and he'd thank me for it later. He started to object and I leaned in close to him and said slowly, "Did you hear me? Calm down. Shut . . . up."

As we made our approach to the ship, the sun was going down and the ship's lights were on. In the area under the landing deck I saw an assortment of lights and shapes. The ship's air controller broke in on his landing instructions to say that the captain wanted to talk with someone in authority on the helicopter, either one of the pilots or somebody else. Hitchman said they had just the man. Mule.

"Mule?"

"A U.S. embassy man is aboard," Hitchman said.

"He's just the man the captain wants to talk to," the radio operator said.

When we touched down, several Marines with guns came to the helicopter door. One Marine pointed to me and motioned me off. They escorted me, as though I were under arrest, up the same flight of stairs I had climbed that morning. The same Navy officer was standing on the bridge.

We went into his cabin and he asked me again, harshly, who had authorized this evacuation.

I said a rear admiral at MACV. I couldn't remember his name.

The captain said nobody in Saigon knew anything about this. No one. I asked if anyone in his chain of command had talked to the ambassador's special assistant, Jacobson.

He didn't answer. He seemed tired of talking with me.

He said that his ship was to be in position in a matter of hours, possibly to lead the Navy up the Saigon River to evacuate the embassy. He was not in the CIA-support business or the refugee business. He was going to put us off at another ship. Now. And he was going to go on with his mission.

"Us?" I asked.

"You and all those ratty-looking people of yours below deck who themselves know nothing about this. They are below deck demonstrating, trying to attack my Marines. You, my friend, are going to

lead those people off my ship. Now, go say good-bye to your helicopter. You belong to me. And to those people of yours down there."

This man, I surmised, was not to be argued with. But I heard
myself telling him that I had to get back to the consulate. I was
thinking about the two children and Loi.

Ignoring my statement, he said, "You take your people to this
merchant marine ship beside us and tomorrow—if we don't go
up the Saigon River tonight—I will send someone over to pick
you up, and your helicopter can come get you and take you to
your consulate. It is the best deal I'm offering, and I have been
very good to you. Plus, you don't have any choice."

He had indeed been very good to me that day, and he had a
point—there were a lot of Marines outside. I went back out on
the bridge and down to the helicopter. I told Hitchman to come
back and pick me up in the morning, that I had to move the KIP.

The people on the flight were already off the helicopter. As it
lifted off, the Marines lined them up and searched their luggage.
One of the Marine officers asked if I had any weapons. I showed
him my 9mm, which he said he'd take and hold for me.

"Thanks," I said sarcastically and, though I was on a U.S.
Navy ship, gave it up reluctantly.

I followed the last helicopter load of KIP as the Marines escorted them off the helipad and down into the ship. We came out
below the deck and saw, under bright floodlights, landing craft
tied up near walkways along the side. All of the KIP, sixty-seven
people, had been herded into a corner of the docking area.
Marines were standing around them with drawn weapons. Some
of the more aggressive of the Vietnamese were staring angrily at
the heavily armed U.S. soldiers.

One saw me and yelled. The rest looked up, and some called
out my name.

"These are not VC," I said to a Marine standing to the rear.
"They are pretty good people."

"Couldn't prove it by me," he said. "They are awfully pissed.
And they were all armed."

I broke through the Marines and went into the circle of Vietnamese. One of them said, "Do not tell us everything is okay
again. It is not okay." Many of the women and children were
crying. Some of the older people were almost frozen with fear.

They had expected to be in Tan Son Nhut that night, not under arrest in the bowels of a monster foreign ship at sea.

One of the Navy men called out that the boats were ready. I turned to see two of the landing craft being prepared to launch from the side docks on the inside of the ship.

I led sixty-six tired, confused, angry, disheveled Vietnamese and one Cambodian past the ranks of Marines and divided them into separate groups for the two landing craft. When we were on board and outfitted with life jacket, the landing craft moved away from the dock and out the back of the ship.

Surprisingly close by was another large ship at anchor. The ocean was calm as we made our way toward her. One of the sailors in the landing craft used a loudspeaker to attract the attention of someone on the ship's deck. A rope ladder came over the side and the end of it dropped into the sea. The landing craft pulled in against the ship and aimed their floodlights up the side. The KIP began to climb up the ladder. A crane boom extended over the side of the ship and dropped a net on a line. Navy seamen filled the net with the KIP's luggage and hauled it aboard. Ros and I were the last ones out of the boats. I was tired and had to labor to climb the ladder.

On deck, one of the crewmen, a Filipino, said the captain wanted to see me. This is becoming a common request, I said. I followed him up a couple of flights of stairs. Lights from Navy ships winked and flashed all around us. It was hard to tell how many vessels there were; there appeared to be hundreds. Below me were the open, empty holds of the cargo ship. In the distance I could see the landing craft returning to the rear of the Navy ship.

A middle-aged, beefy individual welcomed me aboard the USNS *Pioneer Contender*. He said he was Merchant Marine Capt. Ed Flink and asked who the hell I was and who were "these people."

"They are Vietnamese staffers of the U.S. consulate in the delta," I said.

The captain said, "That little four-year-old child down there works for the consulate?"

"Staffers and their families," I replied.

I was very tired and did not want to go through another confrontation. All I wanted was a full night's sleep and to be up early in the morning so I could get back to the U.S. Navy ship and return to Can Tho. I did not want to make conversation or problems.

"Listen, my friend," Captain Flink said, "I was recently told to go up to Da Nang—you know Da Nang—to pick up some Vietnamese staffers of the U.S. consulate there. Didn't get what I expected. Got Vietnamese Rangers who terrorized my ship. Thousands of them. So I don't believe you. I believe I'm getting set up again." He paused. "What am I supposed to do with these people? I don't have enough food. I don't have facilities. I'm being told all the time what to do. So you tell me, what do I do? You tell me. What do I do?"

"I don't know," I said. "They probably have some food with them. They can sleep on the deck. They will be no problem. I will be no problem, especially if you have a spare bunk, or, if you don't I can go down there with my people and sleep."

The captain continued to look at me. "Where's your grip? I've got a room for you, but I'm telling you, I don't want any trouble with those people down there and I don't have anything for them to eat. Maybe some food for tonight. That's it. They can stay in this first hold here. It'll get them out of the weather. And I'll have the galley make them some food for tonight. But that is all. Period."

"Okay," I said. The situation was settling itself.

"Where's your grip?" the captain asked again.

"I don't have one. It was not my plan to be here tonight. I'm here courtesy of the U.S. Navy."

I followed a crewman into one of the forward holds. The Vietnamese followed me. Some were still grumbling. Others were tired, like myself, and just wanted to find someplace to lie down. For all her rust and cavernous space, Capt. Flink's ship was more friendly than the Navy ship had been, and her crew more accommodating.

On instructions from the crew, Ros and a few of the other men went to the galley and came back with pots of hot food. I said good night to the group and went up to the mess hall. After a hot meal, I sought out Captain Flink.

He was standing on the bridge with a cigarette and a cup of coffee. I explained to him about the deteriorating situation in the delta and the danger my people would face when the North Vietnamese took control of the country. I expected the government of

South Vietnam to fall within the next couple of days. There was much work that I needed to do, and I had promises to keep. I was anxious to get back to Can Tho.

He listened sympathetically and then said, "Sure. But like I said earlier, you aren't the first person from the U.S. government to come to this ship from Vietnam and talk about evacuating people. You all act like you're on a deadly serious mission. And you are. You all are. I know. But I think it's beyond you a little bit. Ain't no one in control."

Then he paused and looked toward the ships on the horizon. "I was on my way from Hong Kong to Singapore and was told to lay in near Hue to evacuate some Americans from Hue, only we were too late. So at the end of March, they told us to go on to Da Nang and evacuate some Americans there. Some of your people came on board and said something much like you just did, that they had some people to evacuate because if the Commies caught them they'd be killed. Well, what ended up on my ship were those South Vietnamese Rangers I was telling you about. Wild, crazy people. I took two loads out of Da Nang—thousands of 'em, there were so many they couldn't all find room to lay down—and the Vietnamese Rangers that second time took over my ship. Took over my ship. Killed, raped, robbed. You could hear gunshots all the time. Soldiers were walking around with bloody knives. We had to lock ourselves in the pilothouse. I only had a crew of forty, plus some security, but there were thousands of those wild, crazy Vietnamese people.

"They finally shot some of the worst once we docked at that island, Phu Quoc, and the people got off, but I'll tell you, son, it was hell. We found bodies all over the ship after everyone got off. Babies, old women, young boys. Cut, shot, and trampled to death. And it all started when some of your friends came aboard talking about taking on some good Vietnamese refugees who'd be badly treated if the Commies got 'em. Well, if they were talking about those Rangers, I know why they would have been treated badly. They were crazy."

"It'll be different this time. There are only sixty-seven civilians with me," I said, aware that I wasn't the only one trying to find my way safely through this morass. "I'm sorry about your problems before. We won't be a problem." Flink rolled his eyes and in short order showed me to my quarters, a stateroom with bunk beds and a shower. He said he had taken the liberty of providing some toilet articles out of the ship's store.

I thanked him, shut the door, and fell across the bottom bunk. I was asleep before my head hit the pillow.

The following morning, Tuesday, 29 April, I was up before 0500 and on the bridge.

The *Pioneer Contender* was alone.

There were no U.S. Navy ships around—nothing but flat sea for as far as I could make out in the half light.

"Where's the Navy?" I asked the two men on duty in the control room.

"Left in the middle of the night, I think. Pulled out to the north."

"Oh, give me a break," I said. "Where's your radio? How do I call the U.S. Navy?"

"Sparky's still asleep," one of the seamen said. "He don't have no communication with the Navy, though. We do have this," he said and offered a small portable radio, not unlike a Radio Shack Christmas toy.

"Who do you talk to on this?" I asked, in an incredulous tone.

"Ship Control, I think, is the call sign. It's part of the Sealift Command," he said.

The seaman was not used to a lot of questions from strangers in his control room so early in the morning.

"Yeah, okay, that's what I want, Ship Control; I want a pickup," I said.

I walked out of the room onto the bridge and turned on the radio. The frequency was crowded with transmissions, some weak, some strong.

There was no Ship Control, although a common call sign was Tugboat Control. I made several efforts to call but got no response. Finally a ship relayed to Tugboat Control that the *Pioneer Contender* was trying to reach him.

"Yeah, what does she want?" Tugboat Control asked in a decidedly unmilitary tone.

"What do you want, *Pioneer Contender*?" asked the intermediary.

"I'm an embassy officer on board, and I want a pickup for delivery back to the USS *Vancouver* so that I can get to Can Tho. Where's *Vancouver*?" I asked.

"We don't know. Tugboat Control doesn't know. That's naval operations."

"What does the *Pioneer Contender* want?" asked Tugboat Control.

"It's some guy trying to get on shore. Everyone's trying to get out. He's trying to get in."

It was hard to tell exactly what was going on with Tugboat Control. Apparently it was involved in a massive way with what we had been doing on a small scale the previous day, getting Vietnamese civilians out to ships, and probably operating some distance from the lonely, empty sea around us. Evacuating people from Saigon, I guessed.

There was nothing I could do. I was stuck on a merchant ship sitting at anchor.

I returned the radio to the seamen in the pilothouse and asked them to get me if the U.S. Navy reappeared. I went back to my stateroom, took a bath, and went back to bed. At mid-morning, I awoke, dressed, and went out on deck.

Ros was standing close by and listening to a commercial radio station on a portable AM radio. He said the station was reporting that North Vietnamese troops were entering Saigon. The U.S. embassy was being evacuated. The radio broadcast was crowded with the voices of excited people.

We swayed at anchor. Seagulls squawked overhead, but there were no ships anywhere in sight.

Saigon evacuated. North Vietnamese troops entering Saigon. The best and brightest Americans in Saigon said it wouldn't happen. In the delta we had believed Hai, and he was right, to the day.

The consulate in the delta was also certain to be evacuated. I thought about Loi and visualized him waiting at my apartment with his family. Loi would be quiet, trying to calm his family, and unsure if he should stay at the apartment any longer. He must be wanting desperately for me to show up.

Nearby in another part of Can Tho, the mother would be huddled with her two children as they waited for me. She would not go out; I had made that clear. Don't leave. Don't go to the consulate. Wait for me. She would be crying. I could almost hear her across the ocean. And cussing me. Right now, I thought, she is inside her house looking at the door and pleading, "Where is he? I have been abandoned again by American men, this one leaving my children behind to die."

All those people waiting for me, and I was trapped at sea, sitting at anchor, cut off from the world.

I sought out Sparky, who said he had only shortwave to the Philippines in addition to the tiny portable used to net with Tugboat Control.

"This big boat and that's all you've got? Two dinky radios?"

I ate with Captain Flink at lunch. The evacuation from Saigon was continuing. I suggested that it was an exciting break in his normal routine.

"I ain't set up for all this. I can't take people," he said. "I've got no food, no sanitation equipment. The people making all these decisions don't know this. I'm supposed to carry cargo. That's C-A-R-G-O. Your sixty-seven people are more than I can handle. I don't like people. Especially people who don't speak English. I don't want this ship ever again considered as a people carrier. You appear to be a nice guy, all of you people are nice guys, but I don't want you on this ship of mine. Or those Vietnamese Marines. I want boxes of things that don't talk some foreign language, carry guns, eat, and shit."

Throughout the afternoon we listened to the AM radio station and Tugboat Control. The Americans were on their way out of the country, and evidently thousands of Vietnamese as well.

My anxieties began to drain out of me. There was nothing I could do. The war was over for me. Thinking back over the past few days, I knew I had done all I could do. I wished that Loi and the woman and her children had not been traumatized, and I hoped they would be treated fairly by the North Vietnamese. I'm sorry, I said to myself a dozen times. I couldn't help it that I wasn't there.

There was a certain peace on the *Pioneer Contender*. I had been the subject of so much scorn recently—from the woman and from the 7th Division commander. It was all over.

As dusk began to fall that evening, the newsman on the AM radio station said that all of the Americans had left the country. For the first time in hundreds of years it was under the complete control of the Vietnamese. The Western devils were gone.

—— TWENTY-THREE ——

Air America to the Rescue

After supper I looked over the paperback books in the ship's library, and wandered down to talk with the KIP. By then most of them were appreciative of our efforts to get them out of the country. Still, a few of the older women continued to cry. Some of the men said they would remember the day for the rest of their lives. Ros, as usual, was quiet. He was the only ethnic Cambodian in the group, but that made little difference. He had always been a loner.

I wondered how the evacuation had gone in Can Tho. We had been ready. Jim D. and Tom F. had proved themselves to be very capable. In the face of uncertainty, when the safest course would have been to do nothing—no one would have blamed them if the KIP didn't get out—they had done what they thought was right. Everyone except the base officers and Air America yelled at them. Tough guys, they had probably gotten out without any problems, I thought.

In fact, I found out later that there had been some problems in Can Tho. Early on the morning of 29 April, both helicopters, which had remained in Can Tho overnight, were dispatched to pickup points to get the last of the remaining KIP and take them out to the Navy. Later, in the consulate, Tom was talking with one of the Marine guards downstairs when someone told him that MacNamara had just received a telephone call from the embassy ordering the evacuation of all Americans in the delta. When he got up to the base offices, Jim was reading a flash cable from Saigon with a parallel message ordering the evacuation of base personnel.

Tom said, "We were right. To the day."

Jim didn't comment. He told the support officer to bring his

money to the logistics compound to pay off the last of the base
guards. Turning to Phyllis, he asked her to gather the few sensitive records that were left so he could destroy them and he also
told her to advise everyone to move to Coconut Palms to stage
for the evacuation. Tom was dispatched to the radio room, where
he told the communications operator to shut down and either destroy the coding equipment or take it with him.

Within minutes the support officer was ready with a large
pouch of money, Jim had destroyed the last of the sensitive
records, and everyone hurried out the door. Phyllis was the last to
leave. She calmly counted people off as they left, reached in and
turned out the lights, shut the door, and walked out.

Jim, Tom, and the support officer went to the logistics compound and met up with the chief guard, who had his supervisors
standing by. They all went upstairs in one of the buildings to
make the final termination payment. That had been a major concern of Tom—that we maintain a cohesive guard force no matter
what happened in the delta. He had had long talks with the chief
guard, not unlike my conversations with Loi in Vi Thanh, to get
assurances that the Americans would be protected to the end.
Tom had told the Nhung that neither he nor his men were going
to be evacuated. He had to understand that Tom would not make
any provision to get them out, but he would provide adequately
in the way of a termination bonus. The guard who, with an agency
staffer had received the CIA's highest award for bravery for their
activities during the Tet offensive of 1968, agreed. This would
probably mean that he and his family, in addition to his men and
their families, would have to go into hiding after the Americans
withdrew because they were incorruptible anti-Communists,
supportive of the Americans to the end. But the guard didn't
question his role. Like so many other agency men, he accepted
his last assignment by saying he would do good.

At the Coconut Palms, the guards let the base people inside
and locked the gates. Phyllis accounted for everyone except the
communications operator and radioed Tom.

While Jim and the support officer were paying off the senior
guard people, Tom went down to the dock where several Boston
Whalers (stout, flat-bottomed fishing boats) were tied up. The
Air America choppers had not been seen since they had departed

early that morning with the last load of KIP going out to the U.S. Navy ships. Tom had heard that American officials in Saigon were being evacuated by helicopter. He felt sure that their Air America helicopters had been diverted to the capital. The CIA people in Can Tho would have to leave with MacNamara in his landing boats, which were tied up downriver from the logistics compound, at the State Department club.

After inspecting the Boston Whalers, Tom called MacNamara to tell him that the base people would be coming down the river in their small boats to join his group. MacNamara said he had already pushed off and would wait for them in the middle of the Bassac River. He said the CIA communicator was with him.

The group at the Coconut Palms overheard the radio conversation, and everyone moaned. Now their evacuation would involve moving by Jeeps from the Coconut Palms to the logistics compound and then down the small river in the Boston Whalers to the Bassac River for the beginning of what certainly would be a hazardous trip to the South China Sea.

Tom was squeezing his eyes shut in anticipation of what lay ahead. Around him in the logistics compound, workers were busy with the end-of-the-month inventory, mechanics were doing maintenance work on various vehicles, and other workers unloaded a truck that had recently arrived from Saigon with supplies. A voice broke in on Tom's radio. George Taylor, copilot on one of the two Air America helicopters, was saying that both choppers were returning to Can Tho. Tom looked up and, way off to the east, could just barely see them.

He was almost giddy when he said, "Oh, you are so beautiful."

"Yeah," Taylor said, "we almost ain't here. On the way back, air ops in Saigon ordered us north to help in the evacuation, but we said we had some good customers in Can Tho and had to return there for one last trip before we headed up. You did want us to come back, didn't you?"

"I wish I had as much money as I'm glad to see you," Tom said.

The pilots of the two helicopters, Hitchman and Weitz, said that they were low on fuel and needed to gas up before they did any more flying. Mac got on the radio at Coconut Palms and suggested that one helicopter land where they were and the other in the logistics compound, and he would help direct the choppers to a fuel dump somewhere in town.

Tom ran upstairs to get Jim and the support man. When they left, the chief guard suddenly found himself in possession of all the U.S. and Vietnamese money left on the desk. Downstairs, the CIA men moved to a cleared area in the compound near the front gate, and Hitchman landed—blowing off the roofs of dozens of sheds in the community of lean-tos right outside the fence.

Weitz sat his helicopter down at Coconut Palms and picked up the base people there. Mac had on the customer headset. He had been working the helicopters over the past few days and suggested that they first try to get fuel at the airport. This idea was discounted out of hand by the pilots because no one answered the radio in the control tower there. There was no telling who was in control of the airport by now. The next suggestion was the Shell compound on the road to the airport. Although neither pilot had landed there recently, they knew it had a pump and a landing zone inside the compound large enough for two helicopters to be refueled at one time.

Weitz's helicopter, with the people from the Coconut Palms, reached the Shell compound first and made a pass overhead. No one on the chopper saw any unusual activity below, so Weitz brought it around and landed near several rubber bladders of fuel. Within minutes, Hitchman's helicopter containing Tom, Jim, and the support officer landed behind them.

Once both helicopters were on the ground, a group of armed Vietnamese soldiers came out from behind a building and lined up by the pumps.

"Goddammit," Mac said, "we were so close to getting out of here."

"Oh, shut up," said Weitz, "they probably just want a ride out of the country."

"They ain't got no luggage," Taylor said. "Plus, my bet is people who want out come running up to the helicopter. They don't stand in front with guns in their hands."

Both helicopters settled down, although the pilots kept up full power and the *battey-de-battey* of the blades continued loudly.

Weitz said, "Okay, here's what we're going to do. Two people go over there beside those Vietnamese and pick up the gas nozzles and bring them back to the helicopters and give us a squirt. We don't need to top off. Just enough to get us out of here."

"I'll go," said the flight mechanic in the rear helicopter. "Who's going up there?"

"Mac," Weitz said.

"Mac?" Mac asked.

"Look, we have submachine guns. You go over there and get the gas nozzle and come back to the helicopter. If they try to grab you, drop down and we blast them with automatic fire."

"There is no chance in hell we can get away if we start shooting. There must be a dozen of them. You going to kill them all or what? And how we going to get fuel if everyone starts shooting? This ain't the movies, you know."

"You got a better plan?" Weitz asked. "We have to have petrol. It's right over there."

"Okay," Mac said, "if they try to get me—shit, look at them, some have AK-47s—if they try to get me, I fall down and you guys blast 'em and then I get up and try to make it back to the helicopter."

"Right."

"Okay."

Mac slowly, awkwardly, got out of the lead helicopter and walked stiffly toward the rack holding the gas nozzles. The flight mechanic from the other helicopter was somewhere behind him. The Vietnamese did not show any expression. Hopefully they were going to ask for a ride out of the country, Mac thought. Please don't want to capture me. Please don't want to kill me.

Picking up a nozzle, Mac walked back to the helicopter. He looked one of the kickers in the eye the whole way, as he watched for any sudden movement by the kicker. Anything sudden and Mac was dropping to the ground. But then, he thought, I've got to be sure because if I drop, the pilot and Taylor and the kicker are going to start shooting.

The kicker had removed the gas tank cap on the side of the helicopter, and, as Mac walked up, he went back to lean against the helicopter near his gun.

The flight mechanic in the rear helicopter passed him with another hose and nozzle.

Mac starting pumping gas, and he pumped and pumped. Finally he realized that no one in the helicopter was going to tell him when to stop. They were all intent on staring down the Vietnamese in front of them.

The flight mechanic from the rear helicopter had finished pumping and was screwing on the gas cap.

"Hey!" Mac yelled over the noise of the helicopter to the kicker. "Is this enough?" The kicker didn't hear. Mac stopped pumping and went over and grabbed his arm. The kicker jumped straight up.

"Is this enough?" Mac asked again. When the kicker said that it was, he went back to the nozzle, extracted it from the helicopter, and began to walk back to the nozzle rack. Halfway there, Mac thought to himself, I don't need to take this all the way over to where those men are standing with their guns. I'll just drop it here.

And he did.

When he turned to go back to the helicopter, one of the Vietnamese shouted, "Hey you!"

Mac was facing the helicopter and watching Taylor, who was vibrating because of the high torque of the engine. Mac knew that Weitz had an automatic rifle in his lap. The flight mechanic, the gas hose in his hand, stopped, frozen, and looked wide-eyed at Mac.

Should he drop to the ground? Was this it? Mac was rigid, tense. His face was suddenly wet with sweat.

"You. You!" the Vietnamese said loudly behind him.

Mac turned around, ready to drop.

"You have to sign for the gas." The Vietnamese offered a clipboard. Mac signed it and got back on the helicopter—the last American on the ground in Can Tho, and one of the most thankful to be leaving.

I went up to my stateroom early that night. Captain Flink woke me up around midnight.

"There are planes buzzing my ship," he said. "Why are there planes buzzing my ship? Do they have bombs? You caused all this. They are North Vietnamese jets and they want to kill you and your people, and they are buzzing my ship." Outside, I could hear a jet scream by, low.

"Jets?" was all I could think to ask. A lot had happened during the past few days. I was on a merchant marine ship. A strange beefy man beside me was accusing me of something that had to do with jets. I didn't have a lot of experience with merchant marine ships or jets, and I had trouble putting things into perspective.

Someone came running up to the cabin and told the captain that boats were coming at us from shore.

Still confused, I thought, Boats?

"Goddammit man!" the captain yelled at me. He wheeled around and left.

I dressed and ran outside to the bridge. Standing by the captain, I watched two boats slowly make their way toward us in the dark. The captain ordered the anchor hauled. Jets continued to buzz the ship and the two approaching boats. It was a friendly sort of nuzzling by the aircraft, I thought, and I suddenly realized that the two boats were the landing craft with MacNamara and his staff. I told Captain Flink that everything was going to be all right.

That was clear when I looked at the boats through the ship's binoculars. They were flying American flags.

"The consulate is coming," I said. "You've got more guests."

"Jesus H. Christ!" the captain exclaimed. "I think I would rather be attacked by jets." After a pause he said, "I'll tell you this, my friend, I don't know how you'all did this, but I know if you hadn't been on this ship, I would have been out of here. Those two boats would not have caught me until I reached Singapore. I don't like jets and unidentified boats that come out of a country the Communists have just taken over. You people don't understand. This is a C-A-R-G-O ship."

Talking through a relay, I tried to get someone at Tugboat Control to pass the word to the Navy that the U.S. Consulate group was arriving at the *Pioneer Contender*. Finally, someone netting with Tugboat Control said they would pass the message.

Sparky tried to raise Sealift Command to get instructions on what to do. In his messages, he said the captain urgently requested permission to get under way.

As the boats approached, the captain threw the rope ladder over the side and ordered his crane in position to take on the luggage.

I contacted Tugboat Control again and asked if they were interested in two landing craft to assist in the evacuation. Otherwise we were going to cast them off. Tugboat Control, usually slow to answer any of my calls, immediately came back and said through the intermediary that landing craft were exactly what they needed. They asked if there was any way we could bring them up to Vung Tau, a coastal town near the mouth of the Saigon River.

I remembered that MacNamara had hired some river pilots to drive the boats down the river, so I figured they could drive the boats to Vung Tau. The captain was busy with instructions to get the two landing boats tied up beside the ship near the rope ladder, so I asked someone in the control room, "How far is Vung Tau? How long to drive one of those landing craft there?"

"Eight, ten hours," the man at the wheel suggested.

I went back on the bridge and stood beside the captain. Borrowing his loudspeaker, I called down to MacNamara and asked if his river pilots were up to taking the landing craft to Vung Tau. He answered through his loudspeaker that he didn't think so.

Two of the first people up the ladder were Filipino engineers who had maintained the generators at the consulate. I asked them what was wrong with the pilots, and they said the Vietnamese crew had disappeared before the boats left Can Tho. There were no river pilots on board; they had learned how to drive the boats themselves.

"Good," I said. "We're going to take those boats to Vung Tau. You guys and me."

Most of the Vietnamese who had arrived with me were on the upper deck as they watched the on-loading of the consulate crowd. I yelled for Ros, and he walked quietly out of the crowd. When I told him to get his stuff together because we were going for a ride, he turned without a question and went down a ladder to get his gear from the hold.

I went back to the portable radio, called Tugboat Control, and asked them to confirm that they seriously wanted these landing craft. Was it important or just something that would be sort of nice? Tugboat Control responded immediately and said the boats would make a difference in whether some people got out or not. It was important to those people.

I had left Loi and the kids, but perhaps I could help others. Maybe it was a trade-off. Putting the radio down, I told the captain that a Cambodian, a couple of Filipinos, and I were going to drive the landing boats to Vung Tau.

Flink said Sparky had just gotten word that the *Pioneer Contender* was also to relocate to Vung Tau to help in the evacuation. He suggested that I go in front of him with the two boats. He would hold a straight reading north and pull back to match my speed. All I had to do was keep looking over my shoulder and guide on him.

Ros and the Filipino engineers were on the deck. When everyone had cleared the landing craft except for a couple of men, we went over the side and down the ladders.

The Filipinos got into the rear boat. MacNamara was still in the other boat when Ros and I climbed into it. He put the last items into the net and then motioned the crane operator to lift it. He had the consulate's American flag with him and was wearing his helmet with the word *Congen* and a big white star on the front. I welcomed him to the *Pioneer Contender* and told him of the arrangements to get the landing craft to Vung Tau, but he was exhausted and didn't care what happened to the boats. He was just glad to get to the ship. Coming down the Bassac River, they had been fired on, he said, but everyone was safely out.

"Good," I said. "Go up, take my stateroom, take a shower, go to sleep. See you in the morning."

Ros and I were then alone in the boat, and we didn't have the faintest idea how to drive it.

The captain yelled through the loudspeaker to untie our lines. While Ros did this, I went into the small pilot area and tried to figure out the controls. Gauges on the console indicated that we had plenty of fuel. The throttles and gearshifts for the two engines were prominent in the light from the gauges. With the steering wheel in front of me, that was all I needed, I thought.

The Filipinos threw off the ropes holding the two boats together at about the same time that Ros untied the ropes holding us to the *Pioneer Contender*, and we were free.

I moved the throttles and rammed back into the other landing craft. After I changed gears and gave the boat more gas, I looked up to see that we were heading straight for the ship's anchor chain. It was a long way up to the deck. The captain came on the loudspeaker and told us to stand clear of the anchor, which was coming out of the water.

Easy for him to say, I thought. I finally got control of the boat by putting it into reverse again and backing out some distance away from both the ship and the other landing craft. Ros came around behind me and watched as I played with the controls.

I finally stopped backing up, but couldn't see directly in front of the boat when we were going forward. The controls were in the stern, where all the weight was, and the bow stuck out of the water like a shield. To see straight ahead I had to walk over to the side of the boat while Ros held the wheel, or turn the boat to one side or another. Also, because it was empty and the bow was high, the boat was difficult to drive. Wind and waves turned it from one side to the other. One second I was going due north, then a wave hit the front and I was going due west. I finally moved the boat off the port bow to the front of the *Pioneer Contender*, which had just gotten under way. The other landing craft fell in behind us.

── TWENTY-FOUR ──

Farewell Vietnam

We were a small parade heading north that early morning—my landing craft in front, bouncing from one side to the other, then the less erratic landing craft, and finally the monstrously large cargo ship. I tried to find a good medium speed. The faster we went, the more our bow stuck out of the water and the more affected we were by the wind and waves. The slower we went, the more we fell under the bow of the large ship behind us. I had to turn every minute to make sure we were staying on line.

When I got tired, Ros took the wheel. He struggled with it, and veered off to one side, followed by the landing craft behind us. As we got on line again, I thought that the crew of the *Pioneer Contender* surely must be cussing us as unfit sailors.

The wind picked up around 0400, and we were violently tossed from side to side. Every time I turned around, my neck hurt. I tried to motion to the Filipinos to take the lead, but either they did not understand or did not want the point. Doggedly they stayed behind me.

When the sun came up I had a chance to look around the pilot station after being in the dark all night. I found some lights. Why weren't they on when I got in?

And then I looked at the gear levers. I had only one engine engaged! When I had both engines in gear the boat settled down to the more steady motion I had admired in the Filipinos' boat.

Around 0800, the *Pioneer Contender* suddenly accelerated. Despite our best efforts to stay in front, she passed us to the east and was gone. Nice guys, I thought.

I had motioned the other boat to come up beside us and we were traveling along more or less evenly when Ros tapped me on the arm and motioned to the west. My first thought was that we had come in close to shore. Then I thought we were drifting toward an island, because we were going forward, but it seemed that the island was closing.

I tried to increase our speed, but the more I throttled forward, the more erratic the boat became. And the island *was* getting closer.

The Filipinos' boat moved ahead, leaving me to fight the back-and-forth motion of our landing boat.

The island kept getting closer and I was unable to stop the drift. Then I noticed boats between us and the island. Ros took the wheel while I reached for binoculars and fixed them on the approaching boats. They were filled with people. And that wasn't an island behind them, but many more boats, also filled with people.

The boats were overtaking us. What are those Filipinos doing that I'm not doing? I thought desperately, because their boat was moving ahead. They must have a better boat. That was no consolation, because behind me, maybe a hundred boats were bearing down, straight at us. For what? Who told them I was here? I was taking this very personally. Perhaps they weren't coming at me. Perhaps they were heading to Vung Tau and we were just in the way.

I could barely see the *Pioneer Contender* on the horizon. She wasn't extending the distance between us, and I wondered if I should be so lucky that she was, in fact, at Vung Tau. I had no way of knowing exactly where we were. All I knew for sure was that a haggard Cambodian and I were somewhere off the coast of Vietnam the day after the Americans had been evacuated and that a hundred boats were rushing up to us. Could they be North Vietnamese attack boats? No, they must surely be South Vietnamese boat people heading to Vung Tau, I decided, so I turned the boat southeast to get out of their way. And they turned in my direction. The whole fleet. Why me? The Filipinos' boat continued to move toward the *Pioneer Contender*.

The first boat, lightly loaded with civilians, reached us from the rear. We had no weapons, thanks to the U.S. Navy, but Ros had found a knife somewhere. He looked to me for instructions, but I decided that we could not fend off one boat, much less the many others behind it.

I told Ros to yell at them to go on to Vung Tau, that they would be taken care of at Vung Tau. Ros went to the side of the boat and yelled. I had never heard him raise his voice before and was surprised at how squeaky it was.

The people on the boat ignored him, and someone threw a rope over a cleat on the side of our landing craft. Another boat came up on the other side and lashed on. People from both boats began piling into the landing craft. As other boats arrived, they tied onto the first boats, and their passengers scrambled into our craft. Soon the only place where we did not have boats around us was to our bow. The tongue of the landing craft prevented them from making purchase there.

Quickly our landing craft filled with people, settling the bow into the water, and I could see the ocean in front from the driving console.

More boats were coming up behind, but it was becoming increasingly difficult to see them because so many boats had tied up to one another. I told Ros to get four or five men and bring them to me. Within minutes he was back with a dark, swarthy crew. I told him to say that their being on board was no problem and I would look after them once we arrived at Vung Tau, but we could not take on any more passengers. I wanted them to go around and cut the lines holding the boats to our craft.

As Ros translated I looked up and saw dozens of people, some carrying guns, scramble over the boats toward us. I grabbed two men in the group and pointed to one side. I pushed one of the remaining men to the other side and told them to hurry and cut the ropes. Ros repeated my instructions and the men leaped away, calling on some of their friends to help.

Within minutes we were free of the boats and we pulled forward. It was a wonderful relief to find that the landing craft maneuvered nimbly and could make speed with a full cargo. I located the tall silhouette of the *Pioneer Contender* in the distance and gave the boat full power. It surged ahead and we began to leave the fishing boats behind.

I passed the Filipinos' boat, which had stayed well ahead of the boats that overtook me. By midday on 30 April 1975 we were near the *Pioneer Contender*, which sat amid an assortment of oceangoing vessels, barges, fishing boats, and U.S. Navy ships. The port city of Vung Tau was off to the northwest.

Tugboat Control had mentioned meeting me south of Vung Tau, but no boat came out as I headed north. When I came alongside the *Pioneer Contender*, the captain welcomed me over his loudspeaker. I yelled up that I had some more guests for him. Very special people, every one. He shook his head, but soon the rope ladder dropped over the side.

The first officer yelled down that a U.S. Navy tender was coming soon to pick me up. He told me to hurry with whatever I was doing and get ready to go to the ship, but I said that I had to deliver the landing craft to Tugboat Control before I did anything else.

"Your friends have already left," the first officer yelled. "Come on."

I pretended that I couldn't hear him. After everyone was offloaded, Ros pushed us off from the side of the ship.

With the Filipinos following, we went out into the swirling mass of boats and debris. The harbor was ravaged by the war's end. Refugees were clinging to anything that would float, paddling with their hands and pieces of boards, standing in boats, holding children, arms outstretched to us and oceangoing vessels. Oil spills and litter swirled with the tide.

What looked like hundreds of Vietnamese were standing on a pier as they waited to be loaded onto a barge being moved into place nearby. A U.S. Navy ship, maneuvering in the northern part of the harbor, fired into a hill overlooking the evacuation area. I moved toward shore, past the barge near the pier, and tried to find someone in charge. Four or five large oceangoing tugboats were in the area. As we came alongside one, I yelled out and asked for directions to Tugboat Control.

"Tugboat Control? Are you tetched? Bloody Tugboat Control was in Saigon. The docks at Newport. They pulled out last night." The sailor had a distinctive Australian accent. For a moment I thought I was hallucinating, that overnight I had traveled into *The Twilight Zone*. The voices at Tugboat Control had been American and I assumed the tugboats and other evacuation craft would have been crewed by Americans. I had also expected an organized evacuation of people, where there would be a clear need for the landing boats. But before me was a crowded, chaotic harbor clogged with thousands of hysterical refugees. And a sarcastic Aussie appeared to be in charge.

"Pulled out, are you crazy? Where'd they go?" I asked.

"Out to sea. They're on the *Chitosa Maru*. They brought this barge down the Saigon River. We needed your boats before we got the barge, but that's it. You supposed to meet them, mate?"

"Yeah."

"We're almost finished here. We've only the *Pioneer Contender* left to load."

"You don't need these landing craft?" I asked, suddenly very tired.

"Nope. We did, now we don't."

"You want these boats?"

"No."

"Well, I've broken my ass and was almost sunk trying to get them up here. You hear what I'm saying?"

"We're finished."

"I brought these boats up from the mouth of the Bassac River for you to use in evacuating some of those people over there!" I was getting angrier by the second.

"Okay," said the Aussie. "Okay, tie up to me. We'll use them."

We tied both landing boats to the tug and were taken back to the *Pioneer Contender*. When I climbed up the rope ladder I was coming to know so well and got on deck, I learned that I had just missed the Navy tender. Captain Flink said she probably would be back to pick me up but not to worry if she didn't. I could have my old stateroom back. He said he'd like that anyway, so he'd have someone around to help him deal with all the people on board.

"Thank you for the stateroom, my friend," I said. "I am going to bed. If anyone calls for me, if the Navy boat comes back, tell them to go away."

As I turned to leave the bridge I looked around. With the advantage of the *Pioneer Contender*'s height, I could see U.S. Navy ships out to sea, the chaotic harbor, and the beaches crowded with people and personal belongings.

A tugboat under power held the barge against the pier. The press of people reached from the beach to the end of the pier. As the crowd surged forward, some people near the end were pushed off into the mass of humanity fighting for space on the barge below. The tugboat crew was unfazed and kept the barge steadily braced. The crowd suddenly surged forward again, and more people were pushed off, some falling, screaming, into the water. Two gangplanks were crowded with refugees slowly making their way onto the barge. Everyone was carrying something—women had children in their arms, men had suitcases, boys bags, soldiers guns. Everyone was pushing frantically, desperately.

Suddenly an artillery round whistled overhead and landed in the middle of the harbor. Then another, as if the enemy gunner was registering his rounds. The people on the gangplanks continued to press forward. I saw their mouths open wide in horror when the tugboat reversed its engines and began to pull the barge slowly away from the pier. Men, women, and children tried to jump on board, but many were not successful. As the tugboat and barge moved farther away from shore I could see people in the water behind them. Slowly the boat and barge turned and started in our direction through the maze of smaller vessels—makeshift rafts, fishing vessels, South Vietnamese Navy lighters. More shells began to land randomly in the harbor. A U.S. Navy ship moved by us briefly and fired her huge deck guns in the direction of the North Vietnamese gun position, but the ship soon fell back and the incoming rounds continued. Smoke from fires near a warehouse onshore drifted by us out to sea. A low wail from thousands of desperate people drifted across the harbor.

From Vietnam, ARVN helicopters, singly and in groups of two and three, made their way out to sea in search of a receptive U.S. Navy ship. One helicopter, awkwardly flying alone, suddenly exploded, like faulty fireworks, and debris rained down on the sea south of the barge making its slow way toward us.

Looking over the harbor, back to Vietnam, I thought about my ten years' involvement with the war. I had landed there in Vung Tau during the buildup of American forces in 1965. As a CIA case officer, I was the last American out.

I had been so young when I arrived. I thought about the times I led men into combat, and I remembered battlefield events both frightful and funny. Clear images swirled before my eyes—lost comrades, arrogant American bureaucrats, angry South Viet-

namese generals berating me for abandoning them on the battlefield. I had put so many people into body bags. I was leaving
friends behind.

And I saw antiwar slogans, talking heads on TV, student demonstrations. I remembered coming home as a soldier, proudly
wearing my uniform, and how Dad shook my hand and how
Mom, crying, ran her trembling fingers across my lips. I remembered coming down from the fighting in the hills of Laos—the
kids squealing when I came in the front gate, all the lights on in
the house, Brenda standing on the porch smiling, Disney musicals blaring in the background.

But, mostly, I remembered the fighting. I shut my eyes and
heard the familiar sounds of battle—bombs going off, bullets
whizzing overhead, helicopter blades whirring noisily above me,
men screaming. I remembered the surges of adrenaline as my
body tensed when I heard noises in the jungle night. I remembered holding Goss when he died and saw the young North Vietnamese soldier struggling gallantly to live. I smelled the dead
from the ARVN 21st Division morgue. I felt the tight confines of
the tunnel at Cu Chi when I knew a wounded VC was nearby, underground, in the dark. I saw the VC coming up out of the hole
and I saw the muzzle blast as he fired at me. I heard Slippery
Clunker Six reciting poetry, and I remembered standing by his
body bag at Minh Thanh. And always the civilians—the children
huddling next to their mother in Can Tho, the farmers refusing to
make eye contact, the orphans playing at Vi Thanh, and Loi pro-
tecting my body. I saw the Asian moon through layers of jungle
and the sun rising in the mountains and setting over rice fields. I
could taste the lukewarm, iodized water from my canteen and
Castro's C-ration stew, and I could smell putrid sweat and feel
the rain and the heat and the pain and the anguish and I heard myself yell at Patrick not to die.

My mind was briefly out of control. Everything I had seen or
heard or thought or done in the war merged, then became one
with the chaotic scene before me, and I stopped and looked at the
Vung Tau harbor and the thousands of South Vietnamese refugees
who were trying to follow us home.

What was the value to it all?

Standing on the bridge of the *Pioneer Contender* and looking back at Vietnam, I suddenly sensed—in a startling moment of clarity—that even though we had lost, we had done right by going there to fight the war. History will look kindly on our good intentions to save a country from being overrun by an aggressive neighbor.

We did not win because the government that we came to save, the government of South Vietnam, was incompetent and corrupt and did not represent the people. And we did not win because American politicians and policy makers were guilty of incredibly bad decisions, from start to finish.

It seemed to me that the lasting legacy of the war was the men who had answered their country's call and gave their lives in Vietnam. In a time of shifting values, they reaffirmed the ageless principles of duty and country. They acquitted themselves in the finest traditions of American fighting men. They died young, in battle, with honor. Heroes, every one.

Facing the shore, I saluted them, slowly, with military precision.

I stood silent for a moment, turned, and went below.

The war was over.

Loaded with thousands of Vietnamese refugees, the *Pioneer Contender* heaved anchor early the next morning and pointed her bow east. Vietnam faded behind us.

—— EPILOGUE ——

General Hung and General Hai

At 7:00 P.M. on 30 April 1975, General Hung, the former ARVN 21st Division commander and my friend, called his wife into his office in Can Tho. He told her that ten townspeople had come to him and asked him to not fight the advancing VC in their city's streets. The Communists would shell the city and leave it waste, they said, and many civilians would die. Hung told his wife he understood and had agreed not to turn Can Tho into a hopeless battlefield. He also said a contingency plan to retreat with some of his soldiers to an isolated area of the delta had been compromised and was no longer viable. Surrendering was not an option. He could not bear even to meet with the ranking VC in the area, Major Hoang Van Thach, to discuss turning the delta over to the Communists. And he would not flee his country. He had an obligation to the men who had given their lives in its defense.

He was left with one honorable alternative, he said. He must take his own life.

His wife cried and pleaded with him to reconsider. "Why can't we leave for a foreign country like the others?" she asked.

He reminded her again of his duty to his country and to his soldiers. And he continued, softly, slowly, "Don't let me lose my determination. Continuing to fight now will only bring trouble and loss not only to our family but to soldiers and civilians also. And I don't want to see the sight of any Communists."

He stood, embraced his wife, and wept. Finally he said, "Hurry up and ask your mother and the children to come in to see me."

When his mother-in-law and the children came into his office, he said good-bye to them, kissing each child.

All the soldiers in his outer office came in next, lined up, expecting orders.

Hung told them the fighting was finished. He said the country was lost because of poor leadership in Saigon and asked their forgiveness if he, personally, had made mistakes. The atmosphere was solemn. "I accept death," he said. "Good-bye, my brothers."

He saluted them and then shook each man's hand. He asked everyone to leave. Some of his men did not move, so he pushed them out the door, shook off his wife's final pleas, and finally was alone in his office.

Within moments there was a shot. General Hung was dead.

On the morning of May 1, 1975, at the mobile headquarters of the ARVN 7th Division, General Hai's first lieutenant military aide came into his office.

General Hai lay facedown at his desk. Alone, without saying good-bye to anyone, he had committed suicide during the night. A half-empty glass of brandy was nearby.

Do not stand by my grave and weep:
I am not there. I do not sleep.
I am a thousand winds that blow.
I am the diamond's glint on snow.
I am the sunlight on ripened grain.
I am the gentle autumn's rain.
When you awake in the morning's hush,
I am the swift uplifting rush
Of quiet birds in circle flight.
Do not stand by my grave and cry:
I am not there. I did not die.
—Anonymous
Central Highlands of Vietnam
ca. 1969

"Duty, honor, country."
—GEN. DOUGLAS MACARTHUR

Index

BLACKJACK-33
With Special Forces in the Viet Cong Forbidden Zone

by James C. Donahue

In Vietnam, Mobile Guerrilla Force was the only American unit that truly carried out guerrilla-style hit-and-run operations. Its soldiers roamed for weeks at a time through steamy triple-canopy jungle in areas owned by the NVA and VC, destroying base camps, ambushing enemy forces, and gathering the intelligence Saigon desperately needed.

In 1967, James Donahue was a Special Forces medic and an assistant platoon leader for the Mobile Guerrilla Force's fiercely anti-Vietnamese Cambodian irregulars. On mission Blackjack-33, the Mobile Guerrilla Force was to act as bait, luring VC and NVA regiments into decisive engagements so that the Communists could be engaged and destroyed by the 1st Infantry Division. Well, the MGF did its job, but the 1st Infantry Division didn't show up. . . .

Published by The Ballantine Publishing Group.
Available in bookstores everywhere.

15 MONTHS IN SOG
A Warrior's Tour

Thom Nicholson
Colonel, US Army Special Forces (Ret.)

In Vietnam, the Military Assistance Command's Studies and Observations Group (MACV-SOG) fielded small recon teams in areas infested with VC and NVA. Because SOG operations suffered extraordinary casualties, they required extraordinary soldiers. So when Capt. Thom Nicholson arrived at Command and Control North (CCN) in Da Nang, he knew he was going to be working with the cream of the crop.

Nicholson commanded the four platoons of Raider Company, comprised of nearly two hundred men, in some of the war's most deadly missions, including ready-reaction missions for patrols in contact with the enemy, patrol extractions under fire, and top-secret expeditions "over the fence" into Laos, Cambodia, and North Vietnam.

Published by The Ballantine Publishing Group.
Available in bookstores everywhere.